C000214130

WORTHING AT WAR

The Diary of
C.F. Harriss

Anti-aircraft gun battery just east of The Esplanade.

WORTHING AT WAR

The Diary of C.F. Harriss

Edited by
Paul Holden

PHILLIMORE

2010

Published by
PHILLIMORE & CO. LTD
Chichester, West Sussex, England
www.phillimore.co.uk

Introduction and this selection © Paul Holden, 2010

ISBN 978-1-86077-618-2

Printed and bound in Great Britain
Manufacturing managed by Jellyfish Print Solutions Ltd

Contents

THE DIARY OF C.F. HARRISS

List of Illustrations

Frontispiece: Anti-aircraft gun battery just east of The Esplanade

Illustration Acknowledgements

The Argus, 14, 23, 37; Walter Gardiner Collection: Frontispiece, 2-13, 15-22, 24-36, 38-43; Worthing Museum, 3.

Introduction

In 1938, Clare Fordham Harriss sat down to record his thoughts about the looming threat of war with Germany. He had already lived through one Great War, and looked to the future with foreboding. Mr Harriss, of 10 Rectory Gardens, Broadwater, Worthing, returned to the diary in 1939 and proceeded to record, in remarkable detail, the day to day experiences endured by civilians during the Second World War. His wonderfully vivid descriptions were set against a background of momentous world events, which he weaved like a literary magician into his narrative. The diary's preface stated:

> The following pages are a journal containing the experiences and impressions of an elderly couple living in villadom at Worthing in Sussex, during the whole period of the 2nd World War. It was written daily at the time, and so supplies an exact and vivid record of the wartime life lived by middle-class civilians – by toads under the official harrow as it were. It is this existence of the non-combative side of a nation at war which the student of the past often desires to become acquainted with yet rarely finds directly recorded. Diaries which survive at all tend to be mainly concerned with military or political people. The writer hopes that in the present case he may have done something, however unworthy, to break new ground. Nevertheless, throughout the almost six years that the war lasted, he was conscious of the difficulty of estimating what in the future was likely to be worthy of record. One can but hope that here is a reasonable selection of the grave, the serious and the amusing. In sum, here is a true and intimate example, in the colour of the moment, of what ordinary citizens felt and thought, and above all, said in the slow evolution of this world-racking event. If the pilgrimage described seems more human than heroic, one hopes nevertheless that it may have an interest for the general reader as memories fade, and perhaps, in a humble way, even assist the industry of the future historian probing away amid the mists of oblivion.

The diary, an historical gem, was written with almost religious zeal and commitment. It preserved for future generations many fascinating observations about ordinary life and survival for an elderly middle-class couple during the war. He even recorded the weather on a day by day basis, which will prove of interest to the meteorological historian.

But what do we know of the Harrisses themselves? Mr Harriss, referred to in the diary as 'CF', was born in 1882, the only son of Walter Fordham Harriss. He attended Tonbridge School in Kent, one of the leading boys' boarding schools in the country and highly respected internationally, between 1896 and 1900. The school, founded in 1553 and set in 150 acres, has the motto *Deus Dat Incrementum*, or God Gives Growth. It was at Tonbridge that Mr Harriss gained a classical education, and an expert knowledge of Latin quotations, which often appear in the diary. After leaving school, he became a lieutenant in the 1st Volunteer Battalion of the Royal West Kent Regiment, and served from 1902 to 1905. Mr Harriss was by profession a solicitor, having qualified in 1906, and practised in Newport, Salop and Ely, before retiring to Worthing in 1937.

I have found no reference to Mr Harriss serving in the First World War or, indeed, a photograph of him, which is frustrating, but his diary forms an astonishing legacy. There is a haunting melancholy to his writing; a reflection, perhaps, that he was acutely aware of the passage of Time and of his 'glass filling up'. This is evident in a footnote to the diary's title, 'Hotchpot', which states: 'Created slowly, from the heart, to stand against the claws of Time; still on the Earth, though I depart.'

There is no escaping the fact that Mr Harriss was something of a snob. He and his wife were undoubtedly 'curtain-twitchers', who looked down on their neighbours. They also employed domestic servants to do the house cleaning and gardening. His wife, Florence E. Harriss, or 'F' in the diary, was of Welsh origin, and could be incredibly waspish at times – her caustic comments, recorded by her husband, occasionally scouring the soul of the reader. But she was also sensitive, and often cried at the suffering of others, such as those bombed out of their homes, RAF airmen killed in raids over Germany, or the victims of Nazi concentration camps. F also had a love of shows and films, which her husband did not share, much preferring to bury his nose in a book at Worthing Library, which became his second home. F seemed oblivious of the dairy, although she surely must have known her husband was writing it. They were reasonably well off, and therefore able to eat out most days at the town's restaurants: Khong's, Mitchell's and WH Smith.

Despite being in his late fifties when the war started, Mr Harriss did not volunteer for civil defence duties and succeeded in obtaining an exemption from overnight fire-watching when many others of a similar age 'did their bit'. He felt his role was to record, as highlighted in the following entry, dated 1 November 1939:

> I feel sometimes that in my retired condition I am more of a liability than an asset to the country in the present emergency, and hope that this record may be some justification for my existence through it.

He was, without question, an old-fashioned chauvinist, and regularly made plain his utter scorn for women who smoked in public, wore trousers, or painted their lips red. Mr Harriss and his wife abhorred the idea of child evacuees being billeted on their home, and when a female teacher was installed, in the early months of the war, it wasn't long before the verbal flak started flying. She did not last long, and soon moved out, much to their relief, but they constantly worried about further impositions on their privacy. But any flaws in his character can be cast aside by his remarkably descriptive writing, which recorded every aspect of life during the war, from the drama of bombing raids, the comings and goings of military units, and the ebb and flow of the conflict overseas; to the arrival of child evacuees, the chatter in the food queues, and the passing of the seasons. We learn, in intimate detail, what it was like to wander abroad during the blackout during the so-called 'Phoney War', when pedestrians put life and limb on the line, to scrabble in shops for diminishing rations, to fear the blood-curdling air-raid siren, to hear the crump and vibration of bombs detonating, to view in horror houses and streets wrecked by high explosives, and to witness spectacular dogfights in the blue skies above.

The arrival of the Canadians, and their somewhat dubious behaviour at times, is documented, as is the terrifying advent of the flying bomb and the spectacular sight of American bomber armadas passing overhead on their way to destroy German cities. All set against a backdrop of seismic clashes overseas, from the invasion of Poland, Dunkirk, and the ebb and flow of battle in North Africa, to the sinking of merchant vessels by the U-boat menace, and the destruction of great warships such as the *Hood* and *Bismarck*. Later, the disaster at Singapore, the slow, bitter jungle battles against the Japanese, and, finally, the dropping of the atom bombs. You can almost smell the revellers who packed into Worthing town centre to celebrate Victory in Europe, for Mr Harriss was there to witness the sights and sounds of that momentous occasion.

Most of the diary dealt with Worthing, but excursions to Chichester, Bosham and Brighton are just as enlightening in terms of evoking the atmosphere of the wartime era. Of Brighton Mr Harriss wrote on 3 September 1941:

Fine, but a sea mist of varying density obscured the sun throughout the day. To Brighton by bus to secure accommodation for next week at the *Curzon Hotel*, one of the few hotels there still open. For we require a short rest from housekeeping after 15 months since we were last away. Brighton looked sad in the mist. Each time we go there the barbed wire defences on the front grow greater, and more rusty, and shabby with unkempt grass, so that a scene of utter desolation is produced. People mostly look pale and sad and weary.

Of Chichester he wrote on 3 July 1943:

It was pleasant, in the middle of evening, to sit beneath the lime trees [opposite the cathedral]. Evening parade in Chichester is now an animated and picturesque occasion, a panorama of uniforms and bright summer dresses. There are soldiers (here, too, mostly Canadian), fleetmen, airmen (Dominion as well as our own), navy girls, army girls, land girls, fire girls, police girls – all mingled with the general population. It is a scene, primarily, of sparkling youth, very novel and colourful against the mellow background of this venerable city; a scene unequalled in all of the centuries since first the Romans set out its four square streets. Yet it is a scene which we nevertheless trust will, in no long time, vanish like the rainbow.

In the dark hours after Dunkirk Mr Harriss feared what might happen to him if the Nazis invaded and found his diary. He grudgingly admired the tenacity and bravery of the German Army, and during the Ardennes offensive, also known as the Battle of the Bulge, in late 1944, he even described the 'Huns' as 'a wonderful people'. But he also drew satisfaction from the sight of bombers passing overhead on their way to pound Berlin or the Ruhr, and expressed his delight as the Allied noose tightened around Hitler and his wicked henchmen in the spring of 1945.

Mr Harriss made his first entry into the journal, under the heading 'The Gathering Storm', on Sunday 6 February 1938. His handwriting could be described as neat and tidy, but it did take me some time to decipher certain words. I soon came to regard Mr Harriss as a philosopher with an exquisite turn of phrase. I often had to reach for the dictionary to understand words no longer in common usage, which proved quite an education. The diary overflows with gloriously descriptive prose which lifts the literary soul. Here are just two examples:

4 October 1943:
The sky last night was wonderfully alight with stars. It seemed to glow and flash with a glorious riot of scintillating constellations – a spectacle of serene unfathomable loveliness and mystery, which seemed to bid the war-weary soul look up and be refreshed.

8 June 1944:
Miserable weather for the Allied Expeditionary Force. About 6.15am an enormous armada of Allied bombers began passing overhead. I stood at my bedroom window, chilly in night attire, but enthralled. It was indeed a magnificent, inspiring sight. Coming from the NE and in no formal order, they were moving across this district towards the area of the great battle in the West. They might have been all the bombers in the world unleashed, rising continuously above the horizon and moving interminably in successive waves, black against the newly-risen sun. And the empyrean reverberated with the thunder of a thousand engines in unison. The sky at this early hour (4.15am) was mainly clear, but there was a good deal of light, fleecy cloud and also much vapour streaming from the rear of the planes. At first this appeared golden in the sunrise, but as the sun gained altitude the gold became changed to white. There were magnificent effects of great criss-crossing trails, with vast whirls and streaks across the blue; and, near the sun, cloud-piercing rays of light such as one sees depicted in an Easter illumination. And so from the far horizon ever more planes emerged, cleaving the void in silent majesty. It was time now to dress, but, though I must not delay, in my excitement I could not resist frequent visits to the window to devour the spectacle again. By 7.30am the main body had passed into the SW, and the booming of their engines had declined to a distant rumbling; but a few planes continued to fly over until by 8 all was quiet again. Oh, what combative might does such a spectacle afford; a spectacle never before, nor, ever again, to be seen over England, which I have seen with my own eyes! What stupendous days are those we are living through.

Mr Harriss began transcribing his journal on 17 January 1946, and completed what had become a labour of love on 3 April 1948. He painstakingly wrote out two copies – one presented to Worthing Library, where he spent so much of his time, and the other to the Imperial War Museum, London, in June 1955. The library sent its copy to the archives at Chichester several years ago to save it from further damaging wear and tear, but a photocopy, in two weighty volumes, is kept on the shelves in Richmond Road.

Florence died in 1953, and on 6 May of that year an acknowledgement appeared in a local paper stating that Mr Harriss 'wishes to express his warm appreciation of the great kindness of neighbouring friends on the occasion of his recent bereavement'. Mr Harriss died on 17 July 1956, leaving £14,277 (net). His will, published in December 1956, gave his address as 17 Rectory Gardens, Worthing, though he also lived, for a time, at number 10. His bequests included an album of quotations, compiled over more than 30 years, to the head boy of Tonbridge School. The head boy also received £25 as an encouragement to study literature 'which I have found to be the greatest and most lasting pleasure in a long life'. In addition, Mr Harriss bequeathed his epic diary to the town's public library. It would seem, following a phone call to the Town Hall, that the Harrisses were not buried in Worthing, and the author would welcome details on whether they were cremated or buried, and where. The Harrisses had no children, but the diary does mention several relatives, and hopefully his descendants will get to read this book and fill in the gaps.

To conclude, I hope publication of this diary, or rather extended extracts from it, will prove informative, entertaining and thought-provoking.

Illustrations

Photographs of Worthing during the Second World War are rare. The town was, for large parts of the conflict, a restricted military zone. Visitors were banned amid fears that spies might infiltrate and report to the enemy poised across the Channel. After Dunkirk, Worthing was in the front line, and the authorities were twitchy, fearing invasion at any moment. The seafront was fortified, and soldiers with fixed bayonets patrolled the streets. Anybody caught taking photographs, or even making sketches, faced arrest. They might even have been shot by trigger-happy troops in the tension-filled days of 1940-1. Newspapers took photographs of bomb damaged streets, but were not allowed to print the precise locations. They could not even refer to Worthing being attacked, only a 'South Coast town'. So the town's wartime archive was poor until the Walter Gardiner Collection fell into public hands.

Overnight, more than 200 historic black and white images of Worthing at war were added to the archives. They were taken by William Gardiner, whose son, Derek, said:

> At the outbreak of war in 1939 my father was 48 and too old to be called up. Photo processing was closed down but he kept the portrait side of the business open because it was serving a public need. In fact he only opened a few days a week because he hadn't got the raw materials to be able to do more. Everybody was booked in with very tight appointments. Towards the end of the war, around 1944 I believe, he managed to produce a photographic record of Worthing and its defences. He did this despite the security risks and severe restrictions on photography and shortages of film and paper. The threat of invasion had largely receded by 1944, and my father was well-known in the town as a photographer, so he was able to take so many photographs without being arrested.

William toured Worthing taking historic shots of the beach strewn with barbed wire, signs warning of mines, gun emplacements, sports ground allotments, and the pier cut in half to stop German marines using it as an invasion landing stage. He also documented the giant concrete blocks forming a barrier to enemy armour on the promenade, the air-raid warning siren on the Town Hall, the last parade of Worthing Home Guard on Broadwater Green, and various air-raid shelters dotted around the town. Mr Harriss vowed never to step foot in an air-raid shelter, preferring to take his chances out in the open rather than risk being buried alive, or dead. He didn't quite stick to his principles, however, and ducked with his wife into the shelter beneath Steyne Gardens on one occasion.

William recorded the Manor Sports Ground being dug up for vegetables, the gun emplacements at Splash Point and on the roundabout at the junction of South Street, Chapel Road and Warwick Street. The latter was nicknamed 'Hyam Already', and defied, in the latter days of the war, workmen's attempts to demolish it. They finally had to draft in a crane with a heavy weight attached to crush the concrete pillbox. Mr Harriss was there, making mental notes for his diary, which was written up every day. He also chronicled the final parade of the Home Guard on Broadwater Green, which was situated just yards from his home. The photographs are especially fascinating, and perhaps readers can identify uniformed relatives captured on film for eternity.

These images, and many thousands of others, which form the Walter Gardiner Collection, were purchased by West Sussex County Council Library Service courtesy of a Lottery grant. County Local Studies Librarian Martin Hayes said the collection was extraordinary in quality, scope and scale:

It is the output of a Worthing-based business, founded in 1893 as a high-quality portrait photography firm but which was transformed, after the Second World War, into one of the best creators of commercial and advertising images in the UK. Including material inherited from earlier businesses, the photographs cover a period extending from the 1880s to 2000. The images are mainly of Worthing people, places and businesses, although commercial jobs throughout the South-East and beyond were taken on, particularly from the 1960s, making the Collection of regional and national importance. West Sussex County Council Library Service acquired this fabulous collection in 2007. To put this in context, it had taken the Library Service over a century to collect around 50,000 photographs, postcards, slides, engravings, paintings and drawings. The Gardiner Collection has at least 116,000 originals, including full, half and quarter glass plate negatives and medium format film negatives, old photographic prints and prize-winning commercial prints. Through this one acquisition the County photograph and picture collections more than tripled in size. The historical section contains photographs from the 1880s to the 1940s, taken in Worthing and district predominantly, plus some surrounding towns and villages in West Sussex. There are around 9,000 images in this section and over 75 per cent are portraits. It includes breathtaking, pin-sharp images of streets and buildings, and charming portraits of Victorian and Edwardian families. Technically superb images of rural life in the early 20th century also feature strongly and particularly striking are those of working men in the countryside, such as shepherds, sheep-washers and wood-cutters, just before these occupations largely died out. Well over 200 photographs showing Worthing during the Second World War, plus portraits of military personnel, have survived – one of the most extensive records of a wartime town in the South of England. The commercial section consists of over 107,000 photographs commissioned by local and national companies and organisations such as Automotive Design, Bowers & Wilkins audio equipment, Daewoo cars, Link Miles simulators, Nissan cars, Ricardo engineering, Glaxo SmithKline (originally Beecham's) pharmaceuticals, Southern Water and Worthing Borough Council. Many feature farmland on the outskirts of Worthing in the 1950s just before extensive industrial development, and document the building of these factories as well as major civic buildings. There were two reasons for these commissions: to record new machinery or industrial processes, and to advertise new products. Effectively the Collection could be used to study the evolution of British industry from the 1950s to the present.

1 *William Gardiner, who supplied most of the photographs for this book.*

We must go back to 18 December 1893, when Walter Gardiner purchased the Pattison Pett photographic portrait studio in Bath Place, Worthing. Walter and his wife Annie had recently returned to England, after an abortive attempt to start a new life in Australia. This studio was one of the earliest in the town, having been established in 1859 by Samuel Fox. Later owners were Fox's widow Catherine, then daughters Annette and Blanche, James Russell and Sons from 1873, and Edward Pattison Pett from 1882. Walter paid £200 'in respect of the stock in trade and other working interests of the business alone and nothing has been added for goodwill which, in consequence of the condition of things at Worthing, is of no value'. This was a reference to the recent typhoid epidemic which seriously hindered the development of the town at that time.

Walter's first ambition was to be an ironmonger, and it was his wife who influenced him to change direction and indeed trained him. Annie had acquired an in-depth knowledge of photography, in her parents' portrait photography business, before their marriage, and played an active part in most aspects of the business. While Walter prepared the camera, she welcomed the clients, put them at ease, posed them and offered refreshments. She was particularly skilled as a photo colourist, and taught the art to the girls employed by the business. Walter and Annie were members of the Royal Photographic Society and they both exhibited in London from 1895. Their photographs alone illustrated Worthing's *Souvenir of Queen Victoria's Jubilee* in 1898. Although portraiture was to be their main activity for the next 50 years, the firm also made cartes-de-visite, cabinet format portraits, and photographs for local guidebooks and other publications. Indeed they advertised themselves as 'photographers and miniature painters' in the early years. Two editions of W.T. Pike's *Descriptive Account of Worthing* in 1897 and 1899 are largely illustrated with Gardiner photographs, and many of the drawings in various *Album Views of Worthing* published in the later 1890s are based on their photographs. Geoffrey Godden described the firm as 'a pioneer in the introduction of continental-style photographic-based local view cards in Great Britain', from as early as 1894, at least seven years before the widespread publication of picture postcards in the UK.

In 1899 Walter Gardiner borrowed £2,150 to build new premises on two lots, purchased a few years earlier, at The Broadway, 23-5 Brighton Road, Worthing, opposite Steyne Gardens. The new studio opened on 26 July 1900, and within a couple of years the Bath Place premises had been closed. The glass north wall of the new daylight studio can still be seen at the back of the shops. Beginning in 1909, Walter's sons William (aged 18) and Frank (aged 20) took many personal photographs on 5 inch x 4 inch glass plates or film. Some were of the family in Worthing and

Oxford, others of girlfriends or the town and surrounding area. Those taken by Frank are lost but a number of William's remain printable. Among these are a superb and very rare set of early (1910) aviation photographs showing Harold Hume Piffard and his 'Humming Bird' aircraft, and, most unusually, other pilots, plus views, inside and out, of the first hangar built at Shoreham. Although portraiture remained the main photographic activity, William began to photograph houses (interiors and exteriors), gardens, dogs, horses, motor vehicles, etc. Throughout this period, and particularly after 1920, he experimented with less formal photographic styles, taking informal portraits out of doors.

In 1925 the studio and photographic shop were moved to the Arcade which had just been built on the site of the *Royal Sea House Hotel* and other properties. Here the studio was, for the first time, dependent on artificial, i.e., electric, light. Walter found change difficult and the business steadily passed into the control of William during the 1920s and 1930s. William expanded the commercial and wedding side of the business, and began to sell cameras and photographic equipment. He also identified a new business opportunity brought about by the development of smaller, portable, cheaper cameras and an eventual increase in camera ownership. People needed their films processed and printed, and a larger wholesale photo-finishing department was created on the site of an old ice factory in Chandos Road. A much increased number of people, particularly women, were employed from the 1930s onwards, particularly casual workers each summer, in both the amateur developing and printing department, and in the commercial/professional retouching department. Walter, a former Mayor of Worthing, died in 1938. With the coming of the war, William stayed in Worthing and seized an opportunity to create a unique photographic record of a town in wartime.

1938

Sunday, February 6

A dull day with grey sky but mild enough for sitting on the front in the afternoon. F [Mr Harriss's wife] attended evening service at the Congregational Church, Shelley Road. She reported on her return a dull service with dismal discourse about the militarism and unrest in the world at the present time. I deprecate the present tendency of religious ministers to harp on this subject. We get plenty of this in the newspapers. It is not their province, and what good can it do? It is better for people to forget about it if they can. After all, things are still very pleasant in Worthing, and indeed in England generally, so let us be happy while we can although the future be uncertain.

February 20

A very cold night. NE wind mitigated by brilliant sunshine until 2pm. Spent a very pleasant morning on the front. We were rather excited and taken completely by surprise on seeing 'Eden resigns' on newspaper placards.

February 25

The following noble and comfortable words were spoken in the House of Commons yesterday by Lord Halifax, who is Mr Eden's successor as Foreign Secretary. Having remarked that the conquest of Abyssinia could have been stopped by war, he continued: 'I am not afraid of Italy or of any other power. I am not afraid of war in the sense that I fear defeat because I know the temper of this country. And I know that this country would never embark on war unless it thought it both right and inevitable. I also know that, having embarked on war, it would not let go until, as usual, it had won.' He and everybody else, however, detested war.

March 12

Hitler has suddenly marched his troops into Austria and taken charge there. Yet to judge by the newspaper posters, the fight between the pugilists Baer and Farr is judged to be more attractive copy to the enlightened British reader. We preserve, indeed, an admirable phlegm, but some day we shall have to face up to this bully ourselves. I fear it is only too evident that Germany is once again making herself more and more intolerable, and that events are gradually moving to an inevitable course and to war, just as they did before 1914.

April 8

Sunshine most of the day, but a bitter NE breeze. Frost early. After breakfast sat in our front porch in the sun and tried to think it was warm. The principal item of news was the menacing speech by Goebbels on the subject of Germany's demand for colonies. How is it that the German attitude to everybody else so exactly recalls the typical school bully? Other nations are not like that.

May 18

The Germans keep hammering away at their demand for the return of their colonies, lost as a result of the Great War. Hitler is not yet ready [for war]. When he is, in a year or two's time, I believe he will present us with an ultimatum and then there will be war. No one, anywhere, wants the Germans and their Heil Hitler. They are becoming, indeed, the curse and nightmare of the civilised world.

June 14

Field Marshall Sir P. Chetwode is of the opinion that we shall not get involved in war, that we have rearmed in time and that we shall soon be too strong for any nation to attack us.

August 18

Fine and sunny but a high wind. Sat in a shelter near the Dome cinema on Worthing front and watched the holidaymakers enjoying themselves on the beach. The sea was rather rough for bathers, but very beautiful, with its green expanse merging into the distant blue and the white crests of the waves flashing in the sunshine. But one cannot help seeing the dark cloud rising over these happy holiday beaches in the sudden enormous mobilisation of the Germany army. All this just at the climax of their dispute with Czechoslovakia about the Sudeten boundary. One cannot avoid the deduction that Hitler intends a sudden coup against that country. If so, there will be a general war.

September 11

Newspaper posters today are menacing and lurid. We have never been so near to war since 1914. Yet, as I sit on the front after tea, and watch the promenaders, I can detect not the slightest sign of anything affecting their spirits, or of the situation being discussed at all. People were placid and content, or mildly frivolous, in the usual manner of Britons enjoying relaxation by the sea.

September 13

A brilliant day. Temperature about ten degrees higher than average. Hitler's long anticipated speech has brought a little relief, but not much. Of the usual swashbuckling order, with infinite menace to the democracies. But he did not commit himself to war, at the moment.

2   *Worthing seafront, just east of Splash Point. Note the pier in the background, with the decking blown up to prevent German troops using it as a landing stage.*

Something very bad is bound to happen. Dined at Leal's on roast chicken and ham, with two vegetables, followed by plum tart and cream. All very good, for 1s. 9d. per head, which seems cheap to the point of charity. We spent the afternoon in the band enclosure, listening to the excellent orchestra of one Jon Ralfini.

September 14

As we walked into Worthing we noticed a crowd pressing against the windows of the *Worthing Gazette* office in Chapel Street [now Portland Road] reading the latest telegrams. It was just like August 1914. We were revived by a pleasant tea at the Lavender Lady's in Brighton Road, followed by a long walk on the front.

September 15

A brilliant day with a cool north wind. A dramatic surprise this morning. Prime Minister Chamberlain is today flying to Germany to see Hitler. This seems a noble gesture, for in doing so he is putting his pride in his pocket.

September 16

The Prime Minister, having had 'a friendly talk with Hitler', is returning today to consult the Cabinet so delay, at least, has been gained. The Sudeten area of Czechoslovakia seems to be in a state of pogrom and to be clamouring for incorporation into Germany.

September 27

People here are being fitted with gas masks. An official called at our house to know the number of rooms in it with a view to billeting. Some people's nerves are badly strained.

September 28

This morning I noticed a long queue of people of all conditions and ages outside Broadwater Green Parish Room waiting to be served with gas masks. Small children seemed as pleased with their masks as though they had been toys. Later I observed men digging trenches against bombing on a piece of wasteland at the top end of Chapel Street.

In the evening the star of hope returned. Hitler has invited the British and French premiers to meet him and Mussolini at Munich tomorrow to discuss the situation, so we are postponing fetching our gas masks.

September 29

A beautiful day. But it was sad to see great trenches being dug in the fine old turf of Steyne Gardens. Nationwide preparations for war continue. Today the Royal Navy mobilized. To bed after a preoccupied day, having listened to a long broadcast about evacuation from London and billeting – which aroused unfortunate thoughts.

September 30

As I dressed this morning I felt so little expectation of peace being preserved that I was considering in what form to make an offer of voluntary service in the event of War. At the same time I was dimly oppressed by a prospect of personal financial calamity. Then I picked up the paper and read that peace terms had been agreed and signed at Munich at 1.45am! The turnabout in one's mental outlook was so sudden as to produce at first a kind of numbed sensation. There was, of course, immediate relief, but it took time for this to warm up into a glow of rejoicing. I did so as the day progressed, though to me there remains an utter distrust of the lasting good faith of so ferocious and fanatical a creature as Hitler. However, Daniel has issued triumphant from the lions' den, and for the time being at any rate the lions seem tamed and ready to eat out of his hand. It was pretty to listen to the broadcast of the Premier's wonderful reception by the crowd on his return to Downing Street this evening. He is, at the moment, the most popular man in the World, and deserves to be. He says that he considers it 'Peace in our time'. All today we have been conscious of a feeling of holiday. Our 'help', middle aged but still impulsive, exclaimed to F on arriving for her daily task, 'Oh, I must kiss you because it is Peace!' And she did.

October 1

Unsettled. Sun in and out. Mild. I have not yet quite resumed my normal outlook. I suppose everything is going to be all right, as it was before the Crisis was thought of, but my mind is bruised with the shock of recent days and will not assume perfect quietness. Spent a busy morning shopping in the village, one among a smiling throng sensing a pleasant security again. Today no-one minded waiting in the queue at Sainsbury's while the long knives flashed among the cooked meats.

October 21

Sir Samuel Hoare, Home Secretary, has been speaking of Hitler as quite a peaceable, honourable sort of statesman. On the other hand, Lord Hugh Cecil writes that to engage with him in friendly wise is like stroking a crocodile's nose to see whether it will purr!

October 25

To the barber's. What a change of atmosphere since a month ago. Then the Crisis was right upon us. All the talk was of gas masks.

November 28

It is announced that the Prime Minister is to visit Musso, the least ferocious of the two Allied Dictators, in January. This is part of our poor Premier's policy of 'Appeasement', though he seems too old, at 69, to become a sort of minister on tour. The Dictator most necessary to appease is of course Hitler. But owing to his continuing atrocious persecution of the Jews in Germany, he stands for the present outside the pale of possible approach. This persecution in fact has been such to bring my wife to tears as she reads the details of it.

December 2

The newspaper, as usual now, full of alarm. Europe seems to be in ferment, and the Dictators grow so frantic that I fear a big war cannot long be postponed. When the German man eater roars, the Italian jackal yaps – and we and the French run away. So it has been for the past five years. But some day we must stand at bay.

December 23

It was sad to see today, especially in view of the exceptionally severe frost of the past week, which still continues, the throng of unemployed swarming around the Labour Exchange in Chapel Road. It is the day when they receive their dole. There is great depression in the building trade here. After years of building at high pressure Worthing is now over-built, and there are hundreds of unoccupied houses.

December 31

As this year ends we are left wondering what will befall in 1939. For the heathens, in the persons of Hitler and Musso, rage furiously together, seeking whom they may devour next; whilst the British and the Gallic citizen sit in the valley of the shadow of hated war. Luckily, our rearmament has gone some way. We are no longer in the peril in which we stood a year ago. Nevertheless, owing to the development of the aeroplane, our very hearths and homes are no longer safe, as they have been through the centuries. Life seems more helpless than it used to do. We seem to be borne along like flotsam in a mill-race. What will be the event?

1939

September 1

Today at 6am Germany began aggressive warfare against Poland. Tomorrow, France and Great Britain will join in on behalf of Poland and who knows who else will be drawn in? Thus, at 57 years of age, it is my misfortune to have to face a second World War. This terminates my vision of a pleasant retirement at Worthing after 35 years of toil which only ended on the 31st January 1937. International tension has existed as a cloud over life ever since the Munich affair nearly 12 months ago. Well, we stand in a better position now than in 1914, but bombing from the air has become an infinitely formidable menace to both people and buildings. Today is ordered complete mobilisation of our Army, Navy and Air Force. For days past officers and soldiers have become increasingly apparent in the streets. Today also the evacuation of children and infirm persons from London and the great industrial centres has begun. When will they see their homes again? Many have come to Worthing. Knots of little boys and girls have appeared, with identity tickets tied to their coats, under the kindly guidance of members of the local reception staff. At about 7pm an harassed billeting officer quite unexpectedly called and asked us to take in two or three children, to our consternation as we are quite unsuited to the care of these. After discussion I had to compromise by agreeing to take in a lady teacher, she to make her own arrangements for food, but even so this meant much agitation. Our troubles are further accentuated by an order for the concealment of all lights. Spent over an hour on my knees on the floor, whilst the light gradually failed, cutting out brown paper to fix on to the windows. It was a very sultry evening and I have never felt so hot and exercised in my life. Altogether a very sad day and the sudden shock of billeting, with the rest, has overtired and bewildered us.

September 2

We were glad, after lunch at Khong's Cafe, to enjoy nearly two hours of complete rest on the front. Evacuation children everywhere, looking very happy in their new surroundings. No sign anywhere of jitters. Great increase in Territorial uniformed soldiers. Several flights of aircraft passed over to France in batches of a dozen or so. The holidaymakers hardly heeded them. Half-a-dozen London buses, containing old and infirm people from south London, made a somewhat pathetic sight. All day we have been in dread of the calls of those attempting to billet more people upon us. However no one came. There has been difficulty in finding accommodation as more people appear to have been sent down to Worthing than was expected. In the afternoon called at a shop to order dark curtains but all the material is sold out and unobtainable at present.

September 3

As I was sitting in the garden suddenly an alarm was heard rising and falling in moaning blasts. I felt a little disconcerted at first but then decided it was the Worthing fire alarm. However, we heard later that it was in fact the first air-raid warning of the war, the officials having mistaken the return of a British plane from France for an enemy raider. A few moments after our billetee returned prematurely from chapel saying that the minister had announced the declaration of war by Great Britain and in accordance with official desire had stopped the service and asked the congregation to disperse for fear of bombs. All this caused people in our road to collect in knots to discuss the situation, but there was no appearance of excitement. As the news came through Royal Engineer territorials stationed at Muir House, Broadwater, began singing 'Tipperary' and other martial tunes and a little boy of five years of age was heard to cry out 'I am going over to kill Hitler.' After lunch it was pleasant to relax and rest on the seafront. Many people had brought out for the first time their gas masks slung in their cardboard boxes. There was a fine evening of wonderful calm, with a SW breeze just ruffling the surface of the sea. It was most difficult to realise that a state of war existed as one looked towards Brighton and the long placid line of white cliffs as far as Seaford Head. Yet we went to bed all too conscious that we might experience an air raid before morning.

September 4

Last night the *Athenia*, a liner with over 1,400 passengers aboard, many of them Americans, was torpedoed without warning 200 miles off the Hebrides. Happily the loss of life was small as other ships soon came to the rescue. This outrage recalls the *Lusitania* outrage. Still the same brutal, blundering Hun. All entertainments on the front are stopped to avoid the danger of bombs to massed congregations, but the beach is gay with the crowds of evacuated children glowing in the fine weather. This evacuation is going to effect a fine social reform. Think of the benefit to these children of this escape from the unclean squalor of south east London. Saw trenches for air-raid shelters being hastily dug in Steyne Gardens. The depression on the faces of elderly people, sat gloomily watching proceedings, was very noticeable.

September 5

Another lovely day, which seemed to throw a golden veil over the unseen perils of the time. We were worried, however, by domestic cares. The milk, cut down to a single delivery, did not arrive until almost noon. The laundry was collected but a frenzied woman did not know when it would be returned. War has much stimulated neighbourly intercourse. People seem to congregate more and more about gateways to discuss the latest rumours. The Manor Sports Ground, lately the arena of county cricket, has become a position for Yeomanry artillery, guns, waggons and all. Opposite, in the boys' high school grounds, a searchlight party is installed, with a man lying on his back in a revolving chair searching the sky for aeroplanes. Soldiers in fact seem everywhere to have sprung from the ground at the challenge of Hitler. Everywhere there is marching around in companies. F observes them sadly, as lambs preparing to be slaughtered, but they seem in highest spirits.

September 6

Another fine hot day. At 8.15am the air-raid warning sounded, rather to our consternation. Much shopping today in Broadwater village. There is a temporary shortage of a few vegetables but otherwise business is as much as usual. No brown paper, drawing pins or dark curtain material to be had.

September 7

This war in its beginning is very different from the last. This time there are no patriotic concerts, no flags, no recruiting posters, nor speeches in public places, no long companies of newly-recruited heroes in mufti marching along the streets.

September 9

We went into Worthing to lunch. I spent most of the time in the shade of the trees in Denton Gardens. A flight of aeroplanes passed overhead in the direction of France. The ordinary Briton is much more settled and easy in mind than a week ago, owing, no doubt, to the complete absence of the expected and dreaded air raids.

September 10

The continual ringing of our front door bell by other teachers, and even more by pupils of our billetee, has been a great annoyance to us. Today, Sunday, at 9am, she being not yet down, it began again. We were consuming breakfast in what we expected to be domestic peace. There was a ring, then another ring, and a bang on the door. I lost my temper, went to the door and told the girl that this was no public boarding house. The billetee appeared and said I must not turn her callers away. Then left in a rage. I spent the rest of the morning composing a letter to the billeting officer requesting the removal of the billetee, who returned at 9.45pm, remarking sarcastically that she had arranged to leave tomorrow. Now thank we all our God!

September 11

She departed today after a peaceful and ceremonious leave-taking. How slowly time passes in wartime. We have been at war only a week, yet we can hardly recall what it was like to be at peace. Listened tonight to a fine broadcast by Mr Anthony Eden. He was very stirring and eloquent.

September 12

Lunch at an eating house. Some extraordinarily small fillets of plaice were served, without reduction in price. These, the manageress none too tactfully intimated, were but a first instalment of the privations of wartime. Fish, for naval reasons, is scarce. Still too many women about with painted lips, blackened eyebrows, painted or imitation nails, trousers, and blowing tobacco smoke. There is something disgusting about all this at such a time. Are we decadent? One gathers from the newspapers that the Germans show no enthusiasm for this war as they did, as I remember, in 1914. There are no flags and no cheering crowds. Meanwhile Broadwater resounds with harsh words of command, Territorials tramp everywhere, and the Manor Sports Ground is devoted to the exercises of miniature artillery. For the first time there was mention today, in the evening papers, of British troops engaged on the Western Front. Hitherto there had been no mention, even of any having left England.

September 13

We still have to wait for blackout material, and therefore cannot use either of our front two rooms after dark. Small windows can be temporarily obscured with brown paper, but this is not feasible with large bay windows containing many lights.

September 14

We are still both depressed and therefore tired with the strain of the times. F dreads the appearance of a stranger in the road, apprehensive that he may be the harbinger of further billeting. But I gather we are now marked off as 'unsuitable for health reasons' and long may we remain so. Many billetees themselves are sighing for home, and, to the concern of the Government, trickling back to London on their own account. The martyrdom of Poland continues, but the Poles continue to fight at great odds.

September 15

Tonight's wireless reports for the first time that the Navy had destroyed several U-boats. As we have already lost about a dozen good merchant ships through the attacks of these pests, this news is most gratifying – most of the crews of the sunk U-boats must have perished. Vile as are the German methods of carrying on war it must be acknowledged that these crews are the bravest of the brave.

September 16

Here in Worthing the days pass with leaden steps. However, we are no longer without entertainment, for the cinemas and other shows are now permitted. To our surprise the dark curtains which we had ordered about a week ago were delivered last night so we spent most of this morning taking down the old ones and putting up these. The lighting regulations are a dreadful curse. Banged my knee badly against the corner of the writing table as I was climbing about. Swore! There are many Territorial soldiery, RE, RA and Royal Sussex, billeted in the town as there are as yet no camps for them. Worthing town today was further crowded to inconvenience with civilian people. I have never seen it so full. Mostly, I suppose, evacuated children and their relations. A grand cricket match was to have been played today at the Manor Sports Ground between Sussex County and the Worthing Club, but this, like most other sporting fixtures, has been cancelled.

September 17

Going into Worthing after lunch we were startled and dismayed to read on the newspaper posters 'Russia invades Poland'. One more blow to the gallant Poles and to the Anglo-French Alliance.

September 18

Sad news today of the sinking of HMS *Courageous*, an old aircraft carrier, by a submarine.

September 19

I sat down in a shelter to read my *Daily Telegraph*. But I was soon incommoded by the fervid outcry of two youthful evangelists at Splash Point who orated on the joys of Salvation and on eternal Damnation as the wages of sin, so that I was presently fain to change my seat. So home to tea and to more blackout, which seems interminable.

September 20

To our coal merchants as to registering for our coal ration. Each household is to be allowed two tons per annum. The rationing, as it appeared, had affected the bearing of the female assistant, who, in former days, was amiably obliging, now dictatorially independent. In a dearth of coal our custom is evidently no longer something to be sought after.

September 22

The absence of rain since the war broke out has been a great blessing to the newly mobilized troops, and also to the various Home Defence services. As for civilians, the lavishness of peacetime existence is already being curtailed. Today the milkman asked us to keep the metal tops off our milk bottles. They are to be the subject of weekly collection. People are beginning to ask, with a touch of impatience, 'When are we going to do something in the war?' But I don't know what we can do until at least next summer. Apart from our very small Regular Army we have at present nothing but a mass of Territorials, but little trained, or merely recruits. It is clear that for the time being the French must hold the fort on the Western Front.

September 23

The battery of Yeomanry Artillery (anti-tank) has suddenly disappeared from the Manor Sports Ground with all its little motorised cannon, cars and lorries, it is whispered, to France. They are a fine looking body of men and we shall miss them.

September 24

Thermometer in the north room was at just below 60 degrees this morning, which indicates the changing season. We look forward to the winter with dread, with fuel and light to be reduced. Petrol rationing began yesterday, cars being limited to petrol sufficient for 200 miles per week. As we have no car this regulation meets with my hearty approval. The number of cars in use is an annoyance and a public danger. Curious to witness 'no lights' regulation in force. No street lamps, buses suddenly looming out like dim leviathans, cars showing only heavily obscured lamps. For the pedestrian who leaves the footpath, peril, despite much whitewash everywhere to help them.

September 26

I was amused and interested to notice today when passing along Ann Street that the shop hitherto occupied by the local branch of the British Union of Fascists for their business and display of literature was closed and empty. Their leader, Sir Oswald Mosley, was billed to address a meeting here just as war broke out. It was, however, very wisely for him and his, cancelled. For although the Union seems to have had a certain following in Worthing, the citizens are in no mood to suffer opposition on the issue of the war, which has come to be regarded as a crusade.

September 27

Miss B, our former billetee, who had left us for 'alternative accommodation' more than a fortnight ago, called and asked for the remains of her packet of Typhoo tea. However, her visit was in vain, for assuming that she had abandoned this delicacy, with certain more perishable items, on leaving, we had ourselves consumed them! She cloaked her invasion in a proper guise of amiability, to which we made a suitable response.

September 29

The fine weather enables the Royal Sussex Territorials who occupy Muir House to use the garden to the full extent. This garden has been one of the beautiful old world sort. It still contains a magnificent chestnut tree, a spreading mulberry, and a walnut, the last in the decay of extreme old age. Around about are lawns and undergrowth. Here squads may be seen reclining at their ease whilst an officer lectures to them at a blackboard; or springing about in shorts at physical exercise. Others sit about under the trees cleaning their accoutrements. From time to time a harsh word rings out. The front of the house is sandbagged against aerial attack, and a sentry with fixed bayonet stands always at the gate enduring the battery of many curious eyes. These premises were until recently the ancient vicarage of the Parish Church of Broadwater. What a change.

September 30

The Government keep telling us that there is no shortage of foodstuffs. But although this may be true in a general sense, there are local shortages. Sainsbury's seem to have been without sugar for over a week, and I had to try three shops today before I could get any bacon rashers, and what I did get were indifferent, and dear at 1/6 a lb. Prices are already rising.

October 1

A grey bleak day. NE wind. We sat in until after tea, but were miserably chilly, for, owing to the fuel rationing, we did not feel justified in using our electric fires yet. F went to bed after lunch for combined rest and warmth, while I stayed in the dining room with a rug up to my middle.

October 2

All the talk is about the probable duration of the war. Germany is obviously not so rich, nor her army so well trained as in 1914, and Hitler's position is less assured than the Kaiser's. So many think that the Hun will crack much sooner than in the last war. Looking at pictures of German troops in the papers, I am struck by the melancholy expression in their faces. One never sees a jovial-looking German soldier. All this is not to say that we have not a very rough road to tread for long enough.

October 3

The wind foul, foul, dead foul, as Nelson used to say. Still, eternally, NE, more of it and colder! After lunch in Worthing we stayed on the front in such shelter as was possible against the assault of the wind. Overheard this dialogue: 'God bless you lady! Will you help an old soldier and buy a sprig of white heather?' Lady: 'I am sorry I have no coppers.' Reply: 'Silver will do, lady!'

October 4

Into Worthing to tea at Mitchell's. Here were rich surroundings, cosily illuminated, and well warmed, wherein we found a great content. Afterwards we sought more free warmth and light in the public library; but here again the tyranny of war intervened and everyone was bundled out at sunset (today 6.30pm), although the place is normally open until 9pm.

October 5

We lunched very sufficiently at Khong's, where the only indication of war shortage rested in their inability to provide bacon to attend liver. Afterwards we sought a digestive rest in a shelter on the front, but rain beginning to fall heavily, the abomination of desolation supervened, and we were miserably marooned there for most of the afternoon.

October 7

The Government is exhibiting various red on blue posters bearing texts in white letters such as 'Don't help the enemy – a careless word may disclose a vital secret', or 'Freedom is in peril. Defend it with all your might', and others of an encouraging kind. They appear on hoardings, on the tarpaulin tops of railway lorries, and in banks, and in places where one eats.

October 9

I was awakened prematurely this morning by a southerly gale accompanied by very heavy rain. The gale abated later, but not the rain, which continued practically without ceasing all day. To Sainsbury's in Broadwater and found they had no cooked ham to cut, and no uncooked bacon of any kind.

October 10

Wet morning, but we spent a healthful afternoon on the front, blessed by a liberal allowance of sunshine. It was low tide and there was that delicious pungent scent from the seashore which prevails here with a southerly wind. The air seemed full of ozone. Despite Government injunction many evacuated mothers and children have returned to their houses in 'dangerous areas'. Many people in the absence of bombing seem to be living in a fool's paradise, but evacuation is apt to be as unpleasant for the evacuated as it is for their hosts.

October 11

Prices are rising. Butter has gone up from 1/3 to 1/6, and back bacon rashers from 1/4 to 1/10. We are quite content with streaky, but they are difficult to find. One observes that the days pass much more quickly than they did at first. F no longer remarks, 'Well, that is another day gone. The war is one day less.' We are told that the first 158,000 British troops have been transported to France without casualty. It is distressing to notice the bullying of the Baltic States by Russia, and now it is Finland's turn. Yet nothing can be done about it. Russia is too big to tackle.

October 12

This morning I went for a walk down Forest Road to Upper Brighton Road and home by the Green. Inspected the Territorial Drill Hall with military office in course of erection at the corner of Forest Road. This is very large and was begun a few months before the outbreak of war, being now 20ft high. There were but few men at work, and of those two were engaged with the eternal feminine chatting across the fence. There was every evidence of slow, easy and comfortable building. Perhaps these premises are required rather for the next war than for this one.

October 13

We walked into Worthing in the afternoon. Many lurid newspaper posters, e.g., 'Nazis Rage At Chamberlain', 'Germans Say The War Is Now On', and 'The Air Force Will Speak'. Well, I think everyone is glad to have the decks cleared for action. There can be no end until there is a beginning. The Huns will not have it all their own way, that is very certain. But what a curse they are to the world, to be sure.

October 14

We were faced with the lamentable news of the sinking, apparently by a U-boat, of HMS *Royal Oak*, with the loss of some 800 lives. The loss of this 29,000 ton battleship, coming so soon after that of the aircraft carrier *Courageous*, must arouse acute anxiety as to the protection of our battle fleet.

October 15

It was raining when we rose today, and had apparently been raining for many hours, and it continued to rain heavily without ceasing until 6pm, after which the downpours gradually dwindled and stopped. The constant rains of the past fortnight must have more than atoned for the September drought. Perhaps this record, on a usually superfluous subject, is permissible, since the newspapers are not allowed to make any reference to the English weather, on account of the 'State of Emergency'.

October 16

The sun returned today and produced a wonderful contrast to yesterday. I went out to shop in the village first thing after breakfast, particularly to enjoy the sunshine after being immured all yesterday, but also because in these days the early bird gets the rashers. They are soon sold out. It was a perfect autumn day and War's alarms seemed far away.

October 17

I began to wonder whether the Government policy in the months before the war of pressing the enlistment of Territorials was wise. The physical standard required of Territorial recruits is by no means high. Now that they have all been mobilized one notices many undersized and sickly looking youths in their ranks, and an undue proportion wear glasses. They look as though they would never become soldiers capable of meeting German troops in battle.

October 18

In the afternoon strolled round Broadwater Green, which presented a sight very different from that of peacetime when, at this season, it would have been almost deserted. Now, the triangular prolongation at the village end is a mass of untidy excavation. The grass has disappeared and an elaborate underground air-raid shelter has been in course of erection there for several weeks. There is a network of trenches in course of being lined with cement and fitted with a drainage system and other semi-permanent complications. I do not, however, believe that it will ever be wanted, but the local authority must not take risks. Further on, the Green itself was thronged with hundreds of schoolboys evacuated from London. Some were playing football and others performing physical exercises under the direction of masters. These boys added nothing to the gaiety of the scene, for they wore black caps with white piping, dark coats and dark grey flannel trousers, and seemed mostly to possess dark sallow complexions and dark hair. They looked indeed as though the metropolitan soot had even been absorbed into their flesh.

October 19

A vile day. Thermometer in house down to 52 degrees, the lowest yet. Rain came on about 9am and continued briskly until 2.30pm. As I cannot go out I spend much of the morning with a rug over my shoulders trying to keep warm, as I feared to use the electric stove on account of the fuel rationing. By bus into Worthing for lunch. Afterwards, to escape the elements, we peregrinated to Woolworth Palace, where I purchased a pocket diary for next year, we inspected wonders bright and beautiful, and watched small children with faces just rising above the counter, breathing over the sweets.

October 20

We usually spend this day (Friday) mostly at home, there being household duties of a special kind. So, after lunch, we walked into Worthing fully intending to return home to tea; when F suddenly pulled me into a teashop, and our good resolution became instantly void! The cosy Worthing teashops offer a seductive temptation to tired pawns of war at the fag-end of their day. Arrived home just in time for our blackout. This is a daily ceremony which demands an anxious care since any neglect may attract the lurking constable or air-raid warden. Each night not only do I have to arrange curtains everywhere so that no glint of light appears, but two small windows have to be fitted with cardboard shutters. All irksome, but so far we have frustrated the enemy at the gate.

October 21

Going into the village this morning to shop I noticed a large placard at Sainsbury's window requesting customers to be easy in their demands for butter and bacon, and ending with the wheeze 'Grin and Share it!' Is not such wit unworthy of the firm? On entering was allowed only half-a-pound of rashers after requesting a pound. The Government have rescinded their harsh order

3 *Worthing wartime air-raid wardens.*

reducing the private consumption of gas and electricity by 25 per cent. We are to be allowed to use the same as last year. Thank God!, Thank God!!, Thank God!!! Our worst immediate affliction is removed.

October 22

Sunday. We went for a pleasant walk out by way of Poulter's Lane, and home by Lavington Road. The war has become so uneventful that one is in danger of relapsing into one's ordinary pre-war attitude of mind. Nothing yet is as one feared – no air raids, no ruthless German Army offensive, millions of men stand face to face in arms. It is an odd war. At about 6.30pm we went down to the front and back. It was our first real experience of the blackout – no street lamps; and the long rows of shops, in peacetime even on the Sabbath brightly lit, now blank and shrouded, presented a weird spectral effect in the evening haze. But a three-quarter moon assured us against any inconvenience in walking.

October 23

The company of RE Territorials suddenly disappeared from their headquarters in Muir House. Whither we are not to ask. The war is already hitting small shop businesses. There are more shops than usual empty. Sometimes the proprietor has gone to the war, and sometimes it is a luxury trade that has wilted before the new conditions. One notes with sorrow 'The Lavender Lady' tea house in Brighton Road, which we have known long since to our pleasurable advantage. Alas! That cosy haven is now 'To Let', and the Lavender Lady herself, so cunning at cakes, no more seen.

October 25

Sunny but very cold. The transition from Autumn to Winter has set in early this year. Walked down to Worthing to tea and felt better after roes on toast, with chocolate, negotiated in the luxury of Mitchell's in the Arcade, though one does feel in these days that perhaps one ought not to be indulging constantly in such places whilst there is so much peril on the sea. We seem gradually to be hunting down the U-boats, but I think our ships have suffered and are suffering more than most people anticipated from this pest. It is galling when one reflects that under the Versailles Treaty the Huns were forbidden to have U-boats at all. It is melancholy to read about the drowning of sailors and of innocent passengers. When we had the Huns right down why did we not keep them down? Now all has to be done again at the sacrifice of another generation of young men. How feeble in foreign affairs seems democratic government.

October 27

Shopping this morning I did not succeed in obtaining bacon anywhere. Sainsbury's had two or three lbs of it for a few minutes, but it was soon snapped up by the crowd on the counter, who were like a pack of hungry wolves.

October 29

Worthing at the weekend is lively now with the presence of numbers of the Army, Navy and Air Force on leave, enjoying the delights of England, home and beauty. Yesterday at midday I observed a pair of warriors who had, too obviously, become the victims of each other's hospitality. Such instances of indulgence are rare here at present in spite of too much opportunity.

October 30

Our neighbour, who belongs to the civilian Observer Corps, has been spending part of the night, from 9 to 12, watching and listening for German aeroplanes at the end of the Pier. He also has three evacuees in his house, and runs a one-man business. So we dub him a patriot. Muir House is strangely quiet now that the military occupants of the mobilization have departed for fresh fields.

October 31

A grim day, dark and damp, with a cold E wind. After tea walked down to the Reference Library. Emerging at 7pm, I realise how very black and overwhelming the blackout can be. Until my eyes became accustomed to the darkness I could not see at all. I wandered from the path into the road outside the Town Hall, without being aware of it, and soon had a motor car cheeping warningly at my heel! I felt thoroughly confused and nervous. Presently found some relief in 'shadowing' someone who had a small torch. Without that, and the occasional muffled gleams from the buses and other traffic, I should have had very great difficulty in reaching home in Broadwater. Very shocked today by our Government's disclosure of the fiendish cruelties practised by the Nazis in the German concentration camps, mostly on Jews.

November 1

I feel sometimes that in my retired condition I am more of a liability than an asset to the country in the present emergency, and hope that this record may be some justification for my existence through it.

November 2

The Food Minister, Mr W.S. Morrison, has just made the rather staggering announcement that the long threatened food rationing will begin about the middle of next month, at least as regards bacon and butter.

November 4

An old lady at an adjoining table at Khong's, where we lunched, had occasion to ask us 'is life worth living?' On arrival home this evening was met with a bill of £5 10s. for new dark curtains. Altogether for our little six room house the detestable blackout will have cost me £7.

November 5

We walked out along Sompting Road in the morning, meeting many groups of young evacuees of various shapes and sizes. Returning by way of Broadwater Green we inspected the exterior of the air-raid shelter there which has now been completed. I could not resist the feeling that I would prefer to take my chance of death on the airy spaciousness of the open Green to seeking refuge in this dungeon.

4   *The air-raid shelter on Broadwater Green. Mr Harriss vowed to take his chances out in the open rather than risk being buried alive.*

November 7

Here is a true story of the time. A Worthing resident was awakened one night by a noise outside his premises. He lit up and opened his window to investigate. 'Shut that window there, put out that light', rang out sternly from an authoritative voice. Scenting a police patrol and a probable fine, the frightened citizen hastened to obey. Next morning he discovered that 5cwt of coal had been stolen from his shed.

November 9

Today there came to see us F's young nephew B, who has returned from farming in Canada, anxious for his people in London, threatened with bombing, and has now enlisted in the Royal Artillery. I trust that in this arm he, an only son, is less likely than the infantry to become a casualty. After tea I performed the melancholy service of making his will for him. A serious but admirable young man.

November 10

The paper full of news of an attempt to assassinate Hitler by means of a bomb whilst he was addressing a Nazi crowd in the Beer Hall at Munich. The Queen of the Netherlands and others have sent him congratulations on his escape. In view of the fact that the Huns are massing on her frontier with a view to the invasion of Holland it would seem that the Queen would have insulted her dignity better by saying nothing. Had tea at WH Smith's, as did many others. Altogether the outward prospect was very pleasant, but in view of Hitler's recent threat to this country, and that the posters of the evening papers full of immediate menace to Holland, there was a sense of crisis oppressing people's minds, which has been absent during the recent long lull.

November 11

The Dutch have begun to flood their land to meet the likely German invasion. This is our day of remembrance for those killed in the last German war.

November 14

As the expected air raids have not so far occurred, schoolchildren are to be allowed out without gas masks. The majority of elders at first obeyed the official injunction to carry them, but as the weeks passed more and more of these have fallen from grace until is seems slightly contemptible, nay craven, to carry one.

November 15

Mild, SW wind. Heavy showers until 3.30pm. Gas man called this morning to read the meter and bring dirt into the hall. He intimated that, owing to the shortage of men, he would in future call quarterly instead of monthly. Well, we will not quarrel with that. Bravo Hitler! I noticed this morning one of the motor vans driven by gas generated by a machine on a small trailer. These vans are introduced to save petrol, which has to be so husbanded now for wartime purposes that private cars are allowed only five gallons per month.

November 20

Fine light NW wind. After lunch to a lecture in the Pier Pavilion by a journalist and Socialist MP named Vernon Bartlett on the international situation. He foresees a military stalemate and a revolution in Germany about March. The German people had been led all along to believe that Britain would not fight. Everyone is anxious for more information about this odd war that never begins, but from him [Mr Bartlett] we did not gain any.

November 22

At the boating lake on the front this afternoon we came across a squad of auxiliary firemen in steel hats practising with motor engine and hoses against the time when the Huns drop incendiary bombs on Worthing. A squad of soldiers now lives permanently in a hut on the High School recreation ground in Broadwater Road, equipped with searchlight and machine gun, so we are well protected. It seems an unenviable job for these soldiers out there in the mist and wet, but I suppose they would rather be there than in the trenches at the front.

November 29

As a change from Khong's we lunch at palatial Mitchell's, where the proprietors stand and smile on the proceedings, for which the press of eaters certainly gives them cause. Later F patronised Mr H. Lodge's Orchestra in the Pier Pavilion.

December 1

Very mild. SW wind. It is worthy of note that up to this date the British Army in France has had no fighting and suffered no casualties inflicted by the enemy.

December 3

Sunny morning. Stormy showers with ultimate tempest and downpour afternoon and evening. We had a very pleasant walk about the pretty district of Broadwater in the morning sunshine. Met many families of evacuees with parents, united happily for the weekend.

December 4

Showers and bright intervals. Very cold. Strong W wind. The war is outwardly stagnant, but we know immense devilish preparation is going on behind the scenes. We live in the heavy quietness of a gathering storm. The war is always present at the back of one's mind.

December 5

In the afternoon I escorted F to the Rivoli cinema to view a film featuring dancers Ginger Rogers and Fred Astaire.

December 13

F accompanied Mrs T to a concert at the Assembly Room under the direction of London County Council, with evacuated children as performers. Mrs T took her three evacuees and the concert was a great success. All took tea at WH Smith's Tudor Cafe. The evacuees, boys aged about nine years, were very nicely conducted and consumed crumpets and cakes with silent and deep concentration.

December 15

It is a dismal time of year. Nature seems dead but the exciting news of Commodore Harwood's glorious naval action off Montevideo has supplied some much-needed cheer. Three British cruisers with only light armour and six or eight inch guns drove the German pocket battleship *Graf Spee*, disabled, into harbour there. The *Graf Spee*'s guns are 11 inch and quite able to sink the cruisers if she had hit them. The most gallant action. The best news since the war began.

December 16

Very cold. N wind. Dull. Made my first purchase of margarine since the last war. The two of us are allowed only half a pound of butter per week so have to make up with this substitute. Yet the butchers' shops are groaning under the burden of masses of meat and turkeys. In fact, there seems to be a profusion everywhere except as to butter and bacon. There is nothing visible in Worthing to

5 *The playing field at Worthing High School for Boys, Broadwater Road, was partially turned into allotments as the nation was urged to 'dig for victory'.*

suggest the war except that the police carry steel hats and gas masks. Soldiers are rarely seen since the Territorials left. In absence of important events most people seem to have ceased to worry about the war. Yet I read that a vast massed attack by the Huns from the air is a certainty in the spring, and there is still a sickening daily toll of ships.

December 24

We walked out at noon and sunned ourselves joyously. In the evening listened to the wireless. Carol service from King's College Chapel especially notable. After tea, I went out alone up Hill Barn Lane. The silent depths of the wooded near-Downs country, half illuminated by the moon, was very beautiful.

December 25

N wind. Calm. Temperature well above freezing point. A pleasant morning but about 2pm a fairly thick mist came on, making conditions dismal. People have gone about very quietly in Worthing today, though there have of course been feasts indoors. Monumental events must separate this Xmas from the next. How shall we stand then?

December 26

Lunch at Lyon's since our usual eating places were closed. Worthing seemed like a city of the dead, paced by lost souls treading along avenues of closed-up shops.

December 29

Sunshine all day, but very cold. Three or four inches of snow covered everything this morning and I busied myself after breakfast in sweeping some of it away. The scene was as beautiful as Switzerland in winter. Old inhabitants say that snow rarely lies on the ground in Worthing.

1940

January 1

Cold. Snow gradually thawing away but still objectionable. Wind E. Some welcome sunshine. Actual rationing has not yet begun, but tradesmen have in weeks past been kept in very limited supply of provisions. The war is for the time being overshadowed by a ghastly earthquake in Turkey. 400 square miles in Anatolia in a state of ruin, with over 45,000 deaths.

January 2

Corporation employees, with rather pointless zeal, were painting the electric light standards in our road this morning, for they must not be used during the war. In odd corners of the town it is sad to observe the number of small shops which have had to close down because of the war. 'To Let' notices are becoming all too numerous.

January 3

A very hard job rising at 7am in a room registering 45 deg! All day we were rendered miserable by the cold. Outwardly the war seems to have almost petered out everywhere.

January 5

Dined off what will probably be our last meal of cut ham for the duration of the war, for rationing of bacon and ham begins on Monday, with a ration of only one quarter of a pound per week to cover both. Walked on the front alone this afternoon. A large company parading in the sunshine, many aeroplanes overhead and here and there flocks of seagulls descending for scraps.

January 7

Sunday. Very mild and close. Fog all day. Dead calm. I went out after lunch, but I could not see more than 20 yards ahead. Was able to assist two polite young RNVR sub-lieutenants in Warren Road who had quite lost their bearings.

January 8

A grand day. Slightly colder, sunshine all day. Compulsory rationing of sugar, butter and bacon (including cooked ham) began today and so at Sainsbury's this morning they clipped off coupons from our two ration books in exchange for our week's half pound of butter. I think the bacon ration of one quarter of a pound per week is insufficient at this stage of the war. This is only about 25 per cent of what the average person normally eats. Lunch at Khong's. Here the rationing had caused the withdrawal of the sugar and I had to consume my grapefruit in sorrow and bitterness.

January 13

After lunch to Barnwell's nurseries off Montague Street to procure some kind of floral decoration for the lounge, to honour guests expected tomorrow. After traversing vainly a maze of passages and greenhouses we purchased an unsatisfactory little primula for 9d.; cheap if not beautiful.

January 14

The thought occurred to me today how slowly time passes during a stationary war – how it drags. Although at my age the years are precious, yet, in the present emergency, I certainly wish for the time to pass quicker.

6 *A close up of the Southern Pavilion, turned into an island by the destruction of the decking.*

January 15

Lunching at Khong's, we found that, during the cold, a regular customer was suddenly dead, four waitresses were absent ill, and a good deal of 'barking' amongst those still present. Certain of our water pipes have frozen for a couple of hours or so.

January 21

We listened to Mr W. Churchill, First Lord of the Admiralty, on the wireless last night. He is by far the most effective of the Government speakers, though not the most polished. He is rugged, vehement, bellicose and confident, and fired with indignation against Nazi ideas. He speaks as though he thoroughly enjoys doing so. His speeches kindle one's patriotic ardour and are a good tonic to those who feel that they are brought to the brink of one of the greater cataclysms of world history.

January 28

A grisly day. After about 24 hours of continuous rain it froze again in the early hours of this morning, so that the roads and paths were covered with a sheet of ice. During the morning it hardly thawed. There was no sunshine, and heavy rain fell again from 2.30pm. We went out for an hour at noon to stimulate our circulation, but it was perilous walking. Very few people about, and fewer cars. I have never seen the paths as well as the roads in such a dangerous state. People stepped delicately in constant dread of falling. What a terrible winter we have had, and are having. Many evacuated children attended the Saturday afternoon variety show at the Pier Pavilion yesterday. They were asked to choose a song to sing and they chose 'We'll Hang Out The Washing On The Siegfried Line'. This song, now very popular in England, is said to have given great offence to Hitler. Another favourite song of the moment is 'There Will Always Be An England', which has a sweet air and a real pathos in these perilous days.

January 29

A truly terrible day. Temperature at 9am, 29. On coming down one noticed that the raindrops were frozen, and icicles were hanging from fences and gates.

February 3

My morning was largely spent hunting for sausages, which I failed to obtain. Tea at Mitchell's. Every table in the sumptuous hall filled with eaters – fair women and brave men (in blue and khaki), lovely children (there are many in Worthing). 'You would not think there was a war on,' remarks F.

February 11

This return of the cold has shattered me. Could not get warm all day. We came to Worthing particularly to enjoy warm winters. The two we have had could hardly have been colder. This one seems endless.

February 12

On waking this morning found the land once more completely covered with snow. This for the third time this winter, probably an unprecedented occurrence for Worthing. Snow showers all day.

After lunch at Leal's, F to Odeon picturehouse. Perhaps owing to the severity of the season, the fair sex have adopted a fashion of wearing hoods over the head, pointed at the back, like little pixies in a fairy book.

February 13

A constable called for particulars with a view to billeting a soldier in the house. He stated that 2,000 soldiers were coming to Worthing and remarked, rather hopelessly, 'I suppose we shall have to put them out in the fields.'

February 17

Here is a tragedy of the war, a distant ripple from the stone cast by Hitler. Mitchell's of Worthing have stopped making their unequalled coconut ice, which invariably forms our second course when we lunch at home. This is the unkindest cut. This because their sugar supply has been reduced by 40 per cent.

February 20

Very mild and calm. The Army Service Corps have made a horrid mess of the corporation [Manor] cricket ground. Save the pitch, it is churned up, mud everywhere, a sight to make a cricketer weep. A party of these soldiers has been drilling in our road.

February 25

Many rank and file soldiers about in their sad-coloured khaki. Yesterday, servicemen on the front were much more ornamental. There was an air vice-marshal, now a little stout and elderly perhaps, but his azure uniform glorious with gold lace and medal ribbons; a spruce grey-haired naval surgeon, equally glorious; a colonel of Scottish Rifles, in dark green and plaid; and a Scots Guards captain, with red and white chequered cap band. These touches of the old military glamour alleviated the general drab and warmed the imagination.

March 1

March came in with proverbial ferocity, a bitter NE gale raged all night and throughout the day. People walked with heads down and pinched faces. There was sunshine most of the day but it was a mockery in the face of the tempest. Our garrison, the RASC, having nothing serious to do, continued their squad drills, mostly on the front now, and drove their very numerous lorries constantly about the streets of the town. Officers are rushed about in little motor cars, in what to an uninformed civilian onlooker seems an elaborate facility. Lorries and cars alike are painted a kind of mud colour with darker streaks, and look sadly shabby.

March 4

We sat for a long time in a shelter and watched in glorious panorama of sea and sunshine a girls' school do rounders on the sands and little children casting pebbles about in a usual scene of peace. Yet we know that spring must bring a mighty clash.

March 8

Poor Gladys [the author's home help] came this morning in a tizz about the two soldiers billeted upon her. She says she cannot call her home her own. They are untidy and leave things about, and are often in the kitchen cleaning their equipment. Whenever one of them is away for the night, the beggarly 6d. paid for him is stopped, though she cannot let his bed to anyone else.

March 9

Intense frost at night. The countryside white at daybreak. Lunching at Mitchell's my pleasure much diminished by the filling coming out of a great tooth as I ate, after having stood firm for many years.

March 10

We took two constitutionals about Broadwater. Very little growth in the gardens as yet owing to the constant night frosts. Large numbers of wallflowers have been largely destroyed, and the rest, except where specially sheltered, stand white and withered.

March 13

There has lately been talk of a peace between the Russians and Huns, and now it is announced. After all the gallantry and apparent success of the Finnish Army it comes as a shock. It is yet another victory for shameless aggression and a great encouragement to the Huns.

March 14

A return to mid winter. Heavy snow 10.15am to 1.45pm, much of it thawed as it fell, but the fall was so heavy that it gradually gained on the thaw.

March 15

A very severe frost last night. There has been yet another attack on our citadel. I had just sat down to read the paper at 10am, jaded with cold and matrimonial toils, when a lady called, apparently to follow up the recent circular from the Ministry of Health, and to ascertain our capacity for taking evacuees. Had to go through the particulars of poor F's health once more, and strove calmly and patiently to fend the woman off, but she was very persistent. She made a note eventually and left in peace. Poor F, constantly anxious about these callers, is afraid to be left alone in the house lest one of these harbingers of billeting, police, military or civilian, call and give her a fright. Anxiety wears her more than I like to see.

March 16

We spend the last half of the day in Worthing, but the remains of a headache made me feel uncharitable, and I can find no delight in the madding Saturday crowd, sprinkled o'er with trousered slatterns and scarlet-lipped 'lovelies'. How rarely to be seen now English beauty fresh and unspoilt by low art. Nearly all now proclaim the ugly influence of the cinema.

March 17

Amused to see in a shop window yesterday a postcard displaying a flamboyant coloured portrait of General Sir W.E. Ironside, now Chief of the Imperial General Staff. He happens to have been at Tonbridge School partly at the same time as myself, and is the first of my generation to have become a star in the picture postcard firmament. Such is fame! He was not contemptible as a footballer and I well remember him scrummaging in a field by Tonbridge.

March 18

At last, an ideal spring day. Today at 10.15am the sweep came and swept the chimney of the Ideal Boiler, and we therefore much put about setting out dust sheets and newspapers to prevent the soot. A very clean sweep, but demanded 2s. when we had expected 1/6.

March 19

We began to discuss family economies and F remarked, 'We have only about 20 years to live so why not spend our money and enjoy it while we can?'. 'The difficulty is,' I replied, 'that we don't know how long we may require it. We don't want to end our days in the County Court.' Which amused and silenced her.

March 23

We spent most of the day in Worthing. A bewildering crowd of trippers everywhere, especially in our usual haunts of refreshment. Lunch at Mitchell's, where a polite gentleman of the old school of courtesy ceremoniously tendered to F the sugar bowl for her coffee. She returned appropriate thanks, and then discovered it was empty! Multitude of people around the town who seemed willing, and what is more, perfectly able, to spend freely. The economic frost of war has not as yet apparently begun to touch this fortunate nation. It was fine enough this afternoon for F to sit in the open in the bandstand and enjoy the band of the Royal Berkshire Regiment.

March 24

On the main roads there was no lack of cars, their owners, apparently, having been saving up their petrol ration for this holiday occasion.

March 25

I have never seen a greater crowd on the front than there was this afternoon. A Bank Holiday crowd is always an interesting study. Today, as often before, it prompted in me a reflection that our civilisation fails utterly to produce a good national physique. How rarely one sees a really fine specimen of man or woman. Most seem puny or undersized, with wan, knobbly faces.

March 29

F called at Mrs T, who had three evacuated boys quartered with her. She is middle aged and getting worn out with the work of them. At the pittance paid it is sheer slavery. Yet the Government care not.

April 1

Gladys arrived to her labours a little late and not a little perturbed. For having, soon after 2am, been called downstairs to admit the soldier billeted upon her, she found him about an hour later harbouring a wench in his bedroom. This hussy had brought a cur as escort, which, being left in the garden, became impatient, aroused Gladys by his barking, so that she heard suspicious sounds through the bedroom wall. She, although without her husband, who was on night work, courageously admonished the soldier and ejected his trull. This hero, who had previously been stationed in the Holy Land, pleaded as his excuse his love for the baggage and that it was his last night in Worthing. He and his 1,500-odd comrades of the Army Service Corps have in fact left, with their vehicles, this morning.

April 2

The streets of Worthing seem quiet this morning owing to the departure of the Army Service Corps. They were a very nondescript lot to look at, ranging from men over 6ft high to some less than 5, and having little of the soldierly bearing that we used to know. As I saw them slouching abroad in their ugly drab battledress I could not help mentally harking back to their dashing prototypes of 40 years ago, in dark blue cavalry kit with white facings, very smart and tight, and jingling spurs withal. And indeed it is sad to see the extinguishment of light and colour and pride in arms now that the machine has ousted the noble horse.

April 3

With F to a matinee performance of *The Pirates of Penzance* at the Pier Pavilion, the first time I have been to a play for years. Found this one twaddly and jerky, like others of its kind. But I am no Savoyard. One or two pretty airs, and the rest of the music nothing. Some very good singing by the Worthing Amateur Operatic Society, and pretty dresses. But the play gives no scope for acting; it is but a series of songs. It began at 12.45pm and we were out soon after 4.30 – to my great relief.

April 4

W wind freshening to gale force. It was so rough on the front that after lunch at Lyon's on poached eggs, and a little shop with F, I was glad to seek a quiet retreat in the Reference Library.

April 5

We strolled out after tea and as we were coming home by Broadwater Road three heavy anti-aircraft guns, drawn by lorries, containing their crews, passed us, going north. A couple of years ago, in such a town as Worthing, that would have been a sight to gaze and wonder at, but today it scarcely causes a pedestrian to turn his head. We were amused to notice the white surfaces of the now blank hoardings near the railway station scrawled with crude portraits of Hitler by proletarian youth.

April 7

I notice that Mosley's men, who closed their Fascist shop in Ann Street on the outbreak of war, are again installed there; and meek maidens, and not very virile men, stand at street corners mutely offering to passers-by their newspaper *Action*. This journal they advertise by the surreptitious defacing with chalk of walls and hoardings. But its sale is very small. Fascism makes, and will make, no strides in Britain.

April 8

One of spring's harbingers, the perennial 'Stop-me man', hath lately reappeared on our streets, trundling Wall's ice cream pram. Since his allowance of sugar is now reduced by 50 per cent, I had been in doubt whether we should be so favoured this year. There is a very small popular song of the day, so popular that it is often to be heard, lustily, from the little round mouths of juveniles in the streets. It goes 'Roll out the barrel, roll out the barrel for fun!' Very heartening for all in the present emergency.

April 9

My 58th birthday. It will be one of the great days in history, this day when the long quiescent Second Great War suddenly flared up into intensity. For, just after breakfast, a laundryman brought astounding news that the Huns had invaded Norway and Denmark, and that Norway has joined us in the war. Was there ever such a day! The extraordinary suddenness of these new events! The mind feels the force of violent upset. Yet without any dismay, for the Allies are very strong by now. There are, of course, infinite possibilities including the bombing of Britain.

April 11

It's exciting to watch history being made hour by hour, and to feel the mind insatiable, always stretching out for more and more news.

April 13

F yesterday to the Odeon picturehouse to see *The Stars Look Down*, a film of colliery life in which Nancy Price, an actress having local associations, appeared.

April 14

Sunday. Last evening at 10.15pm, when I had retired to read in bed, F suddenly called out, she being with the wireless in the lounge. So I rushed down and then had to wait about half an hour, chilly in night clothes, since the message was delayed. But, when it came out, it indeed seemed worth waiting for, for it stated that the Navy had forced a passage upon Narvik Fjord, had sunk seven Hun destroyers, and that further operations were proceeding.

April 16

Worthing is honoured by a new garrison: this time it's infantry, to wit a battalion of the Queen's (Royal West Surrey) Regiment. Detachments under NCOs are again to be seen marching about our

7 *Anti-aircraft gun battery just east of The Esplanade.*

streets, their object to exercise or to feed. They seem in the best of health and spirits, and march along singing choruses or whistling tunes. They are youthful soldiers, and most of them, I imagine, a long way from being trained – which, perhaps, is all the better for them! Allied troops, British and French, have landed in Norway at seven points – Narvik has been recaptured and the Huns there dispersed.

April 17

Detachments of the 'Queen's' were drilling this morning on beautiful Broadwater Green, and made a lively picture in the sunshine. I noticed an amusing instance of the modern 'humane' Sergt-Major. A large warrior, attempting to 'unfix bayonets', dropped his rifle, which used to be the supreme barrack-square crime. I can remember when a Sergt-Major would, under such a trial, have begun to curse and to swear, or at least have uttered a withering sarcasm. However, this officer merely remarked kindly to the transgressor, 'Pick up your rifle, sonny.' In the village street there was further pomp of war presented by a tall NCO walking beside a girl of the Auxiliary Territorial Service. The ATS girls looked very smart and comely in their khaki, and honour is due to the authorities for restraining them from wearing trousers, a vile fashion for women, which the looseness of the time so much encourages. 'No people can be safe until this mad dog has been destroyed,' says Premier Chamberlain, referring to Nazi Germany.

April 18

By bus in the rain to Mitchell's, where the increasing practice of the women smoking makes a horrid defilement of the air and hinders enjoyment of eating. Perhaps, before this war is over, we shall be compelled to a less self-indulgent habit.

April 20

For me this was a day of neuralgia, when one is inclined to inquire 'What's the good of anything?' After lunch at Mitchell's F went to Winter Cheer, a kind of music hall entertainment recurring each week at the Pier Pavilion. She was much diverted with an impersonation of Hitler, featuring particularly his shouting habit, and said she never laughed more. Turning into the grocer's on our way home, to buy tea, found it had jumped 4d. the lb in price. I think that bread and milk are now the only basic foods still at their pre-war prices, and they are subsidised by the Government.

April 21

Sunday. A day of brilliant sunshine, with a light S wind. Temperature in N room 57 at 7am, rising to 60 in the afternoon. Temperate for the first time this year. All Nature seemed to rush out suddenly into greenery and bloom after standing long in leash. Our silent guests the butterflies, which, since September, have slept on an upstairs ceiling, have flown at summer's call. My lupins have been wilting in the heat, and half naked soldiery enjoying sun-baths on the roof of their quarters at Muir House. The said soldiery have this afternoon disturbed the Sunday siesta not a little with some of the most execrable 'canned' music of the popular kind, repeated eternally. But to endure it cheerfully is, one supposes, the duty of every patriot at such a time.

April 22

F's nephew from Canada writes that he is gone away to the British Expeditionary Force, but whether it be to France, Syria or Norway may not be disclosed. But as he says he is living in a tent, and has but recently gone, I suppose it must be France. He is a driver of motor vehicles in the RA, and our only military relation that we have to worry about. May good fortune attend him.

April 23

Today we entertained a guest, Mrs A, to tea. On the subject of evacuation it has been usual to stress the hardships of the hosts, but Mrs A gave us a peep at the other side of the lantern. She told us of a couple of hosts who gave their charges a piece of corned beef and a beetroot for their dinner on Sunday, intimating that the Sabbath was intended for cultivation of the soul, and fasting was good for the soul. Having devoured the corned beef the evacuees were immediately sent for a walk, whilst these precious 'hosts', in defiance of their own text, proceeded to enjoy hot roast and pudding! Another hostess forbade the house to her evacuees except at meal times. They were threatened with the stick if they failed to observe this regulation. It is alleged that she even sent a boy out with a pan and sausage to cook his own dinner on a piece of wasteland.

April 24

All the talk today of Sir John Simm's Budget of yesterday. A War Budget is rather like a plunge into cold water, confounding at first onset, but tolerable when one gets used to it. There are usually special consolations for those who do not drink or smoke. Even increased postage can be borne easily by those who rarely write, though two-and-a-half pence for a letter is a sharp thrust. The real menace of this Budget lies in a vague proposal for a 'Sales Tax' to make people save and to reduce consumption of goods.

April 27

Lunch and tea in Worthing. The town very thronged, and mildly entertained, by a Civil Defence exercise. Improvised lorries and ambulances running about, and many special police, auxiliary firemen and ARP people in attendance, adorned with various coloured steel hats and other trappings.

April 28

I went on a pioneering expedition at the call of the wild. I set out to explore the, to me, Terra Incognita at the far end of Dominion Road. I discovered considerable deposits of old iron and broken bricks, and lost my bearings for a time. But presently recognised from the adjoining footbridge the lone paradise of the Eastern Railway Halt. And so, before succumbing to hunger and thirst, struggled back to familiar ground by way of Homefield Park and Broadwater Road.

April 30

Gladys has begun to arrive for her labours with her hair trained to a fringe in front identical with the fashion of F's coiffure. It seems, indeed, copied, the one from the other. F suggested that this is 'cheek', but I say it is a compliment. We agreed that, anyhow, it best to say nothing, we wanting no civil war in the midst of Armageddon.

May 2

With reference to the recent appeal by the town council for householders to take in evacuees in case of emergency it appears that out of about 21,000 citizens here who received the application, only some 1,200 have offered. In vain the net is spread.

May 3

The Italians have been very forward lately with bombast and impertinences. That Musso is knave enough to join Hitler in the war is certain, but that he is fool enough I cannot believe. Yet I feel that it were better for the future peace of the world that a clean job be made of both while we are about it. I am sure the Huns would find the Italians to be more of a liability than an asset as co-belligerents.

May 4

This may be called the first day of summer this year, though tempered by the cool N wind. People began to bathe and paddle, and sunbathe on the beach. Cricket has begun on the Sports Ground in full panoply. But the turf is still scarred by traces of the wheels of the unthinking military, who have had to pay £400 for the amending of the damage done by them in the winter.

May 6

Very busy day at home today. What incessant, never-ending small jobs are being performed perpetually in every house and garden in every street in every land of the busy world, to keep heads above water, to keep in train the inevitable business of this mortal life! I lunched at Lyon's, F at WH Smith's, for she finds too much noise and crush of eaters at the former.

May 8

The war begins to tighten its grip on us. The *Daily Telegraph* now wavers between ten and eight pages only. Chocolate, as a drink, is struck off the menu at Lyon's, and the latest block chocolate appears without its traditional silver paper.

May 9

I read the paper most of the morning on a sheltered seat at the Green end of Poulter's Lane. I could look up from time to time and observe some of the visiting infantry doing bayonet exercises with an energy quite unusual to them. These people are so frequently to be seen lying 'easy' on the sward that I had been led to think, I trust erroneously, that their directors are at a loss to fill up their working hours.

May 10

The real war has begun. The Huns invaded Holland, Belgium and Luxembourg at 2am this morning. I did not know of this stupendous event until about 11am when I went into the village to forage. Then I saw a brief note to the effect scrawled on a board outside the newspaper shop. There was the usual crowd of people in Sainsbury's, mostly women, awaiting their turn for sausages, bacon and butter, but they appeared quite as happy and unconcerned as usual and exchanged no comments on the war at all. Perhaps they had seen the notice and did not believe it. This is one of the great days of history. Now there is to be a life and death struggle for the Channel ports, including Antwerp. The Whitsun Bank Holiday has been cancelled and we have been warned to look to our gas masks. How thankful one feels for our island situation and the British Navy, notwithstanding prospective air attack. As I sit writing this in my front window bay this calm and brilliant afternoon, girls flit by in light clothes of many colours, children played unconscious, and all about is the lovely jingle of busy lawnmowers. The morning's news seems to have made no difference and in our street at least it is the usual summer scene.

May 13

Mostly bright but cold wind. This is Whit Monday but this time it is not an official holiday so nearly all the shops were open. Still, many coachloads of trippers came into the town, many of them parents of evacuees, and I witnessed a pretty reunion at the corner of our road of a little red-haired freckled evacuee and her parents. She held up her arms to hug them and seemed delighted.

May 16

As I was walking in the village this morning I overheard an ancient inhabitant remark, 'Oh, I daresay 'e'll be sending some of them planes over directly.' That is the thought at the back of most British minds now that Hitler bestrides Holland. One feels that Worthing will not be the first place to be bombed and, whenever it is bombed, if at all, it will not be with gas bombs. A nervous lady has been heard to ask 'Ought I go down to the bank and take my money out?'

May 18

When will the Huns' momentum slacken? When will they be stopped? After lunch we walked to The Pantiles at West Worthing, where we took tea at a nice home-made shop. Thence back to Worthing by tramocar. I observed a trader sitting at a table outside a shop in South Street retailing metal identity discs. He seemed to be doing a brisk trade. But since these things find their use only if one is burnt to cinders or blown to bits, it seems to me a too pessimistic commerce.

May 20

The Prime Minister broadcast grave words last night. He preaches attack and hopes, without being sure, that the tide will soon be turned upon the advancing Huns.

May 24

We strolled down to the front after tea and were met by the poster 'Germans occupy Boulogne'. People mostly had grave faces. It was a fine, calm evening, but there seemed a tenseness, a kind of vague perplexity in people's attitude. The pier was under military guard and closed to the public. Outside the Pavilion at the shore end, a squad of Royal Engineers was loading themselves and certain mysterious gear into a couple of lorries. The people were kept moving by the police on the promenade and all seats within 100 yards of the pier had been turned upside down. Out at sea a long grey minesweeper was just discernible in the dusk. One had an uneasy feeling that our world as we had known it was on the point of crashing.

May 27

We noticed today that workmen were removing all the boats from the beach. Also, the evacuation is set in reverse. Children are now to be evacuated to the Midlands from all sea coast towns from Yarmouth to Folkestone.

May 30

The Anglo-French army is retreating to the coast. It is fighting with extreme gallantry but the impression remains that its situation is almost desperate. England's turn is expected to come next by means of parachutists and bombing aircraft, then perhaps invasion. Last evening we watched Corporation employees erecting barricades across Montague Place and South Street and other thoroughfares giving access to the sea. These consisted of bathing machines placed side by side and partially filled with shingle. Outside the deserted pier stood sentries with fixed bayonets and nearby were posted auxiliary firemen. The whole prospect looked menacing. One wondered if one were dreaming.

May 31

The retreat to Dunkirk and evacuation of the Army is proceeding, with fair promise. Many of our men and of the French are already arrived in England. The danger of general capitulation seems to have been averted.

June 1

Seventy-five per cent of our men are already safely home from Belgium and more are coming. Yet there is a tendency to over celebrate a clever retreat as though it were a triumph. For it cannot be thought that the Allies have suffered a great disaster. Taking a walk in the town, met a company of the new Local Defence Volunteers, now being recruited in all districts, to help oppose any landings of the Huns. These were in mufti, not having yet received their uniforms, marching some with rifles, some without, mostly veterans of the last war.

June 2

Fine and hot. At 9.30am the garrison at Muir House held a church parade on the lawn in the shade of ancient trees. At 12.30pm, the peace of Broadwater was broken by a loudspeaker crying out for more recruits for the Women's Land Army.

June 6

Here it has been a sweltering day, but with a redeeming NE breeze. The barricading of all outlets to the sea is proceeding. In places concrete flagstones are being used as a facing, with a core of shingle. The barricades are only about 4ft high. A concrete strong point for guns is being erected at Splash Point and today glass lamps were being removed from the promenade. It seems curious to observe all this grim preparation whilst children played about on the beach as usual.

June 7

At 1.40am we had our first air-raid warning. It was very eerie to hear the scream and blood-curdling siren as we lay in the silent darkness half awake. Our milkman informed us later that one old lady of the district, whose heart was weak, 'pegged out' on hearing it. We rose at once and fumbled about, uncertain how safe it was to use light. Then we heard a warden shout to others 'Put out that light!' We grasped our gas masks and extra covering and cowered in the hall, as the place most protected from splinters. Then nothing happened beyond the occasional passing of official cars and whispered talk outside. There was no sound of guns or bombing. It became dull and we returned to bed.

June 17

A thunderbolt. The French have given up the conflict. Alarm was on every face and one tried to say encouraging things to reassure the women. This news has come, indeed, as a very great unexpected shock. There has been constant talk by their politicians of fighting to the last inch of French soil.

June 18

This for the world was a day of tragedy. Hitler and Musso met to achieve the ruin of France.

8   *On 6 June 1940 Mr Harriss wrote, 'A concrete strong point for guns is being erected at Splash Point.'*

June 19

A grave but inspiring speech by the PM in the Commons yesterday. If France makes peace we continue alone. Our countrymen 1,000 years hence shall have cause to say, 'This was their finest hour.' There is news of the most considerable air raid on Britain since the war began. One hundred bombers over Essex. Seven brought down. But 14 people killed. A sad business, but only a foretaste of worse to come. Yet Hitler will never conquer us in that way.

June 20

Last night at 11.15pm we had our second air-raid warning [ARW]. I was in bed, but this time we were veterans to it. We experienced no flutter, but only annoyance at disturbance of rest. Went to the windows and watched the searchlights in operation along the Downs. There was no sound of bombs or guns. Returned to bed at 11.45, but the disturbance had banished my ability to sleep, and I heard 12, 1, 2, 3 and 4 o'clock strike on the Church clock. I was quite tranquil and probably dozed a little, but my subconscious self was worried about the 'All Clear'. This came at last at 4.15am. Then I slept until 7 but awoke rather unrefreshed. It gave me an idea of the effect constant night bombing must be having on the health of the industrial population in Germany. Attended this morning at the ARP station in the village where courteous volunteer helpers affixed to our gas masks additional mouthpieces to make them more efficient. Lunch at Mitchell's, and then a walk along the front to see the new defence works at the west end of it. The whole promenade and roadway beyond Heene Terrace is shut off with barbed wire, and fairly elaborate fortifications of brick and concrete are in course of erection within this forbidden area. A scene to gaze and wonder at, had we any longer the capacity to wonder at strange sights.

June 21

Almost the whole British Army with many Colonial troops are now in England to form a garrison against invasion. There is no longer a 'Western Front'.

June 22

Under the menace of the Huns civilian life seems to be drying up. More luxury shops are closing. There are no bands playing on the front. The Repertory Company at the new Connaught Theatre, which has run continuously playing for eight years, is in its last week. The Worthing cricket ground displays a notice 'No more cricket until further notice'. Elsewhere the racing has been stopped, somewhat tardily!

June 23

One feels this is the calm before the storm. A dozen lorries containing soldiers in full equipment and armed with rifles passed through the village this morning. The men seemed to be thoroughly enjoying themselves. Very important movements are evidently afoot all along this coast, but we, of course, are not allowed to know anything of them. Most of the soldiers have mysteriously left Muir House. There was no sentry at the gate this evening. But raucous singing indicated that the house was not quite untenanted.

June 24

The French Government has betrayed the Allied cause and the prospect for Old England is very black. After lunch at Lyon's we went about to make provision for a worse time to come, 'whilst the going is good,' as F puts it. Ordered a winter suit whilst there is still pre-war cloth, and coming taxes on purchases not yet imposed. Also ordered half a ton of anthracite nuts against the winter. Half a ton will last us ten weeks.

June 25

Many people near us are very nervous about the risk they have to run from bombing.

June 26

Last night at 10.45pm we had our 3rd ARW. Stayed in bed and managed to sleep most of the time until the 'All Clear' siren offended the dawn at 3.30am. Yet it was not the best quality of sleep. Once again no raiders passed our way, but once gone the broken night condemned us to a heavy day.

June 27

Going down to lunch at Mitchell's, where a great company of eaters. I noticed a concrete machine gun post just erected on the circular open space opposite to the old Town Hall. This area might be described as Worthing's Piccadilly Circus, and it is very strange to see embrasures of guns pointing down each of the four principal streets which meet there. Men say that the chief hotels are about to close, and that many residents have left town because they fear invasion. Which seems unworthy of an Imperial race. Indeed, if the Huns came I am certain that they would soon be very sorry they had.

June 29

This afternoon, F feeling that she would like a drive by way of diversion, we went in a 'Luxury Coach' on a verdant circular route, via Washington, Cowfold, Henfield, and home by Lancing. The modern coach is a sun trap, and our pleasure was much discounted by excessive heat. Everywhere one observes signs of preparation against invasion. Road signs have been removed, and place names obliterated from churchyards, auctioneers' posters, coaches, tradesmen's cars, etc. We passed many barricades, and air-raid shelters made or in the making. On the road between Henfield and Bramber we came across a battalion of the Royal Ulster Rifles, marching in single file, in full equipment, with many Bren gun carriers at intervals. In this extended order they must have covered as much as a couple of miles. The men were mostly short of stature, but looked stocky and strong, and hot! We heard that most of them had been in the Dunkirk retreat. They seemed in excellent spirits, and waved and held up optimistic thumbs in answer to the salutations including wild cries of females from the occupants of our coach. One notices that all the local petrol filling stations have been closed save two or three left under military guard; lest invaders help themselves.

June 30

One cannot regard lightly the fact that the coast of France is become the coast of Germany. Yet I cannot but think that however the Hun attacks, it will be against the East coast and not the South. For it is only from the East that he can get at England's vitals.

July 1

Our *Daily Telegraph* reduced from eight to six pages, just a quarter of what it was before the war. We stopped on the front in the afternoon. There was a remarkable number of pretty children about, looking in the pink of condition. Many of the children were digging or playing on the sands. The sun blazed down, the sky was cerulean and the sea not quite sure whether to show green or blue. But near to the children soldiers were filling sandbags, and constructing gun emplacements on the shingle edge.

July 2

The front this afternoon was crowded with people trying to make the best attempt at holiday they could; without bands, bathing or boating. Among them are brawny, cheery defenders from a Scottish regiment who filled sandbags and stood about in happy converse, apparently without a care in the world.

July 3

Preparations to meet the craft and subtlety of Hitler continue. This morning I noticed that the emergency water tank at the end of our road was being encased in concrete bricks. Also, more and

9 *On 3 July 1940 Mr Harriss recorded, 'This morning I noticed that an emergency water tank at the bottom of our road was being enclosed in concrete bricks.' St Mary's Church, Broadwater, is in the background.*

more householders are sticking strips of special paper criss-cross over their window panes to mitigate the effects of splintering by bombs. I am afraid I am very backward about such precautions. I am prepared to take a chance. Artful traders exhibit these remedies in their shop windows. A few purchase them, and then neighbours follow suit for fear of appearing reckless. Anyhow, if there is a raid, I do not propose to stay near glass, but to get into a cupboard in my hall. After bread and cheese lunch at home we walked into Worthing. Found that, from today, the beach and promenade have been forbidden absolutely to civilians. The effect of this sudden regulation is uncanny. The usual many coloured crowd of children, loungers, lovers, was gone. Pedestrians were confined to the footpath against the houses. They were few, silent and depressed. It was as though a pestilence had descended on the town.

July 4

I broke my normal routine to accompany F to the Denton Assembly Room at the Town Hall, where she purposed to take coffee and listen to the reduced 'Summer Orchestra' of eight performers. The performance having been transplanted thither from the closed Pier Pavilion. The band was very well, though there was an audience of only about 50 including a magnificent but introspective cat, which we caressed. Thence to Mitchell's for lunch. Still very crowded though Hitler be knocking

at the door. But Mitchell's will always be popular since, as Mr Shaw once wrote about marriage, it combines the maximum of temptation with the maximum of opportunity. Joined in conversation with a pleasant but unknown couple opposite; a practice unusual among Anglo-Saxons. So to the Reference Library, but much disturbed by the jabber of an egotistical old woman with the attendant nymph about girls' schools. It was not the nymph's fault.

July 5

Much cheered by the morning paper containing long and anxiously awaited news of the French Fleet; how it has been almost entirely placed in British control, or incapacitated or sunk by our Navy. The miserable weakness and treachery of Petain's Government in agreeing to hand over their fleet to the Huns, in spite of their Alliance with us, makes me feel very hot. What a miserable show the French have made in this war! 'France is rotten right through,' a man remarked to me yesterday; and so it seems. Yet there is the usual talk by politicians about French heroism. Just the conventional gloss, I suppose.

July 6

We are very glad to have been told that it has been decided not to sound ARWs in future until local guns actually have to begin firing. There have been so many warnings that have led to nothing, nerves have been so strained by the blood-curdling moan of the siren, and so much sleep has been lost, that this remedy has threatened to be worse than the disease.

July 7

Everyone knows that peril lies desperately near. However, whilst making no claim to valour, I am quite successful in refusing to worry about personal harm, until it occurs. It may never come. This, I suppose, is the attitude of most Britons. We had 2 ARWs this morning. The first came, at 12.05 pm, just as we were getting ready to go out. In view of the official intimation recorded yesterday, we thought that this time this must mean serious danger. Instantly seized gas masks and squeezed into our cupboard under the stairs. F lost a couple of hair curlers. But nothing happened. There were no guns firing, and we soon took a look round. ARP officials and special constables were cycling about in their steel hats, and there was the distant hum of fire lorries taking up position.

July 9

A man sitting in a shelter remarked that Worthing is unlikely ever to be invaded since the sea here is too shallow for ships of any size to approach anywhere near to the shore, which is very well. Nevertheless the military authorities keep elaborating our shore defences. Today I watched soldiers setting barbed wire on stakes just above high water mark all along the beach, and at intervals setting more at right angles to it across the beach and promenade. Also, Corporation men have been constructing great square blocks of concreted shingle for miles along the front where beach meets promenade, side by side at intervals of a couple of feet, so as to make a complete barrier against guns or tanks or other vehicles brought up the beach from boats. The strong point at Splash Point has been painted to resemble a chalet, tiled and overgrown, with shrubs and flowering creepers; all in the way of camouflage. A very pretty thing, but with gun muzzles peeping out of it. Tea is rationed as from today at 2oz per person per week, as much as we are in the habit of drinking at home. Also, icing on cakes is forbidden.

July 11

Gladys having found it impossible to continue her labours with us, we advertised for another handmaid, the employment being for two hours on four mornings a week. Now there has been a flood of applications in person or by post throughout the past 24 hours. Women aged from 16 to 65, a few displaying raddled lips in the latest mode of allure. I saw a neighbour diligently digging for himself and his a 'funk hole', against bombing, in his back garden, but feel no urge to do likewise. I would rather take it in my snug hall than in his 'funk hole' – cold and damp and cramped, and withal of very questionable security. He is not himself in good heart about it. Cannot procure the necessary steel lining for it: seems to think he may be bombed before he gets it!

July 13

F visited three applicants for our domestic situation. I waited long periods outside their habitations. But it was not in vain, for the third one was engaged. She had a nice clean home with holy texts on the walls; and so we fair hope that she will minister to us faithfully.

July 14

An ideal summer's day. After tea went for a solitary stroll across the Green, up Hill Barn Lane to the Golf Links. All the beauty of high summer about these parts, and a great peace. A few golfers. For once, no sign of any military preparations, unless it be some rather unaccountable tall masts on the fairway; which may have been put there to spoil any landing of enemy planes.

July 15

Ruth, our new 'help', begun her duties, and all is well. To lunch at Lyon's, where we were disconcerted by being allowed but one poached egg on toast each instead of the two ordered. Which is very ominous for things to come. The evacuees to Worthing are all to be cleared out and sent away from the coast, for fear of the violence of the enemy. To our great content that this continuing threat to our home is removed. The PM gave a fine broadcast last night. It was robust and valiant and full of rugged eloquence. He agrees that it will be a long war and hard. He seems to be absolutely the man of the Hour; a great figure towering above the statesmen of other nations, as well as of his own.

August 13

To the front. Things are dull there now behind its barriers of monoliths. The promenade, beach and boating have once more been forbidden. Thence to the public library, and I was just preparing to leave when at 4.20pm the siren again sounded. Immediately from each room the presiding nymph solemnly shepherded its drab inmates downstairs into the cellars of the building. It was like unto ministering angels directing lost souls into the abyss, as we see them depicted in medieval art. I feel a certain qualmishness, which the sense of the unfamiliar is apt to occasion to nervous subjects. We sat in rows in typically British silence, back numbers of illustrated papers being handed out for our entertainment. Presently the lady librarian came along and in answer to her inquiry, 'Are you all right?' a wag ventured, 'Yes, no one has fainted!' and won a titter. After half an hour of this I reflected that the 'All Clear' might not sound for an hour or two and it was long odds that anything was going to happen. It all seemed rather silly. So I decided to leave. In a quiver of daring I crept up to the deserted ground floor, and a bemedalled janitor let me out, remarking by way of encouragement, 'What will be, will be.' However, I felt what is good enough for the buses was good enough for me. Their continued running seems in fact to throw a sense of unreality over the appointed rush to cover. There were also a good many other vehicles and wandering stout hearts about who were disregarding the ordained precautions. A disappointed air-raid warden in steel hat was remonstrating with two women standing at a bus halt. 'Well, you don't want to be caught napping,' he retorted as a final thrust. So home. The 'All Clear' sounded at 5.08pm.

August 14

I am concerned at the heavy loss of merchant shipping we are suffering, partly from U-boat, partly from plane attack. About 70,000 tons per week. Can we endure to lose so much?

August 15

When we were out for a stroll along Sompting Road we suddenly, at 7.55pm, had our 17th ARW. It is a residential district, and many people were standing at their doors enjoying the evening. Many, too, were moving about the road. Immediately a few began to run and some of the children looked scared. The horrible wail of the siren was enough to make them so. The road soon became dotted with steel-hatted officials, special police, ambulancemen, firemen and wardens hastening on their bicycles to their various rendezvous. The drone of planes could be faintly heard, and about a dozen of our fighters were just visible for a little while. People gathered in little knots and gazed into the sky. We strolled slowly home.

August 16

The Huns lost 169 planes yesterday to our 37 in what is beginning to be called 'The Battle of England'. How long can the Hun endure such punishment? A lady friend writes from Lancing, 'It is generally said to be a miracle we are alive after Sunday night's (the 11th), and we are badly shaken up. At 12.40am (the 12th) two of these terrible whistling bombs fell at the bottom of my garden, and I shall never forget it. It was just ghastly. No warning. We just got under the bedclothes and waited for the end. One was a dud, however, the biggest one of 15 dropped on Lancing made a crater 27ft across by 12ft deep. No one was hurt but houses were badly damaged. 18th and 19th ARW today. We were fortunately at home on both occasions. During the second there was a continuous roar of passing enemy planes, of greater or less intensity, for over half an hour. It was almost frightening. The volume of sound was so great that the empyrean seemed alive with planes, though owing to cloud we saw but one or two. One plane came circling around Broadwater at merely some 200ft. I suppose it had been hit and was looking for somewhere to land, but it passed out of sight before I could distinguish whether it was friend or foe. I heard no bombs, but there were occasional distant bursts of machine gun fire.

August 17

Yesterday the Huns attacked the London suburbs for the first time, and lost there and elsewhere a total of over 70 planes to our 17. Generally, civilian casualties have been considerable in the last ten days, which is very sad to see. Spent a pleasant Saturday afternoon browsing in Denton Gardens, or strolling about our spectral front, along the rows of hotels, now, with few exceptions, closed and shuttered against war's thunderbolts. Then a concert of sweet music and tea at the Assembly Hall. A good company there, enjoying comfort after agitation.

August 18

Sunday. The night was undisturbed and the morning passed very peacefully. But peace was not to continue long. Suddenly at 1.10pm, as we were sitting on a seat on the Green, the siren, very close by, wailed stridently, alarmingly, like a thousand souls in anguish. This was our 20th warning. We immediately walked home through the village. Passers by exchanged smiles in the camaraderie of the war amid the cheerful hustle of firemen and wardens running to their stations. Arrived home, we had just finished lunch when we heard planes near. Precisely at 2.30pm there was a succession of explosions, I suppose, two or three miles away. The concussion shook our front door and windows. The sound of the planes seemed to be coming nearer. It was alarming. We went and cowered in our coat cupboard under the middle of the house. Then, after a few minutes, to our great relief, the sound died away and was not repeated. The 'All Clear' followed at 2.35pm. So much for the 'Day of Rest'.

August 19

I find I was much out in my estimate of the distance of yesterday's bombs. They fell at Ford Aerodrome near Littlehampton – 10 miles away.

10   *Troops march past the old library, left, where Mr Harriss spent much of his time, expanding his general knowledge and keeping warm.*

11   *Mr Harriss and his wife took cover in this shelter under Steyne Gardens during an air raid.*

This illustrates the terrific force of these missiles. I hear from one who actually witnessed the terrible scene from a passing bus that there was much damage and some 50 of the airmen were killed. The wreckage of a German plane was brought through the village on a lorry this morning as I was shopping. 'That looks a nice mess, doesn't it?' remarked to me a pretty lady with whom I was totally unacquainted. Camaraderie of the war again! This day workmen were tearing up the iron railings around the public library for fashioning ordnance against the Huns. This single example of what is being done all over Britain suggests the vastness of the forces which are under labour for the final smashing of Nazidom.

August 20

We were outside the Steyne Gardens after lunch, when at 2.45pm we had our 21st ARW. People began to run towards the air-raid shelter there, and F, affected by what is called the psychology of the crowd, began to run there too. I had perforce to follow. We had said that we would never enter an underground shelter, would rather be killed in the open than perhaps be buried alive in the bowels of the earth. However, now we crept down through a dark entrance, apprehensively, and were soon seated on a bench in a long concreted and dimly lit gallery. The air was dry, though stuffy, but luckily the galleries were not crowded. So there we sat just facing a concrete wall, with nothing to distract the mind save the occasional passage of a warden or policeman, until 4pm. How sweetly then sang the 'All Clear' to us entombed. How rejoiced we were to run up into daylight again! Nothing had happened, and we would have done better to have at once taken the bus home. Thence to a chiropodist for a corn-cutting who had been waiting for me three quarters of an hour because of the raid.

August 21

22nd, 23rd and 24th ARW. But except in number they were not remarkable. Thus Worthing was fortunate in escaping once again, in a day of evident aerial activity elsewhere, its dreaded baptism of fire.

August 22

I have grown even to enjoy the excitement afforded by the siren and the consequent bustle. By oft repeated occasion such excitement has become no more than a gentle titillation; nevertheless, when one is deprived of it, the spirit misses this stimulation. Today's warning was a poor thing. It found and left us at lunch in WH Smith's, its duration being from 1.42pm to 1.57pm. One lady showed a moderate alarm, the blinds were drawn and the lights turned on. And that was all.

August 23

This day, Friday, as usual, we spent at home. Going out alone this morning, sat a long time on a favourite seat on the Green. The grass is brown now from the drought, but I can still enjoy the broad spaces and 'the wind on the heath'. The Huns have mounted great guns on the French shore and are begun to shoot hence at our own convoys and on Dover. There never were seen such happenings since the beginning of the World. The British lion is indeed brought to bay; and patience remains the supreme requirement for us all.

August 24

After lunch had a look at the sea. Have never seen it more beautiful; all a deep blue and full of motions, the waves everywhere showing white crests. Eastwards, even Brighton seemed transformed into a golden vision of fantasy in the clear and sunlit distance. But at my feet the long vista of the beach stretched away untenanted, just a dreary wilderness, traversed with rusty barbed wire. On the promenade, too, the only figures were those of an occasional soldier, with his rifle and fixed bayonet. To such a pass are we come!

August 25

Sunday. 28th ARW 12.15 to 1.37am. Tried to sleep it through but hardly succeeded. A lamentable break in one's rest. It was a calm, starlit night, by no means dark. Many planes passed overhead.

I looked out and saw half-a-dozen searchlights criss-crossing over the sky like giant fingers pointing. But the enemy were too high to be seen by us. Had five hours sleep after the 'All Clear' but felt very tired in the morning. In the afternoon we attended a People's Concert on Broadwater Green, consisting of the Salvation Army band, a bass soloist and community singing. The idea was to provide cheer in a time of strain, and those responsible deserve commendation. The company, however, was not large, and whether what they heard contributed anything to their cheerfulness must be very questionable. As to the community singing at any rate, the fact has to be faced that to sing in common under the sky is contrary to the nature of the Southern English.

August 26

At about 11.30pm a string of parachute flares appeared over the sea. Poor F thought they were bombs approaching and about to explode, and she was seriously alarmed. But I was able to reassure her, and then we fell to admiring their great beauty which seemed to illuminate the heavens.

August 27

Yesterday was indeed one of intense aerial disturbance. At 9.18pm the siren sounded the 5th warning of the day and the 33rd of the series. The 'All Clear' did not come until 3.55 this morning, indicating the longest raid of the War, so far at least as this area is concerned. There were at times strange lights visible in the sky, and I heard at least one bomb explode, but at a great distance. The newspaper did not arrive until 11.30am, which suggests serious happenings. Into town to lunch. Home to tea, where F, in very good heart, and naughtily mimicking the dreadful undulating of the siren, until it had to be stopped for fear of scaring little old ladies. But it made us merry.

August 28

The war presses upon us in little ways that have a cumulative effect. The bakers have stopped baking the small 2d. loaves which suit our small need. We must now buy 3d. ones and eat them sometimes very stale. After September 30 there are to be no cream productions. No more cream cheese to furnish a modest supper! Our joint butter ration of 6oz is to be reduced to 4oz per week, but margarine is still unrationed.

August 30

There was quite an exciting incident this morning. About 11.40am I was sitting on the [Broadwater] Green in rustic calm. Mothers and children were playing on the grass whilst elderly men took their ease. Then, suddenly, was heard the sound of planes, and a couple of our fighters appeared, silver in the sunlight, manoeuvring at great height. The noise increased and then a large dark grey bomber sailed into view. There was a terrific din, a mix of the noise of engines and the rattle of machine guns. Then the fighters turned back, while the bomber made off over Worthing towards the sea. But it was losing height rapidly and a man declared he could see smoke issuing from the tail. At 11.45am, the 38th air-raid warning sounded. Firing, coupled with the frantic wail of the siren, caused a scuttle among the shoppers in the village street. Some gaily dressed women looked shaken and many literally ran for cover.

September 2

The motor coaches on the front still take the public for evening excursions, which they call 'Mystery Drives', because, to stimulate curiosity, the route is left undisclosed.

September 3

Today is the 1st anniversary of Britain's entry into the war. We have suffered a succession of reverses in consequence of the overthrow of all our Allies. The British lion is wounded, driven right back on its haunches. Nevertheless he is full of fierce ardour and battle, and presently he will spring. Hitler seems afraid to invade us, and his mass attack by air has been effectively held, with a loss of over 1,000 German planes.

September 4

A big drumming of planes overhead, which persisted. Some distant bursts of machine gun fire. F got excited, left her lunch and ran from the room trying to get a sight of them. 'I should like to see a dogfight,' she exclaimed. But as is usually the case the planes were mostly too high to be visible. We only saw two or three RAF fighters, tiny in the distance, whirling about in the sun. Also, a couple of parachutes, very white against the blue sky, descending towards the Downs.

September 7

Shopping for sustenance becomes more and more difficult though there is plenty for those looking for all the baser kinds of sausages. But for those, like ourselves, addicted to dairy products, the door is gradually closing. No clotted cream cheese and eggs three-and-a-half pence each, and often not procurable.

September 10

I spent much of the morning at the distasteful task of sticking strips of brown paper along the edges of windows to hide possible chinks of light all around the curtains and blinds from our nocturnal constable, who prowls and prowls around.

September 11

53rd ARW began at 8.02pm. Each night now they begin at the same time and continue all night for London's martyrdom. We here are feeling much the loss of sleep owing to the noise of the planes and of the nearby searchlight apparatus, but still have very much to be thankful for. The perfect weather is helping the Hun to destroy London, so that one longs, for once, for the weather to break and bring a respite. All these warnings, with their grisly sequels, constitute what is called The Battle of Britain, which began on the 8th August.

September 14

At 6.20am we heard the distant explosion of two or three bombs followed by the rattle of machine gun fire. On walking into Worthing I was astounded to find it no longer unscathed. The whole area in front of the new town hall, between Stoke Abbott Road and Richmond Road, was roped off, the front of Mitchell's premises opposite was gutted and a naturalist's shop next to it completely destroyed, and there was further considerable damage to windows and roofs in the vicinity. Luckily, casualties were few. All this was the result of the bombs which we heard at 6.20am. It was something to provoke thought. It might have occurred in our road. It brought the air war very near home.

September 15

There has been much going and coming of planes all day, especially towards the west. At about 1.30pm we enjoyed the stirring sight of 24 RAF fighters moving in formation in that direction. We fear that the Huns might be attacking Portsmouth again.

September 16

Another miracle is the escape of the Town Hall and library in Saturday's bombing. One bomb dropped on the officials' garage at the back, and another in the road in the front. Yet the main buildings are unscathed save for a few tiles and windows broken.

September 18

Cloud with bright intervals. Soon after 1am we heard a loud explosion and thought it was a bomb but heard later that it was a landmine on the beach against a landing by the Huns which was exploded prematurely by the waves. There are now several 'Danger – Landmines' notices to be seen along the front.

September 20

Half-a-dozen explosions in the early hours. They followed one another in quick succession, and were certainly bombs.

September 21

The Orchestra resumed today after a week's cessation owing to the damage to the Assembly Room, which is still awaiting repairs after the hurtling of lumps of concrete through the roof.

September 22

This afternoon drafted with F her will, she envisaging the possibility of our both being bombed out of life together. Found this a complicated, exacting and exhausting process for a Sunday afternoon.

September 23

When, after lunch, we were sunning ourselves in Montague Place, F suddenly remarked, 'Let's go to Brighton for a trip!' So we went, on the bus. We found Brighton without her former sparkle, tawdry though that was. Though, more fortunate than at Worthing, the public still allowed upon the promenade. Most of the great hotels are closed. The famous lawns at Hove are become a position for men-at-arms, ringed with barbed wire and sown with landmines. The only gay thing we saw is the electrically activated sailor in the window of the Waxworks opposite to the East Pier. He writhes with laughter eternally, at an undisclosed joke, and is a marvel of art.

12   *An air-raid shelter at the junction of Montague Street and Montague Place, with the Odeon cinema in the background.*

September 24

'The French have let us down,' I heard a lady observe today. That seems to be the general opinion.

September 25

We had a visit from a constable who complained that I had left a chink of light beside one of the bedroom curtains. He said he would have to report me next time. The blackout is now being enforced by draconian penalties so that one dreads the hours of darkness. There has been a tragedy at Brighton. A cinema has been bombed and about 40 children killed. This morning all Nature looked bright and beautiful, but the Devil was active in the sky. Heard the rattle of machine gun fire. Later in the day there was the sound of bombs exploding uncomfortably near. So the Battle of Britain continues and one can see no end to it.

September 27

There is an epidemic of looting from bombed houses in London. Even Civil Defence workers have rendered themselves execrable in this way.

September 28

We heard two or three disconcerting explosions at 9.30pm which I found were bombs being dropped on Goring. Yesterday, apart from the night attack, about 800 Hun planes came over to attack London and lost about 130 to 34 of ours (15 of our pilots saved). Another great day for the RAF.

September 29

At 9.30pm there had been two bomb explosions near, so that our kitchen door shuddered as though someone was knocking rudely upon it. My heart came into my mouth as I supposed it was another policeman calling about our lights. The blackout has indeed become a terror worse than the bombs, for the regulations are being enforced to the point of persecution.

September 30

About 5pm we suddenly saw about 30 of our fighters which were making a tremendous din. They were all scattered over a vast area of sky and seemed to be in no regular formation though moving generally from the Downs towards the sea. They were at a great height and kept darting about in the sun like a swarm of little silver fishes outlined against the blue. It was a rare and beautiful spectacle.

13   *Goring seafront, which was turned into a minefield to slow invading German troops.*

October 9

Showery. SW wind of gale force. At 7.05pm yesterday without any warning a plane seemed suddenly to rush over our road dropping several bombs. The noise of the explosions was alarming and I feared our house was going to be hit. F saw sparks falling in the darkness outside. Soon the front doorbell rang and the warden requested that the gas be turned off at the mains. Heard that the bombs fell about a mile from us, hit the gas works and two or three houses nearby. I fear five persons are killed.

October 12

Myself and others, by the front this afternoon, were diverted by watching Home Guards (until lately called Local Defence Volunteers) practising the throwing of hand grenades. This they did with beer bottles containing some chemical fluid which went up in smoke when the bottles crashed on to the shingle.

October 15

Walking in Brighton Road, at Beach House, came across a notice 'Danger – Unexploded Bomb' and felt no wish to approach nearer.

14   *While on his travels Mr Harriss regularly bumped into Worthing Home Guard, seen here parading at Woodside Road, home of Worthing FC.*

October 24

We hear Londoners [enduring the Blitz] are coming down to Worthing at night just to get sleep and returning in the morning to their labour.

October 25

Coming home in the dusk we passed many knots of newly arrived Scottish soldiers, fresh-faced and gay in their red and white chequered caps.

October 27

92nd ARW. There was a considerable noise of planes but none of that awesome drumming which announces the passage of great numbers en masse. Shortly after 5am heard a couple of bombs fall some distance away. This day has been disturbed by incessant warnings, probably indicating several small raids. For the Huns no longer risk hundreds of planes at a time as they did in August.

October 28

We are decidedly more easy in mind than we were a month ago. For we seem at last to have satisfied the Blackout Gestapo. Also, the menace of billeting seems to have passed from us owing to Worthing being now considered a Defence Area, where both civilian adult and child evacuees are barred from it. Soldiers seem fewer here than a year ago. We have only some searchlight engineers and a few infantry to defend the front, and anti-aircraft details.

October 30

Dull with a tendency to drizzle. There was a bomb explosion uncomfortably near at 10.18pm last night. In spite of all, people are maintaining their flower gardens. There is a good demand for plants, and the nurseryman's principal anxiety is how to meet it in the labour shortage.

October 31

Very mild. S Wind, reaching gale force. Lunch at Khong's, whence we emerged into a violent storm so we were forced to seek a draughty hermitage against WH Smith's shopfront, waiting for a break in the tempest, which didn't arrive. Home by bus, disconsolate. 'Cemetery Path,' cried the conductor, [which was] his name for Carnegie Road. 'We are all bound for that,' rejoined a melancholy wag. Sad wit, but it suited the day.

November 1

The siren causes us no agitation of nerves now. One is just conscious of it and then falls asleep again. Such is the effect of constant repetition. Fine weather meant more raids. As I was returning home soon after noon I noticed many people gazing into the sky, which was picturesquely streaked with long tenuous lines and wreaths of white vapour from darting aeroplanes. Someone said, 'There is a battle going on up there,' but unfortunately the planes were too distant to be either seen or heard. 'Are they Jerries, mister?' a little girl inquired, which found me at a loss.

November 2

The worst weekend for catering that we have yet had. No brawn, no sausages, no pies at Sainsbury's. Ham and tongue have long been absent. To tea and orchestra, 4-6pm, at the Assembly Room again, having been repaired after bomb damage. A goodly company and sweet music.

November 5

Cloudy with bright intervals. Walked on the front this afternoon where a mournful spectacle of concrete blocks and closed dwelling houses was rendered more so by hundreds of shattered window panes, caused by a mine which floated ashore two or three days ago and exploded on the beach.

November 6

Had to venture right into Worthing and back this morning (early closing) to obtain cut of tongue for supper, and that at great price. Tried to procure an egg but could not and so F and I must tomorrow consume the second half of our bacon ration with an egg between us. Bread and milk are now about the only victuals which can still be obtained as plentifully as the consumer wills.

November 8

Worthing for weeks past has been made to look silly by labels pasted everywhere, even in windscreens of cars, bearing the words 'Join the Spitfire Club'. All become members who will pay 6d. and undertake that when one member meets another he will say 'Spit', to which the other must reply 'Fire' and represent with his hands the motion of a diving aeroplane. Any member who fails in these antics must pay a fine of 1d. I have yet to observe any public demonstration of the absurd ritual.

November 13

Cloudy, mild, SW wind. At about 7.30pm last night we suddenly heard the vicious thud of several bombs exploding near. The bombs fell on Hadley Avenue, within a mile of our house, and we hear that four people were killed and 15 injured, four houses being demolished. The noise made us rise in some alarm. At 10.50am came the 245th ARW and, very soon afterwards, bursts of machine gun fire. Looking towards the Downs we could see a fight in progress between a raider and two or three of our fighters. Ever so much wheeling and rushing around in enormous arcs. It was difficult to distinguish friend from foe but soon one plane fell away towards the sea, flying very low. It was pursued by two others which seemed to take turns to fire into its tail. Then it disappeared below the rooftops fronting the sea, with black smoke pouring from it in a very long streak, and the others flew away. That Hun will never trouble us again.

November 15

After lunch at home we walked down to Hadley Avenue to inspect the ruin there. Four nice little villas reduced to a chaos of boards and plaster and bricks, perhaps 6ft high. Pitiful little household goods, wireless set, fenders, bric-a-brac, peeping out everywhere. I even noticed a paper bag full of wallflower plants, purchased for the garden. But now the garden is totally extinguished under the wreckage. Nearby workmen were repairing shattered mains in a great bomb crater in the middle of Sompting Road.

November 17

We were lucky, in this season of abnormal wet, in enjoying a pleasant stroll just after noon, in sunshine. Went along Upper Brighton Road, where we met so many soldiers who are quartered in the empty houses in that district, mostly Royal Engineers and a few of the Tank Regiment, looking like Frenchmen in their black berets.

November 20

I took a stroll during the blackout to get some fresh air and enjoy the stars, for it was for once a terrific night. There were so many soldiers about and I heard one of them remark in an aggrieved tone to a comrade, 'I took a girl out the other night. I thought she seemed a nice girl. And then I found out she was married and had a youngster and she wanted to bring the youngster too next time.'

November 26

Find rapidly increasing difficulty in obtaining that modest supply of chocolate upon which, as a non-smoker, I greatly depend. Shortage of sugar is the cause. Yet there is no curtailment of beer which consumes much sugar.

November 27

To tea at Lyon's, which is always a resort interesting to the students of humanity. For there one meets all classes, from the fur coats of those only a little lower than nobility down to the fustian of the workers.

December 5

No grapefruit served out with lunch at Khong's today. They say they cannot procure it. Also there are no lemons or onions to be had. Tried to buy some chocolate in the town but could not find any.

December 7

It is pleasant, when the turmoil of the day is over, to sit around the electric stove, otherwise in darkness, and listen to the golden-voiced announcer [on the wireless] broadcast the day's news. Duck's eggs were available to the wealthy in the village [Broadwater] today at 6d. each. No oranges visible but my greengrocer, as a favour to a regular customer, sold me 1lb of them, which he produced covertly.

December 9

Very mild, wind SW, heavy rain until 1pm. I went for a walk last evening at 6.30pm – it was an utterly lovely night. The moon and stars shone brilliant in a clear sky. But the droning of aeroplanes scarcely ceased and the spectral fingers of searchlights were continually busy probing the vast area of the sky in the attempt to discover them. Then, presently, I heard an explosion. The night's work of death and destruction had begun.

December 18

There is a good deal of poultry about but at daunting prices. Xmas cakes look rather dismal without the traditional icing. Confectioners are using, as an indifferent substitute, grated nuts sprinkled on jam or syrup.

December 21

The town today was thronged with Xmas shoppers, including many officers, and men and women of the three services, on leave. Mitchell's restaurant in the Arcade was crowded to inconvenience.

December 25

Xmas Day. Today there have been few people about the streets. Blackout soon reigned. In fact one meets the shadow of war everywhere. Dined at home on bread and cheese and margarine, rounded off with Bath buns and washed down with tea.

December 29

When we went out on our usual Sabbath walk in the back parts of Broadwater we found some kind of military exercise in progress on the roads. Regular soldiers were taking part with the Home Guard in operations apparently designed to meet a hypothetical landing of the Huns. Sentries with fixed bayonets and in some cases wearing gas masks appeared on corners, while barriers of barbed wire were thrown across harmless residential streets, where in places the ominous words 'land mines' were chalked. Motorists were stopped and questioned. It all seemed very realistic.

December 30

Today I saw the mayor and Corporation in robes, attended by bewigged town clerk and mace bearer, police, etc, march in procession to their annual civic service at Broadwater Church. Let us rejoice that there is still an England and we have still an ancient state and pageantry to assure us of the fact.

December 31

So ends a dismal, tantalising year, a year where our forces have suffered much yet with little opportunity to hit back. Now we feel that we are on the eve of stupendous events which we hope and believe will result in the complete rout of the Hun. The immediate future, nevertheless, remains obscure.

1941

January 1

Fine but cold day. Bitter NE wind. It was a day to make one feel one would rather be dead. Hitler says he will drop ten or 100 bombs on Britain for every one dropped on Germany. There is just one gleam of gold in this stormy sky. There is once more a tiny trickle of oranges. Today in the village I was allowed to buy two.

January 3

Fine sunny day made miserable by the same atrocious wind. Our hot water supply, part of which is situated in the roof, has frozen, so that we can have no baths and all hot water must be heated in utensils. The thermometer has fallen to 40 degrees in the bedrooms (overnight) and was no higher this morning although the boiler fire was kept alight. The meat ration is reduced and now is to be deemed to include hitherto excepted offals.

January 4

F to pantomime *Little Red Riding Hood* at the Connaught Theatre. She found it a very good show. It was produced by amateurs in collaboration with certain enterprising members of the Home Guard. A valuable relaxation at a sad time.

January 6

NE wind. A dark day with a tendency to sleet. Cold thaw in the morning, but frost again at sunset. This last week has been a real purgatory of evil weather. Wherever one has gone one has felt cold, and the south of England is in the throes of a most unhappy fuel shortage.

January 7

Even Mitchell's eating house has begun to show the frost of war. There are more vegetable dishes and fewer meat ones. Grapefruit has disappeared from the menu.

January 8

One notes the decline of the sandbag as an instrument of civilian defence. When the war started, in the uncertainty as to what was going to happen, enormous recourse was had to them for protection of windows and doors of important buildings. But the war has already outlived most of them. Many have burst from rottenness and returned to the dust from which they came. Others have become a nuisance and been dumped out of the way, their owners preferring to take a chance.

January 10

There were many anxious eyes directed at a lone ham, at Sainsbury's this morning, being sliced up, for ham is a rare visitor now.

January 13

The conscription is becoming very severe and causes greater hardship as it reaches the older age groups. Our milkman told me this morning that his firm had just lost six men to the forces. Also, my neighbour, a clerical worker of 35 years of age, with wife and child, reported that he has to join an anti-aircraft unit in the Midlands.

January 20

F to the Rivoli cinema to see *The Dictators*, a film by the famous Charlie Chaplin. A skit directed at Hitler and Musso, it is the most discussed film in the world today. But F found herself bored. The fact is Chaplin, the supreme comedian of the silent film, has lost his way by the invention of the talking film. He is become a spent force.

January 23

As I was walking about the village this morning I was rather concerned to see squads of soldiers digging makeshift strong points covering road junctions. There was one on the north west corner of Broadwater Churchyard, another at the top of the Green and a third on the main street opposite to Beaumont Road. That such work should still be in progress with the war nearly 18 months old, and six months since the French collapse, proclaims the peril of the time. I must not mention this to F or she will be alarmed.

January 24

The post brought me two walking sticks which had belonged to my grandfather and then to my aunt, both now with God. They seem sad little relics, shabby somewhat, altogether less consequential and meaner than I remember them when in use, over 50 years ago.

January 25

Tobruk, the best harbour in Libya, has been captured by our troops, together with 25,000 Italians. Our losses negligible. On other fronts too, in Africa, we advance. It is wonderful warfare, though it has to be admitted that Italians flatter the attack. To Mitchell's to lunch. A pretty, merry, lady opposite said that she and her husband had come down [from London] for a short rest after much bombing. They lived at Ealing and had fitted up a bedroom in their cellar. She added that she would rather die than face the conditions in London's deep air-raid shelters. She could not even bear to see people huddled on the platforms of the Tube stations.

January 26

Sunday, mild, with overcast sky. Walk at noon. Usual soldiery taking their ease about the residential streets where they dwell in requisitioned houses. Poor F indisposed after lunching off some of the execrable tough and tasteless cheese which is all (if any) that we can obtain nowadays. The eating problem, for delicate stomachs, becomes more and more insoluble. The war, indeed, superimposed upon the ordinary burden of life, hangs upon us like a heavy enveloping outer garment, all the more grievous because it cannot be discarded.

January 28

I am kept busy in the engrossing matter of hunting after our diminishing victuals. Thus I had to go three times today to the purveyor of bacon before I could obtain our half-a-pound ration for the week.

January 29

The Corporation has placed mounds of sand about the roads, where from citizens may take sand at pleasure to have ready for extinguishing incendiary bombs. Children are making great sport with spades and pails fetching it. Nevertheless we hear of enterprising wretches who are demanding as much as 6d. for a bucket of this stuff.

January 31

We noticed today that the local newspaper was placarding as its titbit for the week 'Moral Danger of Girls'. F commented, 'That I suppose is meant as a knock at the Army.' What nonsense. These modern girls with their scarlet lips and scarlet nails are asking for whatever they may get. It would be far more sensible for the paper to write, 'Moral Danger For Soldiers'.

February 2

Statesmen on both sides of the Atlantic are stressing the probability of an early invasion of this country by the Huns. Every hour of our constricted existence is clouded by the consequent feeling of tension. The local soldiers are busy at their strong points and lay a vast abatis [defensive barrier] of barbed wire along the seafront.

February 3

Called at the bank to leave particulars of our next-of-kin against our being both destroyed by the same bomb. A gloomy errand.

February 5

I continue to improve but now poor F is under the weather and cries in her distress, 'What with the war and this weather and the pain in my back, I feel I don't care if a bomb comes. I throw up the sponge!' The scene outside was very gloomy at this, the dead end of winter. And the lingering patches of snow seemed to increase the impression of desolation.

February 10

Last night we heard a stimulating broadcast by the PM, who, though nearly 70 years, has a kind of boyish zest about him. Though he warned us again as to the gravity of our situation, with the undefeated Huns ranged against us across the narrow seas, he seemed, somehow, as though he were enjoying the shindig. In fact, he was in his element. He was made for the present pass.

February 14

This morning the band of the Royal Scots Fusiliers played on the Green. Half wore kilts and played on the savage instruments of their nation, but the rest, as though to admit that unrelieved bagpipes were intolerable to most, were garbed as Christians and constituted a normal brass band. In wartime, when one has the perils and hazards of military life so much in mind, martial music seems to touch the heart with specially exalted plaintiveness which is sweet to listen

15 *On 2 Febrary 1941 Mr Harriss notes, 'The local soldiers lay a vast abatis of barbed wire along the seafront.'*

to. This detachment, it seems, has just completed its tour of duty here, and is now bound for Eastern parts. They are a fine looking body of young men and have been very courteous and well behaved.

February 15

This afternoon witnessed the procession to celebrate War Weapons Week, the mayor taking the salute outside the Town Hall. The procession consisted of Navy men, soldiers, tanks and other military vehicles. It took half an hour to pass the saluting point. Crowds, silent, but here and there hand clapping, lined the street as it advanced up Chapel Road from the front.

February 23

Local preparations against invasion go forward most energetically. Barbed wire fences, about 3ft high, have recently been laid in many of the side streets near to the front. More and more temporary strong points of sandbags are being set up.

February 25

The odious Japanese try to emulate Hitler, saying they want the Western Pacific and Oceania, and have been bullying Siam and the unhappy French in Indochina, as they do, periodically, the Chinese. One hopes and trusts that they will one day receive from the Americans the thrashing which they deserve. Worthing War Weapons Week has raised £590,700, lent to the Government for the purchase of armaments. Half-a-million was the aim – so it is well done.

February 26

Chocolate is so scarce in the shops that we have to allot ourselves only a small portion for each night's refreshment. After a bread and milk supper, poor F awoke in the early hours feeling as she says 'ravenous'. I was greatly tempted to eat the pieces for tomorrow night. I had them beside me, but I was firm. I buried my face in the pillow and told myself that I must not think of them.

March 1

There are many subscription dances being held in Worthing just now. And, indeed, it seems very proper and useful for the young people to have such distraction. Having regard to the number of men under arms, casualties so far have been very few, so that there are still plenty of people in good heart for such exercises. Being mostly at home, the military are very comfortably situated and seem not overburdened with the toils of their profession, though one fears for the time when the Army will have enough to do and suffers.

March 3

Our governors are urging us once again to carry our gas masks. We do not carry ours, my view being that if the Huns do use gas, which is unlikely, they will not drop the first gas on Worthing.

16   *Previously horrified by vehicles from the Army Service Corps churning up the cricket pitch at the Manor Sports Ground, Mr Harriss also witnessed its conversion into allotments.*

March 10

A strip of coast from Brighton to Littlehampton, including Worthing, has been decreed an area to which visitors may not come, which is grim news for towns which rely on trippers. A day or two since I noticed that workmen were knocking little pegs into the surface of the borough and county cricket ground [the Manor Ground, off Broadwater Road]. I imagined they might be making tracks for sport but today, to my dismay, I read on a newly erected noticeboard 'For Spaces for Allotments apply to the Town Clerk'. Once again, it is the war, and land must be found for home-grown vegetables.

March 11

On Sunday there were 14 killed in Brighton and two at Ferring, so Worthing, unscathed, has much to be thankful for.

March 12

Last night I noticed a sad uncommon sight in the town. A strong, rough, young man was pushing a go-kart containing a spotty, unhealthy-looking infant. He seemed none too amiable towards an anaemic worn female dragging along hopelessly beside him. They appeared to be tramps, a kind of people very rarely seen now. I wondered how the man had escaped conscription. As they were, what possible prospect of well-being or happiness had any of the three.

March 15

To Brighton by bus, to meet my brother-in-law, from London. We had not seen him for nearly two years. But these lightning reunions are a little sad. There is a straining to make the most of a few short hours. A couple of meals in the din of an eating house and then 'Goodbye' as the evening train swallows the visitor and steams away.

March 18

I was astounded to see at Sainsbury's this morning a ham on cut! But the hungry generations trod me down – I could not secure any. The allotments on the cricket ground have been instantly taken up and the fair arena is dotted over with industrious vandals, hacking up the turf.

March 19

The news this morning is gloomy enough to shake the most steadfast. Ninety-eight thousand tons of shipping sunk last week, following 141,000 the week before. The Battle of the Atlantic is at its fiercest and it is difficult for the uninformed civilian to feel confidence that we can endure such losses long and maintain our food supply.

March 20

Between 9pm and 10pm there was a continuous murmur of planes overhead, which indicated, I fear, a big raid on London. Our elementary and high school children have now been evacuated to Newark and Mansfield. Strange to think that for the first nine months of the war this district was a sanctuary for children from London, but now, through the conquest of France, it is come into the forefront of danger.

March 21

In the afternoon we visited the boating lake by the front. There, and in the adjoining Beach House grounds, were enough children to prove that by no means all parents have availed themselves of the recent Children's Evacuation Scheme, which we were glad to see, for the prospect would be indeed gloomy without any youngsters.

March 22

People are instructed by the Government to form bodies of fire watchers at night to see that the Huns don't drop incendiary bombs on houses unobserved. And, if needs be, males between 41 and 60 may be pressed for this service. So a party of volunteers has been formed in our road, engaged to give up most of one night in seven.

March 23

This was a day fixed by authority for national prayer in all places of worship for deliverance from the Huns. We lay low all of the morning. By a remarkable coincidence, the 372nd air-raid warning sounded at 10.55am, just as the last people were entering the church, and continued until 11.47am. The 373rd sounded at 12.20pm just as the worshippers were emerging, which seemed as though these two raids, so exactly timed, were Hitler's gestures of derision at today's observance.

March 24

Very cold night. The ground was white with frost this morning. I rose in a temperature of only 40 degrees. To the Assembly Room where the band played a selection from the old time musical play *The Belle of New York*, which I suppose was chosen out of compliment to the Americans for their giving us 'lend lease' [a donation of destroyers to reinforce the Royal Navy]. The pretty frolicsome airs of it brought a glow to my heart.

March 27

F this afternoon could not find any meat or fish paste but I found a shop not yet sold out and so we secured our breakfast tomorrow. Yet my Lord Winterton, our MP, hath said that our foodstuffs must be further reduced, for which it is hard to feel kindly towards him.

March 28

Today there is astonishing news of a *coup d'etat* in Jugoslavia. The ministers who have bowed the knee to Hitler have been put down from their seats, and the young king has headed a new government determined to resist enslavement by the Hun. The kaleidoscope of foreign affairs shows strange mutations and combinations. We now seem, jointly with Russia, heroes of these devoted people, yet Russia has lost no opportunity in slandering Britain all through the war, and we look upon the Russians as the ravishers of Finland and the disrupters of Poland.

March 29

A grey and bitter day. Went red-eyed and miserable about until lunch at Mitchell's restaurant restored and fortified me. The press there was so great there was no room for us among the elect and we were relegated to an upper chamber. On emerging we noticed a concourse in Market Street. These souls sought cat and dog meat. Here was a little emporium of horseflesh open for an hour or two, for clearly when a mere shilling's worth of meat in a week must suffice for those made in God's image, there is not much over for the brutes.

March 30

Thought for the day: in this age, for naming of female children, the quality seem to favour Jennifer; the common Valerie. Well, either is better than the Maria or Susan of the days of good Queen Vicky.

March 31

There is much activity in gardens in the endeavour to provide vegetable food. What is more surprising is the continued survival of flower-growing. There are the usual packets of flower seeds, and the usual boxes of bedding plants, exposed for sale, and these do not lack purchasers.

April 1

The new month opened most dismally, heavy rain with a very cold south east gale continued all last night and today until 4pm. Air-raid warnings today were incessant, which seemed strange in view of the tempest.

April 2

We spent half-an-hour trying on our gas masks. While I regard it as unlikely that we shall ever require their protection, it would be foolhardy not to be familiar with their use. We had a successful rehearsal, and appeared in them like a pair of equine hobgoblins – very comical.

April 3

'What a life!' quoth a saturated coal-heaver as he staggered up an entry under his heavy load. But his cheery face indicated the undaunted spirit which we like to call British. F had previously attended the Dome cinema to see *Pinnochio*, a fantasy by Walt Disney, the American master of puppetry. She called it 'a sweet thing' but thought the music nothing approaching that of the immortal *Snow White and the Seven Dwarfs*. Last night, for the first occasion since the war began, we had to go without any chocolate confection for our refreshment. Therefore consumed some Horlicks milk tablets as a substitute, but without any joy.

April 4

At 8am, ran down the street after the vanishing milkman to beg of him three eggs, but he had none. Then, later, an angel from heaven appeared in the guise of a gentleman farmer bringing baskets of eggs to sell and so I joyfully took six from him.

April 5

Benghazi, the chief port of Libya, has been recaptured by a mixed force of Huns and Italians. This news has shocked and depressed people more than anything for a long time, for the civilian in his blindness had been led to expect that our seapower in the Mediterranean was sufficient to prevent any but negligible numbers of Huns crossing over into Africa. But now we have to turn about, burn stores and 'retire according to plan'. Hitler is a wonder. He always succeeds. It is indeed clear to everybody that the Italians were powerless against us but the Huns appear and beat us at once. These are the dominating facts of the moment, and they are disquieting.

April 6

Sunday, mainly cloudy, strong and bitter north wind. At 10.20am, just as the devout were beginning to move churchwards, a low-flying airplane passed overhead and then returned, making a great noise with its engines. Then it went off in the direction of the sea, dropping bombs and eliciting retaliatory machine gun fire. A young man told me that several small houses and a doctor's house in the Park Road district, near the gas works, had been demolished. Happily, the only casualties were six injured. This appears to have been a moderately successful hit and run raid by a single plane. Curiously, there was no warning to announce it but the noise brought many to their doors.

April 9

A few gleams of sunshine this morning but for the most part a grim, grey day. The night much disturbed by the noise of aircraft passing overhead. Heard some explosions of bombs at about 6am. This day is my 59th birthday. I do not feel to be so old and have much to be thankful for in these perilous times, especially good health.

April 10

We were shocked to hear on the wireless last night that the Huns had penetrated into Greece as far as the port of Salonika. A lady told me this morning that it had made her feel really ill. 4,259 were killed in Britain last month by enemy bombs, more than the total figure for the previous month, reflecting the improving season for raids, which is terrible to observe.

April 12

A delicious return to warmer temperatures at last. This being the Saturday before Easter, foraging was a racking and troublesome affair. Throngs in the shops lining up for very little, displaying an admirable patience. Strange to say I saw the longest queue at a dog and cat meat shop in Broadwater Road. Wanted some cheese for dinner tomorrow but could have none, having already had our three-and-a-half pennies worth for the week. We had also consumed our permitted six eggs. Had to fall back on soup and peas from tins. We think it proper not to draw our meat ration since we feed at restaurants on four days and have our share of meat there. Besides, for two it is so small (two shillings worth) as to be scarcely worth the trouble and mess of cooking.

April 13

This afternoon, a dozen great tanks passed through Broadwater towards the town, breaking our peace with a shattering roar and rattle. We walked into town later and noticed a crowd looking over the railway bridge on the upside, watching them being entrained. Many were already in place, on long flat drays, each containing two, the others being with difficulty coaxed into position by their crews, very picturesque and foreign-looking in their loose black berets of the Royal Tank Regiment. All the men seemed in very good spirits, and some were returning from town, where, in spite of the closed shops, they had somehow obtained bags of delicious treats. What was their destination? Out of the void they came and into it have disappeared. We may not know. This is, above all, a war of concealment.

April 14

Bank Holiday. A grey, cloudy day. People just wandering about and shivering and contemplating the rusting barbed wire on the seafront. Many of these holidaymakers had next to nothing in their insides, for there are no sweets to be had, and about half the still existing restaurants are closed. This resulted in those that were open being overcrowded and soon eaten out. F incensed with courteous friends who have intimated a desire to entertain us to tea but propose to postpone the function until after the War. I regard it as a fortunate let off.

April 17

From about 9.50pm there appeared to be a continuous flight of planes overhead, no doubt hostile, for more than an hour. I feared for London, and in the morning men who were in touch with the telephone were talking of one of the worst raids there of the war. Victoria Station destroyed and St Bart's Hospital set on fire. Many casualties. The Hun planes seemed to escape again with negligible loss. There were no newspapers on sale in Worthing until 1pm. Soon after 2am we were awakened by the explosion of several bombs. They fell near Findon, about three miles away, but did little damage and there were no casualties.

April 19

Unsettled. Dark, with drizzle at first, and then considerable sunshine. F by unusual good fortune acquired a slab of chocolate, which she proposed to make do for two nights but could not resist devouring in one. The present plain and meagre diet, coupled with the extreme dearth of sweets, creates a craving. One notices that the official injunction not to talk about the war in public,

17   *Wartime diarist C.F. Harriss regularly walked into the town centre along Broadwater Road and Broadwater Bridge, as did the Home Guard, pictured here.*

lest we help enemy agents, is being admirably observed. One hears few references to the war in restaurants and the same reticence is even observable in private letters.

April 20

I have just seen a picture of our Prime Minister, while inspecting bombed areas, brandishing his hat on the end of his stick to encourage the downhearted. Which shows indeed how he is the man of the hour, differing from all his predecessors, for Neville Chamberlain could not have done it and kept dignity, nor Ramsay Macdonald, nor any of them.

April 21

Lunch at Mitchell's. Although meat is very limited, even to them, it seems remarkable that these caterers ought still to be able to supply a daily choice of seven or eight first course dishes and a like number of sweets to adorn their 2/6d. lunch.

April 24

A really terrible day. We move in a cloud of anxiety about Greece, an anxiety which presses on the mind every hour of the day. The position is uncertain. All that is certain is that the Huns triumph, so that evacuation by sea seems imminent. In Libya, however, they seem to have been effectually stopped, but on the brink of Egypt.

April 25

This morning, at 7.30am, I heard the noise of a plane passing over; then of the dropping of a couple of bombs followed by several bursts of machine gun fire. At present I know no more. There were no casualties posted at the Town Hall.

April 26

Incredibly cold. Yesterday's bombs fell near to the *Three Horseshoes* at Lancing, some five miles from here. Some damage to houses and a few persons injured. One of them, an old lady, has unhappily since died of shock. There is an element of cheer in this story – the raider was brought down in the sea by our fighters.

April 27

At breakfast we were thrilled by the music of a military band accompanying troops on church parade. F exclaimed that the music made her wish to run out and rush about waving a flag. But people here are very depressed about the general situation of the war. I retain full confidence in the ultimate outcome. We shall win!

April 29

Last night some alarm was caused by the dropping of a flare from a German aeroplane. For this was Worthing's first flare. It illuminated the sky with a lovely uncanny white light as it descended slowly to earth, suspended from a dainty white parachute, details of which we could distinctly see. To our relief the plane sped on and nothing untoward followed.

April 30

In the garden more equable temperatures enticed forth the delicious scent of wallflowers. Yesterday there was a ham on cut at Sainsbury's, a rare event now, but the press was too great for me to secure any. So ends this April, a very evil month and the coldest for the season I can remember.

May 2

Heard a whirr of a low flying aircraft just after the sound of an explosion. Ethel [the home help] reported that a friend had seen a ball of fire descending into St Lawrence Avenue. I suspect it was only a flare. Later I heard that last night's plane was a German which, hit and set on fire by one of our nightfighters, fell in flames into the sea after skimming over the town. What a sight we missed.

May 5

Heard a concert for the local troops at the Assembly Room by the string band of the Royal Artillery. The troops were numerous and well turned out. They looked, indeed, too superior for murderous encounter with the barbarian Huns. A large assembly of our soldiers at this time of grave national danger is to me an awful and impressive sight. So much excellent healthy young life, and tragedy waiting around the corner.

May 6

Mainly cloudy. Cold. The fact that cheese rationing, at 1oz each per week, began yesterday did nothing to lighten our darkness. This is the last straw for us and means another restaurant lunch which we can ill afford.

May 10

Last night to the Assembly Room to hear the concert version of *Merrie England* by the Worthing Municipal Choir and Orchestra, with four professional singers in the solo parts. The theme seemed a paradox, England being so far from 'Merrie' just now. Nearly half-a-million tons of shipping was sunk by U-boats or planes last month. We feel that this cannot go on. The only relief to the anxiety lies in the hope that this peril on the sea may soon bring the Americans into the war, which seems more and more likely to judge from the utterances of their politicians.

May 11

Soon after midnight I was awakened by the roar of many raiders passing overhead, and this continued with varying intensity for quite an hour. I fear that this meant another heavy bombing raid on London, which has been spared for several weeks. 'How terrible,' little F kept on exclaiming in an agony of sympathy for the suffering of the imagined victims of this hellish assault. It is Hitler's weather again, fine, calm, unclouded nights with a full moon, and he is taking full advantage of it.

May 12

As was to be feared, the raid on London on Saturday night was calamitous indeed. Many dead, and Westminster Hall, the Commons chamber and Westminster Abbey precincts all badly damaged. A future generation will wonder at the utter calmness with which we have grown to contemplate the ruin of so many irreplaceable ancient buildings throughout the land.

May 13

We were excited this morning to read that Rudolph Hess, Hitler's deputy and most intimate friend, one of the inner gang of Nazi criminals, had fled by aeroplane to England. He is now in hospital at Glasgow with a broken ankle. It is difficult to imagine anything more dramatic. Why did he come? We have been longing all day for more news.

May 14

The flight of Hess fills every mind. It is the most astounding event of the war so far and is likely to remain so. All the world is trying to guess why it happened. To me it has not seemed ludicrous but most encouraging evidence of discord in the German war leadership. Fell to imagining the reactions in the parallel case of one of our ministers suddenly fleeing to Germany.

May 16

F was moved to remark in the tone of a moralist, 'I am surprised Mrs X is wearing her skirt so short.' I mention the matter only by way of recording the prominent female fashion at this historic hour. Like so much else in the War, skirts are going up. It is necessary, in fact, to save material.

May 17

Much noise of planes overhead and explosions from time to time, some of them rather near. It appears that two German bombers were shot down at Charmandean, on the northern fringe of Worthing. I was startled by a violent burst of machine gun fire about 4.35pm but I could not see anything. They seemed to be too high up. Hear there has been a battle at Tarring. It has just occurred to me that in all the dozens of photographs of Hitler which I have seen, he has never been depicted on horseback. The inference must be that, like most house painters, he cannot ride a horse. He is probably the first of the world's dictators to labour under this disability. It is far otherwise with his henchman Mussolini, who cuts a brave figure caracoling on a white charger, like Napoleon.

May 19

I noticed that much of the cricket ground of the boys' high school, on the opposite side of Broadwater Road, is to share the fate of the town cricket ground in being cut up for allotments, save a part reserved for the boys to play on. The turf, after nearly two months of drought, seems like rock. It is pitiful to see elderly men as they wrestle with this stubborn surface and strive to transform it into filth fit for planting. Could not the Corporation have in mercy had it ploughed?

May 20

As we were returning this afternoon from the town a couple of lorries passed us containing the mangled remains of the German 'fighter' plane which was brought down nearby on Friday. A crowd of enthusiastic boys was following.

May 21

The greengrocers' shops present a strange spectacle. Just potatoes, carrots and greens, with a few tins of peas or beans. No fruit or onions whatever. There has been a lull in air raids over this country during the past week. This coincides with the massing of German aeroplanes in Greece for the attack on Crete which has begun.

May 22

The attack on Crete by aeroplanes and parachute troops and boats continues. The PM stated that it will be defended to the death, and without thought of retirement.

May 23

We are amused at recent photographs of the PM showing him clutching a great cigar, glaring with fierce eyes and long drawn sad mouth. This, I suppose, is to stiffen our resolution. However it may be, he provides a rich material for F's imprudent mimicry.

May 24

The battle for Crete continues. It is the most extraordinary, the most thrilling, event of the war so far. The result is still in doubt. The Huns are attacking a well-defended island without ships. But the defence is being plastered with bombs with little remedy against it. There was quite a riot at Mitchell's sweet shop today with a surging queue reaching out into Montague Street. One feared there might be an accident. 'What is it?' cried a nervous lady. 'It looks really dangerous. There ought to be more discipline.' F had a laughing fit. For it was only the sale of a few mixed sweets, unexpectedly arrived after many days of 'Confectionery counter closed'.

May 25

Heard last night of the loss in action off Greenland of the great battlecruiser HMS *Hood*. Few, if any, survivors of a crew of 1,200. I felt stunned by this news. This morning some of the Home Guard paraded outside our windows, ready to be conveyed into the country for their weekly exercises. The coldness of the season was demonstrated by their still wearing their greatcoats. Presently they were ordered to put on their gas masks. And so they were borne away, looking like a lot of hobgoblins.

May 26

Very wet and stormy. High wind with constant heavy showers. If I were asked what is Worthing chiefly to be distinguished from other towns, I would reply, 'Its pretty children.' One rarely sees a small child here that is not charming. Their rosy healthy faces are a credit to the climate and to their mothers. They are everywhere about with their fair, fluffy Saxon heads, their limpid solemn eyes and their little mouths so ready to relax into a smile.

May 27

News has arrived of the sinking of the German battleship *Bismarck*, which sank HMS *Hood*. Behind our daily lives for the past three days there has been the recurrent consciousness of an historic chase going on in the Atlantic, in the Nelson tradition.

May 28

Having heard, on the 1pm wireless, the substance of a much advertised speech by President Roosevelt, I am disappointed. It seems very much the mixture as before. If the Americans feel so strongly about it all, why do they not join us?

May 29

The affair in Crete goes badly. Our men have continually to give ground and I fear evacuation is looming. The Huns seem like mechanised savages.

May 30

Only three survivors from HMS *Hood*. This wholesale elimination of so great a company of the nation's finest manhood is too terrible. And all from a chance hit at 13 miles range.

June 1

The sunk *Bismarck* seems to have been the largest and most remarkable battleship ever conceived. It is difficult not to feel a certain alarm as one ponders upon the extraordinary aptitude for war of the German nation. They are so desperately earnest for their cause, so clever, efficient, thorough, self-denying. We seem happy-go-lucky compared to them.

June 2

Whit Monday. This was kept as a general holiday, except that munitions factories were kept running. It was mainly cloudy, with a raging bitter NE wind. Short of being wet, a worse day for a summer holiday could scarcely be imagined. The long dreaded blow has fallen. Our forces have had to evacuate Crete. We have lost many men and the Navy several fine ships, but the Huns have lost much more heavily. A most gallant sacrifice has not been quite in vain. But the Nazi avalanche rolls on. Where and when will it be stemmed? All clothing is subjected to rationing as from today. Each person is given 66 coupons which are to suffice him for the year. This scheme will cause weeping and gnashing of teeth among the more frivolous type of woman, but it seems very useful and sound. Why, certain women have actually been writing to the Ministry of Supply to complain they cannot get enough lip paint.

June 3

Worthing had but a forlorn holiday yesterday since the town is a militarily forbidden area to visitors from outside.

June 5

Thunder throughout the night, accompanied by torrential rain. To lunch at WH Smith's, wherein a great company of eaters. All sorts and conditions of men and women now throng the restaurants. For who can satisfy his pangs at home on the one shilling worth of meat and one ounce of cheese allowed weekly?

June 6

This morning purchased two undergarments and had to surrender eight of my 66 annual coupons. If I had purchased a suit I must have given up 26. The allowance seems meagre, but, being no Beau Brummel, I shall manage. Spent an hour on glorious Broadwater Green as the sun descended in splendour, bathing the scene in ethereal radiance. More than a score of pleasure motor coaches went by. However, they did not contain pleasure seekers, but workmen returning from the day's toil. Their labour is of a secret kind. The purpose and place of it is undisclosed. It may be restoring destruction at Southampton or elsewhere, or the far flung business of constructing camps for troops on the Downs.

June 8

This morning we found a drumhead service in progress on Broadwater Green. It embraced the Royal Engineers stationed locally, with the sea and air cadets. The mayor was present in chain of office, attended by the robed and bewigged town clerk. The ceremony, in the absence of sunshine and instrumental music, was not impressive. For the unaccompanied singing was excusably weak and fainthearted, and the preacher too remote for most of the company to hear him. So in due course the congregation dissolved without enthusiasm.

June 11

Registered at my grocer's for egg rationing. It is whispered we might be allowed two per week each.

June 13

This year we enjoyed (as much as we could) a protracted rhubarb crop. One still observes that accommodating vegetable peeping out of shopping bags, or bundles of it hugged under armpits as though it were a treasure. And so it is a treasure now that we can procure no fruit. Generally, the supplies of almost all foods are fragmentary and fluctuating. Each appears for a space, becomes unobtainable for a space, and then reappears (not always) but usually in diminished quantity. All this makes for weary and baffling shopping. Never before has the recurrent necessity of shopping to eat been so forcibly and unpleasantly brought home to us.

June 16

Very fine. Summer at last. This afternoon we went for a coach drive to Chichester. The coach was held up on the road near Arundel for quarter of an hour to allow passage for dozens of armed lorries packed with troops. Manoeuvres are in progress. Last night, soon after 10pm, there was a roar of heavy tanks passing along Broadwater Road which lasted for half an hour.

June 17

On the whole, throughout England, there has been, for two or three weeks, a most blessed respite from any considerable bombing. There have been none of those fearful mass attacks. The Hun is evidently preoccupied with other matters. Thus, there is tension between Germany and Russia. Rogues seem to have fallen out. The Huns want the Ukraine and have lined up an enormous army in order to assure themselves of that and more.

June 18

There was disclosed in the news sheets today for the first time a new invention for the detection of aircraft by radar. This, it appears, was in full development in Britain before the war but only now perfected. Which, I suppose, accounts for the mysterious assemblage of gigantic steel spars pointing to the sky, with buildings at their foot, which grew up in a field between here and Littlehampton.

June 19

Visited the boating lake on the seafront but found it to have been wired off by the military since I last came that way. So to watch the bowlers in Beach House Park but found two of the four greens out of use, having been bombed by the Huns in the spring.

June 20

Just now the absence of air raids and the inactivity (or should one say veiled activity?) of the Huns has an uncanny effect on the mind. We are experiencing a kind of specious sweet Nirvana just at the time of year when we had expected a racking anxiety and an intense clash of arms.

June 22

F yesterday to the Rivoli cinema to see *Little Nellie Kelly*, featuring Judy Garland and George Murphy. She returned enthusiastic. 'The prettiest piece I ever saw.' And she has seen her share.

June 23

Last night, when listening to the 9pm news broadcast, we experienced a thrilling moment. The PM was unexpectedly introduced to tell us that the Huns had invaded Russia. One felt a sense of awe and bewilderment. It was as though, in a moment, we had arrived at the crash of worlds. However, as the minutes passed, and the PM made his very forceful commentary, the numbed faculties returned to normal, and we began to reorientate our shaken outlook and to grip reality again. The Soviet government is to be our ally, certainly an unlovely one, and of doubtful military capacity to judge from the recent Finnish war. Yet, on the whole, I think this news is good. It must mean a shifting of part of the burden from John Bull's weary shoulders.

June 24

The invasion of Russia fills the mind. We don't like the Bolsheviks but are very thankful that the Nazi 'creative pause' is not terminated in our direction. Still one feels the horror of the impending gigantic clash.

June 25

This afternoon at 6.30pm we walked out into an exercise for the ARP and fire brigade services. We carried our gas masks as we had been warned that tear gas might be used but did not meet with any. Half-a-dozen aeroplanes supplied by the RAF kept circling over the town, and gave an exhibition of dive-bombing (without bombs!). There were many fire appliances moving about. People were standing in their front gardens in quite a state of effervescence, expecting to see rather more than there was to see. All seemed glad to have the opportunity for a little excitement.

June 27

Lunched out, after intending to lunch in off an egg salad, but found we could only have one egg each this week and this must be saved for Sunday's dinner. So, as we have no cheese this week, and there has been no cut meat obtainable for many weeks, we had after all to seek more expensive refreshment at an eating house. Then, F being seized with wanderlust, we went on a bus to Brighton. The interdict on trippers has hit that delectable city very hard. She is but a shadow of her former self. Even the sailor before the waxworks by the East Pier, who formerly laughed and writhed, now sat motionless in his chair – to save electric current. Brighton and Hove promenade and lawns are now a tangled wilderness of stakes and wire sprinkled with notices: 'Beware of mines.'

June 28

For the first time I saw a bus conductor of the fair sex. She a well-looking wench enough in her dark blue uniform, but spoilt in her lower part by abominable trousers. Then again, in the town, saw for the first time a car driven by a woman chauffeur, peaked cap and all. Thus do women, in the absence of the stronger sex, take more and more part in our public life at home. Coming to the seafront, saw for the first time merchant ships running past with barrage balloons fixed to them by ropes and floating high above them. There were half-a-dozen small ships with three balloons, and they were running close inshore, which is a rare sight here, and people about Montague Place were very interested, craning their necks to see over the wire defences of the promenade, and asking one another what the balloons might mean.

June 29

Sunday. It was surprising to see so many motor cars about in spite of the petrol limitation. Their owners must save up their ration for a burst at the weekend. Also many military vehicles.

June 30

Nearby a great temporary reservoir is building against the possibility of the Hun invaders destroying the normal water supply. Which shows how seriously the Government still think the threat of invasion. If the Russians go down, Hitler will have nothing else to do. So ends June, the best of the months. At another time it would seem sad but now one month is very much like another, only the war matters.

July 1

The feature of recent days has been the daylight raids made by the RAF on Germany and northern France. The air above us has been filled this evening with the hum of our planes returning to roost. Our shores are little troubled now with German planes. They seem to be all busy against the Russians. Long may it be so.

July 2

Too hot and the ground is parched. To the milk factory to pay our monthly dues. Here, in a large, cool upper room sit a score of damsels diligently employed at desks. They are pretty to see in their light summer frocks of many colours.

July 3

Another day as lovely as the last. The fine weather has effected the usual dissolution of sartorial convention. Stockingless females are to be forgiven, for her diminishing coupons are a canker on every woman's heart. But me turns the head away from elderly men in little shorts, like boy scouts. To High Salvington by bus and drink tea in a pleasant little tea gardens, amid splendid views and a sufficient company of others doing likewise. Only the passing planes remind one of the war.

July 6

High Salvington again, which is Worthing's Hampstead Heath, to tea and ramble. But buses were very hot and overcrowded.

18   *Could that be Mr Harriss and his wife seated outside the old library at the junction of Chapel Road and Richmond Road?*

July 7

Very warm. Cloudless sky. The grass is losing all colour and the plants are withering.

July 9

A torrid day. The shade temperature in Chapel Road at 3pm reached 85 degrees. Lunch at Mitchell's but in this heat the best eating house loses all charm. One's fellows seem to glisten and the food becomes untempting. Custard is being served there now of a greenish tinge.

July 11

These sweltering humdrum days sap one's energy and make one long for the night. The war drags. In Russia, on a 1,000 mile front, there is no decision. Yet all the time I feel in my bones that there, at last, the clouds are breaking to disclose the light of eventual victory. There, at last, the Hun is being drained of his omnipotent strength, as Napoleon was before him.

July 13

This day opened very dark and close. Dead calm, then there were thunderclaps and finally, at 8.45am, heavy rain which continued in torrents for over four hours. The most precious rain after four weeks of drought. Then fine and hot again. To Sompting Church for Evensong, a walk of a couple of miles. The pretty little ancient church crowded and hot.

July 19

Cloudy with bright intervals. Showery. SW breeze. This morning heard a short burst of machine gun fire. Heard later that it was directed at a raiding German plane. The combat was a matter of seconds. Having shot down his enemy into the sea, the RAF fighter pilot was seen directing his plane serenely homewards. Pastrycooks' cakes are very much deteriorated in appearance, succulence and quantity during the past quarter. It is a poor drab display in windows now, yet soon snatched up.

July 23

There is a strange movement suddenly started, and growing apace, to use the letter V as a symbol of coming victory. Thus one sees it ad nauseam in public, in shop windows, in the middle of the backscene on the stage where our orchestra plays. This craze threatens, in effect, to become a public nuisance, for little blackguard boys are making the symbol with chalk on pavements and fences and everywhere about the town.

July 25

After five weeks of intense fighting in Russia the Hun onslaught appears to have been brought to a standstill. What is Hitler thinking now?

July 26

Very hard work this afternoon shopping in the heat and crowds. No cut meat, no cornflakes, no sweets, no biscuits, no meat or fish paste. The smug utterances of the Food Ministry in

Parliament give no idea of the hardship that people are undergoing. Man does not live by bread and potatoes alone.

July 30

40,000 Japanese are landed in Indochina to 'protect' it, quite in the Hitler way. And the French, whose country it is, are grown too feeble to deny them. And so we may soon expect to see the Japanese knocking on Singapore and Burma, and doing God knows what mischief in these parts. Lunched at Mitchell's. Two middle-aged ladies were at issue as to whether women should wear trousers. One argued that they are unsuitable for women, men did not like seeing women in them, and all but the slimmest are too broad in the beam for them. Her primmer and meeker companion took the opposite view.

July 31

This afternoon by bus to Sullington, near Storrington, to visit friends whom we had not met for 15 years. Called at the Rectory to ask the way, found a pretty little serving maid who blushed charmingly as she made reply, which is a sight not often seen among our misses now. W [the author's friend] is in the Home Guard and teaching bayonet fighting. He instructs that it is not enough to dig the point into the kidney and liver and turn the weapon round. It is necessary to cultivate also a brutal and ruthless spirit while it is done. So home after a pleasant tea-drinking. Noticed that some of the fields and hills near Findon are scarred with gigantic trenches dug against the coming German tanks. It was little comforting to reflect that we reside on the wrong side of that fortification.

August 1

We were told by our friends yesterday that about 1,000 bombs had fallen in the Storrington district since the war began, though damage and casualties had been very slight. This because the Huns, to their credit be it said, do not deliberately bomb that rural residential area, but it is convenient for them to jettison their remaining bombs on the Downs before setting off across the sea on their return from raids. It is diverting to sit on public seats and listen to the talk. On the whole, people seem to pay great regard to the official injunction not to talk publicly about matters possibly useful to the enemy's spies. So there is little talk directly about the war, and very little grumbling.

August 4

We have this month 1lb of jam and, in addition, 1lb of marmalade, for the pair of us. It is the first marmalade we have tasted since Xmas, for, until recently, there has been none in the shops. This extra 1lb of sweet spread is most welcome and mitigates a little the dismal monotony of our diet.

August 7

Ethel has been able to buy four oranges, and desiring but two, sold us the rest. I cannot remember when we last tasted oranges. They seem to belong altogether to the remote past. This sudden appearance of these fruits is inexplicable but certainly very nice.

August 9

Sabotage in the conquered countries of Europe seems to be on the increase. In one way this is a good sign. It shows that the oppressed peoples are ready to loose their chains, that the cauldron is boiling up. I think we in this favoured land live our lives too easily and do not regard enough the agony in Europe occasioned by the Huns. There are no Bank Holidays over there. I do not forget our bombing, but our island situation still saves us from suffering as others do.

August 13

We are having calamitous weather, just when a bumper harvest is greatly desired and seems actually in prospect. Today was early closing, which, with the weather conditions, caused the town to look especially forlorn. Many empty shops and this is constantly increasing one by one as their proprietors succumb to the frost of war, and the rest closed. A few people abroad, in dull wraps, struggling, with heads bent to the raging tempest, and striving to preserve their headgear.

August 14

As I was sitting on the edge of the Green, looking down Broadwater village, a column of tanks came along amongst the civilian traffic. It was 12.30pm, and the pavements were lively with busy shoppers. The tanks formed what seemed like an endless procession of ugly monsters. There must have been about 50 of them, with several ancillary vehicles. Each had its central turret open, from which emerged the bereted heads of two or three sunburned warriors. The procession took half an hour to pass and was a most impressive display of England's growing might. There were 500 killed in sporadic [air] raids last month, rather less than the number of our fellow citizens who are in the habit of being killed in the same period by means of motor vehicles.

August 17

Thought for the day: each generation of mankind tends to hug the illusion of having reached the culmination of human achievement. Yet, as we scoff at our groping ancestors, so our descendants will surely scoff at us.

August 18

Heavy showers in the night and up to 9am. Autumn is in the air. The wide expanse of Broadwater Green is speckled with little puffballs and the feathers of moulting seagulls. The German juggernaut creeps on into the Ukraine, always a little further. Oh, that Democracy should have voted through the years for statesmen ready to permit this beast to grow from defenceless infancy to fearsome maturity.

August 19

Into the town to order coal. Anthracite is up again at 4s. 3d. per cwt. But, peace or war, coal always goes up. What will our descendants have to pay for coal?

August 22

The position in Russia has deteriorated much in the past week. The Huns gain ground both in the south and in the north, and the fate of Leningrad seems to be in the balance. They appear to possess so much resourcefulness, daring and endurance that one begins to wonder whether anything on earth can stop them. After the mess of things we have made in Libya, the Huns make us look second rate as wagers of war. We sat this afternoon on one of the few seats still adjoining the front and regarded the barbed wire and concrete blocks. 'A most depressing sight,' as a gentleman remarked.

August 24

Kippers for breakfast, a striking event, for none have been obtainable since last winter. They are more welcome since potted meat is become scarce and of poor quality, if not made of 'cat and camel' as I heard a waggish shopman suggest to an anxious lady customer. Poor F diligently mended disintegrating sheets, to put off as long as possible a necessity, now forbiddingly costly, of buying more.

August 25

On the wireless last night a fine eloquent speech by the PM about his meeting with President Roosevelt in the Atlantic. His chief point seemed to be a scarcely veiled invitation to the USA to come and fight beside us.

August 27

I hear that much of the corn on the Downs is sprouting and showing mildew. It seems probable that much of the greatest crop of corn ever grown in Britain will be lost through the rains.

August 31

Two squadrons of fighter planes in formation, a dozen in each, passed over here, one this morning, the other at 6.30pm. A common sight now. They were moving from the west to the east, the direction of the fighting. There is sadness about these passages of youth on silver wings. One always feels that some are not destined to return.

September 2

After lunch in Worthing, F, who loves trips, insisted on an excursion to celebrate the fine day. So to Arundel by bus. Bus frantically crowded. We wandered about the hilly streets in this little township slumbering around the castle walls, till it was respectable to seek tea at the Warming Pan tea house.

September 3

Fine, but a sea mist of varying density obscured the sun throughout the day. To Brighton by bus to secure accommodation for next week at the *Curzon Hotel*, one of the few hotels there still open. For we require a short rest from housekeeping after 15 months since we were last away. Brighton looked sad in the mist. Each time we go there the barbed wire defences on the front grow greater, and more rusty, and shabby with unkempt grass, so that a scene of utter desolation is produced. People mostly look pale and sad and weary. The newsboys were calling out 'Biggest RAF raid on Berlin' and 'Russians attack all along the line of front'. Nevertheless, the figures huddled along the seats remain listless on this, the second anniversary of the outbreak of the War.

September 4

It is said that about 500 workmen are to be brought over from Portsmouth to do engineering work here for the Navy. I have noticed a local garage being fitted up with machinery, and have heard of others. It is done privily, windows being obscured. This is an effort to avoid concentrating labour of this kind in large industrial areas where it is likely to be bombed. The men are being billeted in private lodgings. People with rooms vacant can apply at the Town Hall.

September 8

Our rest much disturbed last night by the constant passing of aeroplanes. Today we heard that they were going to Berlin which again received the heaviest raid since the war began. Today we have taken up residence at the *Curzon Hotel*, Brighton, after a consolingly easy railway journey. Only about a score of people at the hotel, and they elderly. A feeling of suspended animation about the place. After lunch we wandered about until teatime and then sat on the front, just by the West Pier. Through many feet of barbed wire we surveyed a shipless sea, which looked as smooth as

19   *Desolate New Parade, East Worthing, with the boating pool in the foreground.*

a duckpond. Presently along the road at our back came a long line of tanks returning from the day's exercises.

September 9

We spend most of the day outdoors 'resting and getting the fresh air', as F puts it. Which is about all life in a holiday resort now amounts to. And it was rather difficult to kill time. Meals in the hotel are very much curtailed and somewhat meagre. We ate the whole day's allowance of butter at breakfast and then had to wrestle with the management to get a tiny dab of margarine as supplement.

September 10

Brighton front is looking shabby and dilapidated for lack of painting and some of the adjacent squares look quite derelict, with peeling paint, uncurtained windows and many 'To Let' posters. The famous *Grand Hotel*, with many others, is closed. It appears particularly desolate, with many broken windows, which are neither being repaired nor even boarded up. There is no visible destruction from bombing near the front.

September 12

A cereal followed by a single egg was provided for breakfast this morning, which seemed inadequate even in present conditions. In general, however, even now, one certainly enjoys in an hotel articles of diet which the ordinary citizen cannot obtain in the shops – cornflakes for instance, and ham and tongue, also poultry, only to be had elsewhere at a prohibitive price. There is a middle-aged woman in the hotel who appears to have decided to dress in men's clothing from head to foot. This sight I find disgusting and repulsive. It makes me desire to leave the hotel.

September 13

This afternoon we sat in the grounds of the Pavilion and listened to the Royal Pavilion Orchestra. It seemed an improvised medley of professionals and amateurs, male and female, mostly veterans, who produced mildly pleasant music under a capable conductor whose face expressed sardonic resignation. It seemed scarcely worthy of a town the size of Brighton but doubtless reflected the difficulties of the war.

September 15

This morning, while F took a look at the shops, I sat in the Pavilion grounds intent on the newspapers. A tall, gaunt, kindly-visaged railwayman was feeding the pigeons. They approached him where he sat, nearer and nearer in eagerness for their meal. He appeared a veritable St Francis as he stooped to break up a fallen morsel which seemed too large. He regarded intently his feathered friends as they pecked away until a few inches from him then, suddenly, with a lightning lunge, his right hand shot out and seized a bird, thrust it into a bag produced from nowhere, and hid that away in a capricious pocket. Then, his dastardly purpose achieved, the treacherous fowler rose and strode away. After lunch, our holiday ended, home to Worthing.

September 16

A police officer knocked on front door as I was undressing. Full of dread, I shuffled down to him in dressing gown and slippers. He complained that light penetrated the dining room curtains. They have satisfied the police during two winters so I was the more confounded. What an ending to a holiday. There were only 169 people killed by air raids on this country in August last, the smallest number killed since bombing began. That is the measure of the assistance rendered to us by the Russians in their magnificent resistance to the German hordes. Hitler cannot spare planes against us – at present.

September 21

Being a few months short of my 60th birthday, I had to register myself for civil defence, which means compulsory fire watching. This ordeal was unfamiliar and rather disturbing but there was nothing 'Prussian' about it, just a row of clerks at a table in a school in Chapel Street who asked me one or two questions and filled in a form. But I think a man of my age might have been excused. Even the Russians take men for this duty only up to 55. However, I was asked whether I wished to appeal against enrolment. I do, and so in my turn I filled up a form.

September 24

This afternoon we went on a coach drive to Ditchling. On our way back the coach was suddenly held up and boarded by a posse of constables, civilian and military. This attack was so unexpected and strange as to be somewhat alarming. However, after curiously inspecting a few identity cards, they seemed satisfied that there were no enemy agents amongst us, and we were allowed to proceed. It was just one of war's sideshows.

September 27

Ethel left our employment today, and we bade her farewell – not without sentiment. For she has served us for over six months and leaves only that she may undertake a more war-worthy toil. At parting she gave us three rock cakes made by herself and she makes them well. Spent the afternoon in Steyne Gardens, where people lounged on deckchairs in the summer way. Lawn tennis was in progress on the hard courts there. But all the time the RAF were overhead, performing their ceaseless evolutions.

October 1

Sunny morning, cloudy afternoon. Was mystified this morning by observing a spheroid object high in the sky, shining like silver against the blue. It did not appear to lose height, as a parachute would, so I marvelled much until someone explained that it was a barrage balloon which had broken loose. At noon, as I was walking into Worthing, eight RAF fighters flew over in the direction of the French coast. A long queue outside a grocers in South Street who had disclosed that he had biscuits, a rare thing.

October 5

On the continent the ineffable Huns keep slaughtering innocent hostages in the attempt to suppress constant sabotage by resistance movements. These brave rebels at present have no chance, but vengeance must be ever in their thoughts, and will one day come to a terrible fruition.

October 6

Very fine, slight SE wind. The sun was so hot at midday as we sat in Montague Place that we had to seek shade in Steyne Gardens. To tea and band at Assembly Hall, but we did not receive a fair allowance of the former in the pot. 'That tea was miserable stuff,' remarked F in a fervour of indignation as she fingered the bill. But the girl has forgotten to charge the extra 2d. for 'china'. I am always glad when that happens. It is God looking after us.

October 7

One comes to the conclusion, after much observation, that even with the country in a state of total war, each citizen remains primarily concerned with his own private affairs. That is to say, provided his country is an island with a sufficient protection of sea power!

October 8

I have a heavy cold. Also, apprehension as to the result of my appeal against fire watching, to be heard on Friday.

October 9

Blackout is now at 6.52pm. It is weary work to come home tired and have to adjust blinds or screens to every window in the house. Our weak spots are still unremedied as the upholsterer is so pressed that he cannot yet complete the order. So the rooms concerned cannot be used after dark.

October 10

This, the dreaded day of the hearing of my appeal against fire watching, has ended in anticlimax. Half an hour before I was due to set out for the Town Hall I received notice that the sitting of the Hardship Committee had been cancelled. I was actually disappointed, for the impending ordeal had been poisoning my life for days, yet I feel I had a good cause and wanted to get it over. This fire watching is being carried to an extent excessive for this, comparatively safe, area. But in this war it seems to be the way of our rulers to rush to extremes without reasonable discrimination. The repeated exhortations to carry gas masks is another instance but there the solid British public decided 'no' and set up an effective passive resistance.

October 13

Cloudy with bright intervals. Here in England there is a peacefulness passing understanding about these calm, mellow, autumn days and one feels there is something not quite right about it. For the situation of the Russians grows ever graver. The Huns mean to have Moscow. Russia's armies are being destroyed. Should not our army be fighting too? Year after year we prepare, yet, save in the air, what do we effect? This feeling of leaving the Russians in the lurch is a continuing gadfly, likely more and more to prick the conscience of this proud and generous nation.

October 14

The wireless news last night was interrupted by a mysterious voice which made an impudent pro-German commentary on the war situation. However, it caused more amusement than annoyance.

It appears to be a retaliation for a similar but friendly voice on the continent which has been interfering with the German wireless.

October 16

Stood in a long queue outside Mitchell's this afternoon hoping to obtain some chocolate, a hope which was ultimately realised. Each customer is allowed only 7d. worth, with one quarter of a pound of mixed sweets if desired. It is difficult to arrange for enough nourishing meals now. We get very tired of the sardines or 'paste'. I remarked to F that my dentist had eulogised the sausage meat now in favour with many. It is cheap. But she replied, 'I would not eat it, he must be very hard up if he eats it. Who knows what it is made of?'

October 17

There were 217 killed in air raids over this island last month, another low figure for which we again have to thank the Russians. Today was the hearing of my appeal against fire watching. It has been allowed, most courteously, by a triumvirate, and I feel a different being. But I had a bad 20 minutes in a bare room at the Town Hall, awaiting my turn with a dozen other unfortunates. I felt under a torture of nerves. But all is well.

October 18

The Huns are within 65 miles of Moscow and the Russian government has moved its seat from there, further east.

October 19

Our walk this morning took the form of a vain hunt for a Sunday paper. The newsprint shortage is such that retailers are allowed very few unordered copies. A quiet morning at home, the peace of which was presently broken by the roar of a procession of tanks down Broadwater Road on their way to entrain. The noise which these monsters make when there are several together is prodigious.

October 21

In the afternoon we went to take tea with two ladies who live on the front. They feasted us in a way to recall former days of peaceful plenty and had the kindness to remark when we left 'that this little meeting had been a pleasant oasis in the desert of this dreary war', and so it had. The anniversary of Trafalgar. There a combination of genius and circumstance consumated a gigantic climax and a sublime tragedy, which more and more, at the growing distance of the years, avail to rend the heart and light the patriot's way.

October 22

Went down to Worthing this morning early and enjoyed the sun on the front. One may not walk or sit actually on the promenade because of the defences there, but seats in the front gardens of closed hotels opposite are now open to the general public. Today these were crowded mostly with persons of what is called 'the non productive age'.

October 23

The mysterious interrupter still cuts in upon the evening wireless programme. His origin is undiscovered. He speaks with a robust fluency and affects to be a British critic of the Government. The other night the announcer tried to defeat him by running on without pauses, but ineffectively. One hears such remarks as 'Britain is doomed'. The announcer is often countered by 'Lies! Lies! All Lies' when he has any good news to publish and there are repeated ejaculations such as 'What has Churchill been paid by the Jews?', 'Churchill has lost the war', 'The Russians are beaten', 'We want a second front in the West', 'Churchill is afraid to attack', 'Roosevelt has bought him', 'Roosevelt won't fight', 'Eden makes us sick'. As the orthodox news now is either bad or stereotyped, one feels a certain gratitude to this voice for providing light relief. His rather jovial delivery has a certain attraction and he is decidedly amusing. But he will never sow dissension in our ranks with this rubbish. Tea at Lyon's, where a poor man at the table next to ours was seized with a fit and I thought he had died. Presently four policemen arrived with a stretcher and with calm, kindly efficiency carried him away. Poor F, with her abundant sympathy for suffering, was brought to tears and I wish infinitely that she had been spared such a ghastly sight.

October 24

This morning bought a quarter of a pound of new Government bacon, which is given by the Americans under their Lease and Lend Act. Nevertheless the British consumer has to pay for it. Two shillings per pound, ready cooked. It is very fat and rather rank flavoured, yet I welcome it, for it is additional to the exiguous bacon ration and provides an alternative to the inevitable sardines and paste.

October 25

House temperature only about 50 degrees. Women are beginning to appear in fur coats and the military in great ones. Hudson's soap, that time-honoured helpmate of the housewife, is no more. This is the extinction of a familiar friend of old men's childhood days.

October 26

Cloudy with bright intervals but a glacial NW wind, which made walking a penance. This morning met a detachment of Royal Welch Fusiliers, our present garrison, with their traditional mascot, a fine white goat, and a few fifes and drums leading them on church parade to Broadwater Church. The show was not impressive, men being but few, and, besides, the new khaki battledress is hideous enough to damn the show.

October 28

The Huns appear to be held back from Leningrad and Moscow – for the present! But they are sweeping over the Ukraine like a vast swarm of locusts, devouring and wasting that fertile land.

October 29

As one goes about the town, one notices that more and more shops, for various reasons arising out of the emergency, are 'To Let', but this is not the case as to dwelling houses. There are more of these tenanted now than a year ago. Many of the birds who took flight in the early days have returned, new residents have come to what is increasingly regarded as a safe area, and some houses have been taken over by the military.

November 1

The meat supply seems to be causing the Food Ministry a great deal of worry. There are communal feeding establishments set up where a hotpot can be had for 9d. Met a lady from London who has seen much of the terrible air raids there. She mentioned how there had been non-stop bombing for 12 hours at a stretch and people had got no proper sleep over a period of weeks. Yet, after the worst experience, even women say they would go through it again rather than negotiate a peace with Hitler.

November 2

Sunday, cold and cloudy. Showers. Last evening at 8.55pm we were startled by the sudden explosion quite near of two bombs which whistled shrilly in their descent. The effect was particularly confounding because we had heard no bombs since last winter. Poor F was thrown into great distress of mind not only from natural alarm but also on account of her lively feeling for other possible sufferers. Then, at 9pm, the tardy siren signalled our 517th air-raid warning, which lasted until 9.36pm. It nearly always happens here that the warning follows the event, which is certainly unfortunate. Planes rushing about, but no more bombs.

November 3

The air raid here on Saturday night was the worst we have experienced. Two heavy bombs fell in the Haynes Road area near West Worthing station, about a mile from our house. Eight persons were killed and 30 injured. Nine good class houses were destroyed and there was damage over a large area. A crowd of people was to be seen today inspecting the casualty lists outside the Town Hall but otherwise life flowed on undisturbed and mainly, I am afraid, unconcerned. War undoubtedly blunts the higher sympathies.

November 5

Guy Fawkes Day passed unobserved. Fireworks are not allowed. I rise at 6.45am and find the world then cold and dark. The ever-victorious Huns continue to prevail against the Russians, who, one reads to one's amazement, are outnumbered. The Ukraine is nearly all gone and most of the Crimea. The continued Russian defeats are perplexing and disturbing.

November 8

We discuss the effect of war upon conduct and decide that war produces in man extremes of excellence and turpitude, which, under normal conditions, to a great extent lie dormant and concealed. Thus we have on the one hand many instances of sublime goodness and heroism, and, on the other, multiplied examples of the worst greed, cheating and license.

November 10

To the Food Office in Worthing to fetch new ration books relating to tinned meats and fishes. Crowds thronging around pigeon holes. It might have been a booking office on the Underground in the rush hour. We now have in use four ration books each, as has every individual in the land. One is sorry for large families. Housewives must carry a score or more of books when they go shopping.

November 11

Armistice Day in the last war. It seems now but a pallid wraith, void, purposeless. But there was the usual sale of poppies. A leading photographer has filled a window with portraits of those local warriors who have already given their lives in this present conflict. A mistake, I think. The PM made a great, heartening speech at the Mansion House yesterday. He directed the plainest words at Japan, now hovering on the brink of war, and seemed to hint at the enforced ending, one day, of the abominable Japanese aggression in China. He was in fine voice and spirits, suggesting one who revels in crises, and thrives on anxieties. A tireless master of events, in fact.

November 13

Heavy rain from dawn until night. Life pulsated limply in the stresses of a watery desolation. Satisfied eaters tended to linger indefinitely amid the cosy glamours of Mitchell's. 'Those two over there have been in here nearly an hour and a half, they seem to think it is a library,' remarked a disapproving waitress.

November 14

By a majority of only 18, the American House of Representatives has agreed to the arming of their merchant ships and the sailing of these ships into Allied ports. So the USA are halfway into war with Germany, but they come with cold feet. The orchestra at the Assembly Hall this afternoon played a selection from 'The Belle of New York', presumably to celebrate this most important occasion.

November 15

U-boats seem to be more numerous than ever but their activities are being more successfully met. Losses of merchant ships, though still serious, show a considerable decline. Hitler's designs of starving us out seem less and less likely to be realised. It must be admitted, though, that the war still goes badly. The Huns stand on the doorstep of the Caucasian oilfields and, altogether, the future remains portentous and dark.

November 16

After the rain stopped, a walk down Dominion Road. Stood alone on the tall railway bridge there looking across the roofs to where the towering Onslow flats are bordered by the sea.

November 21

To my solicitor in Liverpool Gardens. He showed me, hidden in the laurel hedge fronting his premises, two or three holes dug by the military wherein to place machine guns in case of invasion. For this, to his surprise, the War Office has agreed to pay him £40 per annum commission.

November 22

Yesterday we were put in a flutter by the blackout. We came in after dark and, going into the dining room, I instinctively turned on the electric light, not realising that I had not yet drawn the curtains. There was immediately a harsh shout from someone in the road. We remained for long in miserable dread of a call from an irate official.

November 23

A grand day, whereon Lord Woolton hath cast his shadow by suddenly cutting down our milk to two pints a week. This is less than half what we have been having and we are also deprived of so much else.

November 26

The shops in Worthing are again making a brave attempt to celebrate Christmas. A good show of calendars, cards and children's books.

December 4

I notice that our garrison of Royal Welch Fusiliers has secretly departed. In their place we have some very sturdy, stocky successors, Canadians, mostly of the West Nova Scotia Regiment.

20 *An Army lorry, possibly Canadian, in Montague Place. Mr Harriss's wife was a regular cinemagoer, and frequented the Odeon.*

December 8

Japan has declared war on Britain and the USA, having a few hours previously suddenly made treacherous air attacks on American naval bases in the Pacific. One feels that we are on the brink of the gravest events. For the Japanese will fight like devils, regardless of losses, to oust the European from East Asia. As I was walking towards the front in the blackout last evening, one of our new garrison stopped me and asked if I would like to buy some 'Canadian cigarettes'. However, to a non-smoker it offered no attraction. On going a little further, I was astonished to be held up by another soldier who desired to unload on me 'a nice pencil'. These colonial cousins of ours seem to be a very impecunious lot. I have never been accosted like this by any of our own troops. Yet the Colonials receive double their pay.

December 9

The position in the Pacific is of absorbing interest. There has been no situation to compare with it of such dramatic intensity since the war broke out more than two years ago. Quick developments are certain, but they are veiled and the area of operations is vast. Life in England is, of course, not affected.

December 10

The *Prince of Wales* and the *Repulse*, two of the greatest of the King's ships, sunk by bombs from Japanese aircraft off Malaya. The little waitress attending to our lunch at Mitchell's told us this with hushed concern. This frightful news has since been announced by the PM in the Commons. The loss of life we don't yet know. Never before did the Empire receive such a blow in one day.

December 11

I happened to be free of shopping this morning and much enjoyed strolling about on the Green in the sun's rays. By midday we were much consoled by learning that there are over 2,000 survivors of the two lost ships. Which is far better than anyone could have expected. It is further consoling that the German invasion of Russia seems to have reached high tide, and the barbarians are now being gradually rolled back. Moscow and Leningrad appear to be safe. At last the Americans, willy nilly, are in the war, not only against Japan, but also Germany and Italy. Another consoling thought, but it has been a long, long trail to get them there, though not through any fault of that grand champion of liberty – President Roosevelt.

December 16

Bad news from the Far East. The Japanese are invading British Borneo, they have already invaded the Philippine Islands and the hinterlands of Hong Kong and Singapore, and have entered Burma. Our whole East Asian Empire seems to be imperilled. And all this coming to pass in a week. It seems like a nightmare.

December 17

The disappearance of familiar younger figures from the shops into the abyss of the services is becoming very marked. I have today observed a maiden from a shop parading in the smart azure uniform of the Women's Auxiliary Air Force. 'Her skirt is too short,' remarked a correct lady, reprovingly.

December 18

Yesterday I stood in a chocolate queue for 45 minutes outside Mitchell's in the Arcade. Obtained a slab of Terry's Bitter, a rare prize in these days. The queue was 30 yards long and constantly reinforced.

December 21

The Russians keep pressing hard up on the withdrawing Huns. This retreat seems to me to be the outstanding event in the war to date. The Russians are doing what we have not enough men to do, and doing it magnificently. The German army is suffering so that it can never be the same again. Walking out in the dark this evening I noticed that the blackout was being well kept on the whole. Two serious exposures of light which I did notice were both on premises occupied by the military – as usual!

December 23

Xmas will be a grim festival this time. The usual display of holly, holly wreaths and flowering plants, but nothing extra to eat. Dog owners are having an anxious time. I noticed a very long queue outside a dogs' meat shop in Market Street.

December 24

The ban on visitors to this coast was removed a few weeks ago, so that a certain number have arrived for the holiday. But they are not many and there are no extra trains anywhere.

December 25

The streets have been strangely quiet all day. A few soldiers strolling about, but most of the civilians kept indoors. We dined on part of our cheese ration and a mince pie. The latter suffered by absence of lemon peel. There are no lemons now. Xmas cards have been fewer, and of poor quality, marked by crude colouring and an absence of gilt. We were glad when the day was over. Xmas Day for elders is too charged with melancholy. It is like an old family photo album in recalling wistful memories of the dear departed.

December 26

All shops closed, but the banks open. Hong Kong, so far and yet so dear, has capitulated to the Japanese. A bitter humiliation for Britain.

December 28

I walked in the afternoon to Haynes Road, near to Tarring, to view the devastation effected there by enemy bombs two months ago. Seven persons unsuspectingly engaged in normal household occasions were in an instant blasted out of life and a score were injured. I saw where near a dozen large houses once had been, or still stood merely as dismembered shells.

December 29

To my solicitor. He is troubled, having much business but most of his staff gone. Only women and boys left.

December 31

Thus ends a weary year, a year which leaves an impression more of patient waiting than of progress in a military sense. But it leaves us still a well-nourished nation, completely united, determined and confident, conscious, moreover, that the partnership with the USA, and Russia, crowns the year, and makes complete victory only a matter of time. All the greatest events of the war are still to come. Vast preparations are in train.

1942

January 1

This week there is a 'drive' in Worthing to induce more women to engage in the making of munitions or [joining] the women's services. Saw a shop window in Chapel Road being filled with different kinds of ammunition from 8in. shells down to .303 cartridges, and machine gun belts, which were intended to enlist the interest of the fair patriot. Nearby another window was equipped to display the activities of the Auxiliary Territorial Service. Recruits to it are badly needed, and are enticed with a feminine official promise of 'lots of fun'. This afternoon the streets were full of Canadian soldiers strolling about at a loose end. They were mostly come over from Brighton, the headquarters of these warriors. In addition to our resident party of the West Nova Scotia Regiment I noticed representatives of 'Hastings and Prince Edward', 'Carleton and York', and '22nd Royal' regiments, also artillery, engineers and Army Service Corps. These cousins look fine raw material for soldiering, but they tend to be wilder than our own men, and their presence is causing anxiety. There has been window smashing and other offences, and they are over quick to cry 'Honey' to our girls. I observed a couple of them by no means certain about either their steps or reality in general. 'What is it today, Saturday or Monday?' one huskily inquired. 'No Toosday,' came the reply. Now the best authorities hold that today is Thursday!

January 4

Sunday, rain early, then fine. Very mild. In the afternoon went for a walk up Warren Road to Durrington Corner. On the way took rest on seats, absorbing the sun's precious rays. Many comfortable, tranquil citizens abroad on the traditional Sabbath promenade, same the flower bearers on the traditional pilgrimage to the cemetery. The fine weather had also brought out many aeroplanes to practise evolutions. For the RAF never rests.

January 5

It is very noticeable how in the past few months girls have been taking the places of men in the shops and on the buses. The national war effort seems to be gaining a great impetus at last. The Government makes more and more outcry for the salvage of all paper and card. Yet the streets remain littered with it. We are a slack and untidy people. Our democracy does not include much sense of public duty.

January 6

The news from Russia is very cheering. The Huns continually give ground, much more than they intended. One begins to see a point of daylight at the end of the world's dark tunnel.

January 7

Fine, frosty all day in the shade. The position in Singapore seems threatening. The Japanese keep advancing down the Malay Peninsula and our men cannot stop them.

January 9

Be it remembered what comfortable words the paltry Spanish dictator Franco addressed to Hitler early in October last, when disaster threatened the Russian armies, 'In my own name, and in the name of the Spanish people I wish to express my enthusiastic congratulations on the final decisive victories of the glorious German army over the enemy of civilisation.' What a fool he must feel now as he sees the German hordes rolled back with terrible losses and suffering.

January 10

The first snowdrops have appeared in the garden, though the little white pearls of flowers are not yet opened. These comely pioneers of Nature's cycle seem at once to induce a happier outlook.

January 13

Today was the abomination of desolation. The wind was strong and still immensely cold. Snow fell most of the day and though the temperature was slightly above freezing point it accumulated faster than it could melt. Everywhere one felt cold. At the Reference Library I realised that one cannot improve the mind with body crying out for warmth. And later we had to leave the band concert at the Assembly Hall at half time because we found ourselves becoming chilled. Weekly rations are reduced again, sugar from three quarters of a pound to half a pound, butter-cum-margarine from 8oz to 6oz, and cheese from 3oz to 2oz. Milk is now down to one and three quarter pints and all this is decreed by reason of the new Japanese war. As to that mystery reigns. The situation is very tense.

January 14

Cloudy and cold. The snow was three inches deep this morning and most of it remained at nightfall.

January 15

Docile though the British public is nowadays, there has been a good deal of murmuring about the recent extremely drastic curtailment of the milk supply. The Food Ministry gives no explanation save by casting in our face that we drink more milk than before the war. So one is left to suppose that there has been official miscalculation. 'Lord Woolton must go!' agrees F in properly democratic condemnation. Only 34 killed in air raids over this country in December.

January 16

The curse of the blackout presses heavily upon us now. Thus we have to breakfast by artificial light, and even when daylight comes, the brown paper fixed along the top of the window often renders the rooms too dark for comfortable reading. In the evening brown paper cowls over the lights, greatly limiting their efficiency in illuminating rooms. Emerging from lunch at Mitchell's I was struck by a contrast in the visible consequences of a world at war: 1 Honourable – a female horticulturist sweeping up the leaves in Steyne Gardens; 2 Not so honourable – an elderly Army subaltern tipsy in Montague Street.

January 19

The thaw continued. Lunching at Mitchell's today, I was struck, as I have often been before, by the contrast between the plenty in eating houses compared with the privation in people's homes. I think that this contrast is too marked, and hardly fair to people of small means, though for them, it is true, there are cheap communal feeding places, run by the Government, and known as British restaurants.

January 20

Life was rather a misery. Four inches of snow fell last night.

January 22

It froze all day and we suffered much tribulation. The WC early went out of action and at midday the hot water supply followed suit. In a garden in Poulter's Lane I noticed a large bird unknown to me which I was later able to identify as a fieldfare, at Worthing Museum, which much pleased me. Saw a queue of animal lovers standing outside a dogs' meat shop in Market Street, withering in the cold. It is difficult to imagine greater love.

January 24

In Malaya the war goes very ill for us and Singapore is imperilled, while in Libya the very able German general Rommel keeps bobbing up against our forces most disconcertingly – long after he was supposed to be reduced to headlong retreat.

January 25

This afternoon about a score of tanks were entrained here. Worthing, where in peace they were never seen, is become quite a centre of the Royal Tank Regiment. Some clutter the fields about the new drill hall in Upper Brighton Road, and many have for months been gathered in the woods around a pseudo-Gothic castle [Castle Goring] on the road to Arundel. Lately others have been parked in a residential cul-de-sac off the Broadwater Road.

January 26

Bright morning, cloudy afternoon. Very cold NW wind. It seems that since the war began we have already lost by enemy action nine million tons of merchant shipping out of 21 million tons which we had at the beginning. The provision of enough ships is become the crux of the war.

January 27

Intensely cold. Snow fell in the afternoon, later turning to rain, and bringing woe to man and beast. The first portion of the American Expeditionary Force has arrived in Northern Ireland, which is writing on the wall for Hitler. The Americans inspire confidence with a certain divine fervour lacking in us, an older and tireder nation.

January 28

A side of the war's hardship which receives little advertisement is the lamentable plight of old people left without domestic help. In our small circle we know of two such cases. One venerable lady, having been deserted by her housekeeper, must shut up her house and go into lodgings until she finds another – a remote prospect. Another, left alone with her daughter in a house too large, is becoming despondent in the struggle to maintain existence with lessening strength.

January 29

Three members of the West Nova Scotian Regiment hilarious drunk in South Street this afternoon. They attracted much notice as they reeled and embraced and sang. I caught the lyric 'We'll get no promotion, this side of the ocean, and so cheer up me lads!' Which indeed seemed highly probable. But pity it seems that the rude sons of New Scotland are not better protected against the allurements of our more advanced civilisation. A Canadian soldier has been heard to remark that he first learned to drink when he came to England.

February 1

It was rather astounding, for these parts, to wake up this morning, and, for the third time within a month, to see the ground blanketed with a considerable fall of snow. Snow continued to fall until about 11am when rain took its place and persisted during most of the day. Did not go out save to sweep snow away from our curtilage.

February 2

A dark and bitter day. Took tea with a lady whose mother-in-law thinks it wicked to go and listen to the Municipal Orchestra. We know another who disapproved of her minister attending the mayor's musical reception. Perhaps these stalwart Puritan examples may be comforting to those who fear that this nation is drifting into general godlessness. On the other hand, the fact that an 'ankle competition' has just been held on Sunday evening at the Assembly Hall, under the auspices of the town council, indicates the trend of the time.

February 3

Awoke this morning to see for the fourth time the ground concealed under a thick canopy of snow, but by midday a rapid thaw set in, thank God.

February 6

Found at my bank this morning a lady installed on the front counter as cashier, who counted out my notes as well as her cold fingers would let her. I have hitherto seen only girl clerks.

February 7

Same bitter weather. All the news, though scanty, is bad. Our fighting prospect has never been so black since Dunkirk. Nevertheless, the average Englishman is not worried, save about the blood and tears and the waste, because he has no doubt about the ultimate outcome. How different must be the outlook of the more intelligent German. He must think sometimes of the possibility of defeat, and of the awful nemesis which must certainly follow it.

February 8

Sunday. The temperature hardly rose above freezing point. We took a walk along Sompting Road and Upper Brighton Road. We passed on our way a mother of England who stood outside a tavern with one hand rocking a perambulator and the other hand brandishing a glass of stout.

February 13

A mass meeting in the Assembly Hall this afternoon to inaugurate 'Warships Week'. The various celebrations of this will, it is hoped, stimulate the citizens of Worthing to lend £500,000 to the Government for the purchase of a destroyer. We took tea at Khong's Coffee House. There in soft light, sitting on divans and ministered to by glamorous hosties, we absorbed the divine beverage and consumed toast in a scene of Oriental lavishness. But, going forth, we found ominous placards outside the newsagents: 'Two Nazi battleships escape from Brest. Navy and RAF in chase.'

February 14

The two German battleships which, with a heavy cruiser, escaped from Brest yesterday, are arrived in a German port with no more than superficial damage. There was great gallantry by RAF pilots in trying to stop them, 42 planes being lost, which is very sad.

February 16

The PM broadcast a gloomy speech last night announcing the surrender of Singapore to the Japanese. He seemed anxious about the effect of this and other recent reverses on the national spirit.

February 17

A dark, grey day. NE wind, strong and excruciating. The temperature only just above freezing point. In fact the emergency reservoirs have hardly been free of ice since Xmas. In the Singapore disaster we have lost over 50,000 men as prisoners, and masses of stores. It is Hong Kong repeated, but the loss ten times as great. In a civilian's breast the thought arises, what purpose is served by throwing large garrisons into places which cannot be defended and from which they cannot escape?

February 23

To Mitchell's to lunch. On arising, found to my horror that some villain had appropriated my coat. Took a bus home, put on another, all too thin. So back to Mitchell's, when joy! my warm coat had been returned. So all well, but it was a nasty jar. F, however, indecently merry at my discomfiture.

February 26

A dark day with snow threatening. Same torturing NE wind. Each morning a couple of auxiliary firemen pass our road to the emergency reservoir to break the ice along its edge so hoses can be introduced if required. They stand precariously on the narrow top of the 5ft parapet and jab at the ice with steel spikes attached to long poles. It looks hazardous.

February 28

Startled after blackout by a ring on the front door and the looming of a uniformed figure – immensely relieved on tardily recognising it was the harmless uniform of the Salvation Army. Troubled about our eating, for we can no longer obtain sardines, our chief support. One feels a craving to break out, and really eat one's fill of jam just for once, or to consume the whole 6d. slab of chocolate in one afternoon.

March 2

Saw five great Canadian soldiers happily drunk in the town this afternoon. They kept trying to enter places where they had no business. And there were two sergeants among them, one of whom kept trying to climb lampposts. Then they entered a grocer's shop in a body and asked for wine, but went out good humouredly when told there was not any wine. These soldiers are kept idle here as part of our assurance against invasion, and find it boring. They have nothing to do in their leisure time and this is our way of entertaining them.

March 6

Last night we heard on the wireless the topical song 'The White Cliffs Of Dover', a little exquisite, haunting thing.

March 7

Many British soldiers about the town on leave. I was struck with the pallid, weakly look of many of them. Our national physique seems to be suffering from the artificial urbanised life most of us lead. These men do not look equal to standing up to primitive healthy Huns and Japanese. The Colonial troops look bigger and sturdier.

March 9

Heard two bombs exploding at a great distance at about 5am. The Hun still sends occasional raiders, who come apparently for practice rather than for serious business. But, unhappily, some people are usually hit.

March 10

The Japanese now have Java and much of Burma. India and Australia are in peril. Such calamities were inconceivable only six months ago. Is it all a nightmare? What would the great Victorians have thought of it? We see the British Empire tottering and disintegrating before our eyes. Are we, too, going the way of old Rome?

March 17

We have had no biscuits for months. By a kind of irony what are called 'cereals' have reappeared in the shops after about a year's absence. Plenty of them, but now we have no milk to spare for their embellishment.

March 20

There is talk about the misdemeanours of the Canadian soldiery, which by no means abate as the days of their sojourn amongst us multiply. A lady stated today that 300 of them are awaiting trial at Lewes Assizes, which seems to be scarcely credible. Nevertheless, there have been bad assaults and window breakings here, so that many would be relieved to see our garrison changed again.

21 *On 9 March 1943 Mr and Mrs Harriss were forced to fling themselves to the floor as a German bomber, targeted by anti-aircraft guns, passed overhead and dropped bombs into the sea.*

March 21

The uncomplimentary epithet 'Croaker' is becoming more and more common as applied to those who express dissatisfaction with our military misfortunes. There seems, in fact, to be a great effort by the Government to stifle criticism as much as possible. Hence this term in the mouths of its henchmen and hack journalists. Yet there does seem a danger of our becoming case-hardened to defeat. With our 'successful withdrawals' and 'retreats according to plan' we are becoming past masters at euphemism. For we never admit defeat. It would seem that this glossing over of calamity is breeding distrust among the people.

March 22

We are depressed by the monotony of our diet. Sardines and kippers have been long stopped and instead we are offered salted cod and American chopped pork, which we relish not. So it is fish paste ad nauseam.

March 23

To the barber's, where I am always in hopes of hearing news (uncensored!) but there was no talk save of the weather. People seem tired of mentioning the war.

March 25

The postman delivered this morning a communication headed 'Invasion – notice to householders', telling us what we are to do if the Huns come. It has sadly alarmed some of the old ladies in our road. There was a tremendous droning of planes overhead at about 4.30pm. The noise recalled alarming moments during the Battle of Britain in the autumn of 1940. But this time the planes were ours.

March 26

One hears of an ingenious citizen who has exchanged fire watching, which offers no compensations, for the Home Guard, in order to obtain the use of a good overcoat gratis. I was concerned to hear that he is also supplied with ammunition too, to keep at home! Ammunition may so easily become fatal in inexperienced hands. I am reminded of another local Home Guard who had a round in his rifle which would not go off. So he decided to treat it as a dummy, pointed the rifle at his sergeant and pulled the trigger. This time it went off. An inquest followed.

March 27

On the afternoon of the 25th there was a very heavy attack on the Ruhr by hundreds of our planes, which accounts for what I heard overhead.

March 28

To Brighton with F. The *Metropole* and *Grand Hotels*, last summer derelict, are now occupied by the RAF. The front was gay with airmen and with young naval officers from the training establishment at Hove [King Alfred]. But there were few soldiers about. Four United States naval men presented a novel and cheering sight.

March 30

Question of the hour is as to when and where we are to take the offensive and open a new battlefront in the west to assist the Russians.

April 4

A crowd of shoppers urgent to procure goods still unrationed crammed the buses into Worthing and often met with disappointment. Cakes, especially, very short of the demand. A pile on the counter would vanish in a flash, like a handful of corn thrown to chickens.

April 5

Save for a short constitutional around Broadwater in the morning, we remain in or around our premises all day, which seemed impressively tranquil after yesterday's battling for provisions.

April 8

Here in Worthing the calamitous effects of total war on the small shopkeeper becomes more and more evident. Shops in the main streets still hold their own and even maintain a semblance of affluence. But in the lesser streets there are rows of empty shops, and 'To Let' notices are constantly apparent.

April 9

A torrid tempest raged all last night and today, and rain fell heavily from before dawn until 3.30pm. My 60th birthday. There is a solemnity in this entering upon the last decade of anything near a full efficiency. When I had just descended, at 7.50am, and was watching the milkman's tranquil, solitary round, the stillness was suddenly rent by a whistling noise and then a terrific explosion followed by a burst of machine gun fire. When we went down to Worthing we found that once again the gasworks had attracted a bomber. There were two people killed and half a dozen injured. The hospital nearby was damaged. Altogether a birthday more memorable than happy.

April 10

We were inspecting the casualty list outside the Town Hall concerning yesterday's raid when a girl exclaimed 'only two dead', as though the affair lacked thrill. Little F, incensed, cried out, 'All the same it is bad enough for those who were killed, and their relatives.'

April 11

F intervened valiantly today in protesting from the queue against a selfish lady being served with a dozen cakes, contrary to the beneficent rule of the shop that each customer may receive no more than six of the very limited supply. Forgetfulness was pleaded, but the blushes of shame betrayed the guilty countenances of both server and served. And F went forth triumphant, 'not frightened but elated!' as she said.

April 13

Yesterday afternoon saw two squadrons of our fighters pass over in succession on their way to the continent. From today's paper I gather that they went to some of the bitterest fighting of the war. Eleven fighter pilots missing, though not all, presumably, from those two squadrons, comprising 26 planes. All Nature is at full speed. The verdure is bursting forth, the birds are twittering amid the branches and the women are chatting over the garden fences, the really modish ones, of course, with cigarettes in their mouths.

April 14

This afternoon seats in Montague Place were crowded with people basking in the sun. Montague Place is now almost the only refuge left in Worthing with seats.

April 16

Saw three Canadian soldiers in a state of happy intoxication in the fashionable quarter of Worthing this afternoon. We have been unable to procure any chocolate at all for the past week. Why this excess of alcoholic drink everywhere?

April 17

Today was notable for my obtaining half a pound of digestive biscuits, for the first time, I think, since the first year of the war.

April 19

We were taking the air this morning on Broadwater Green when the Sabbath calm was suddenly broken by the rattle and dust of a long procession of tanks along the main road. Soon they were succeeded by dozens of private motor cars, now normally so little seen upon the roads. Apparently, exercises were in progress on the Downs.

April 23

F to the draper's to buy cloth for a coat. For this she had to give up just over 15 coupons out of her 50 for the year. Which does not leave many for other things. As to our points ration, while formerly we were much limited by the paucity of points, foods are becoming so limited that we cannot find enough to exhaust them. Sardines and all nice meats are quite stopped and we are driven back upon supplies of bread and milk. Our milk ration is aided by dried milk obtained from the chemist's.

April 24

There is much anxiety among leaders about the defence of India against the Japanese, who continually penetrate more and more into Burma. This seems of little concern to people at home, for the British have given up 'thinking imperially' this many years past. In this district, indeed, there is little besides our stomachs and the high income tax to remind us that we are at war.

April 25

A ferocious gale blew all through the night. Then I fell asleep and dreamed that the Huns had taken Worthing! All the buses stopped running and I found myself under the direction of a young German officer. I experienced a lively dread as to what was going to happen next and was hugely relieved when I awoke and realised that it was a dream.

April 26

Our garrison of Canadians are gone, it is said, on a 300-mile route march, which to some of them at least cannot but be a salutary and corrective exercise, for their transgressions are many.

April 27

Both annoyed in last night's news broadcast at the sarcastic inflection of the announcer when reporting the Huns' offensive operations. It is surely his duty to convey the news just as a passionless automaton. We don't want any expression of his personal feeling, patriotic or not.

April 28

Having observed in the shops lately a great plenty of pineapple chunks, which the loss of Malaya, whence they came, made a perplexity to me, I inquired of my grocer the cause of it. He explained that all existing stocks are being thrown on the market at once to make an end of them quickly, since the Government wished to remove Malaya out of people's minds, so many having had relatives disappear in that disaster. So there is to be a clean sweep of pineapple chunks before they can become a vehicle of despondency, which is very strange.

May 2

There was heavy gunfire at intervals last night from 11pm to 12.30am. The fearful might well have thought it was the Germans come, for we had had no warning. But we know that it was but practice firing of our own troops.

May 6

A glorious spring day, but one feels that the drought is becoming very serious in view of our special wartime agricultural necessities. I think we have had no appreciable rain since March.

May 7

Another brilliant day. Lunch at Mitchell's, where F was roused by seeing a lady give her plate of meat to her dog to finish off. Disgusting, to be sure. F near to calling the management but, to my relief, subsided after letting off steam on our friendly waitress.

May 8

Today a lady in the queue outside an eating house, gazing through the crystal doors at the paradise not yet gained, suddenly exclaimed in astonishment, 'Why, there is my husband inside! He is supposed to be in Brighton today.' What an opening for a thriller novel!

May 9

Much heartened today by news of the defeat of the Japanese in the Coral Sea in the greatest sea fight of the war so far. This was mainly by American ships and planes and seems to have saved Australia from the menace of invasion.

May 10

To our great satisfaction, rain began to fall at 12.30pm and continued, though in a half-hearted fashion, for the rest of the day. Rain is now becoming a matter of extreme urgency for the crops, as sinkings of food ships by U-boats continue.

May 11

Last night we sat down to hear a 9pm news broadcast with feelings of special expectancy, for the PM was to speak. He said he did so to mark the 2nd anniversary of his appointment. He was confident and restrained, and almost commonplace. There were no 'fireworks', no disclosures, and no flowers of eloquence. He seemed tired. One noticed particularly that he avoided altogether allusion to awkward things – Singapore, Burma, and the heavy shipping losses. In sum, he left us disappointed.

22 *Writing in his diary less than a month before D-Day, Mr Harriss noted: 'Saw on the front, extending from Splash Point to the Beach Hotel, a line of military vehicles.'*

May 12

At lunch, an estimable man, and wife, informed us that bombs had fallen at Rustington, five miles away, on Friday last. A bomb cut off half a house. There were several killed. He showed no more concern than if they were chickens. This war induces a callous outlook. Rather strangely we had heard nothing of this bombing. Saw in a greengrocer's window, to my surprise, what looked to be fresh gooseberries. On approaching nearer, I read 'grape trimmings 8d. per lb', which I have never seen before, and arises, I suppose, from the present dearth of fruits.

May 13

There was some good rain late yesterday evening so that the agricultural situation is much eased. Went out to tea at the house of a naturalized Frenchman and his English wife, and were kindly entertained. He said that he was worried by the feeling that his nation had betrayed Great Britain. We parted after a secondary refreshment of dandelion wine, a very ill drink.

May 14

The Huns seem to have begun their long promised spring offensive against the Russians, attacking them in the eastern Crimea. They claim to have taken 40,000 prisoners and much booty. Our men in Burma continue their hazardous retreat. So the news in this war seems always bad, and we feel always depressed.

May 17

Awakened at 3am by an explosion which made the window rattle and was followed by machine gun fire.

May 18

The last day of Daphne, an admirable handmaid at Mitchell's, who is joining the ATS, and hopes to be posted to an officers' mess. F has given her a nice topaz scarf pin. A little honey has appeared on sale after months of absence.

May 20

New ration books have to be applied for, this time in person. Arrangements for this primitive, to the point of scandal. Too few booths, too few clerks, and no allocation of persons to particular booths. Hence much congestion and loss of time. I to Dominion Road Infants' School at 10.30am, but the queue so great that after a quarter of an hour in it I abandoned hope and left. Returned at 1.50pm and my turn did not arrive until 3.20. A woman had fainted in this queue in the morning. Some of the infants provided light relief, little mop-haired creatures coming to stare at us intruders with great wondering eyes. The British public, as usual, admirably patient and good tempered under hardship.

May 23

Saw the first postwoman on regular round. Female Xmas 'temporaries' in civilian clothing we have had long since, but this one was evidently recruited for the duration. She was uniformed, wearing an official sombrero hat, blue overcoat and blue trousers with a PO red stripe.

May 25

Whit Monday. Cloudy, cold and boisterous. Rain from 4.15pm. Today has been observed as a general holiday, a respite from the war effort. There has been no holiday traffic permitted, and Worthing, subject, in addition, to the ban on visitors, has been about as gay as a concentration camp.

May 26

Wind greatly freshening into a most horrid tempest. Very heavy rain from 1.30 to 6pm. This morning I overheard this exchange which illustrates 'defence' from the feminine viewpoint. Phyllis, pausing in her polishing, to F, superintending, 'My husband says that the Home Guard are to practise with live ammunition. It makes me quake rather for him.' F (consolingly), 'Well, of course they ought to be careful, still, I think it is best they should practise with them, for then they won't be so frightened if they have to shoot at the Germans.' The gale today was exceedingly violent. The rain was driving up South Street from the sea almost horizontally. Much damage done to gardens, umbrellas and hats. Pedestrians flung themselves exhausted and half-drowned into buses.

May 29

The Japanese have driven us from Burma, and now we have only to hope that the monsoon will keep them out of India until our forces are more ready to join battle with them. At 8pm stirred by

23   *The Home Guard at bayonet drill on the Woodside Road pitch of Worthing FC.*

the magnificent appearance of three RAF fighter squadrons flying abreast at no great height above the house. They were returning unscathed, after a daylight sweep over the French coast, doubtless leaving something behind for the Hun to think about.

May 30

Cloudy with bright intervals, showers, strong SW wind. 554th air-raid warning, 7.10 to 7.24pm; 555th 9.30 to 9.45pm. We can get no chocolate. F has just stood in a sweets queue at Mitchell's, but the greatness of the multitude in front of her was sent empty away. Watercress is to be no longer sold in bunches as of yore, for lack of labourers, nor is wrapping paper supplied for it. So this morning my shopping bag filled with loose wet sprigs. Next time I must remember to take a piece of newspaper.

May 31

A not unprofitable day. This morning repaired some blackout cardboard disintegrating in the long duration of the war. In the afternoon sat cross-legged at the front door repairing with needle and thread rents in the sunblind occasioned by the recent tempests. Execrable Bath buns for tea. These are now so bad through war stringency that they become drier than stale bread in 24 hours after baking.

June 1

On Saturday night, the 30th, occurred what may well come to be regarded as the turning point in the war. The RAF bombed the Cologne district with over 1,000 bombers, more than twice the number which the Huns have ever used over here on any one day. The damage has been enormous and our losses small. One is sensible of an unholy joy that the Hun, perhaps the cruellest animal in the Universe, is meeting with a fitting punishment at last. And the PM promises that all other German cities shall suffer alike; while the Americans have not even begun yet! Who would be Hitler now? This afternoon a large convoy was to be seen proceeding down Channel. This is a rare sight off Worthing, and people were balancing themselves on the bank of the seafront to get a view of the ships, peering out to sea over the festoons of barbed wire. I made them out more than 20 vessels, some four miles out to sea, stretching irregularly from beyond Brighton as far as Worthing Pier, and others kept appearing. Among them I could just discern some flat grey shapes which I took to be escorting warships. High in the air, here and there, floated barrage balloons silver in the sunshine. Nature's share in this inspiring spectacle was indeed exhilarating, for sky and sea were both brilliantly blue, and the fresh breeze supplied just enough motion to the water to make it seem gently alive. As one regarded the black unlovely shapes of these tramp steamers as they ploughed slowly past, one felt how precious they are become to us, and in what perils they move. Even as I looked, the air-raid sirens suddenly moaned forth their portentous warning. But this time nothing untoward occurred.

June 3

After a cold March-like May we seemed suddenly to have jumped into the heats of summer. Today was brilliantly fine; the sun intensely hot. There has been another raid of over 1,000 RAF bombers on Germany, this time over the Ruhr. We seem suddenly to be exerting a tremendous power in the air. I feel apprehensive about the Huns' response to it. For they must realise that, failing effective response, they are lost. So their comparative inactivity is perplexing. One is anxious of the possibility of an unpleasant surprise in store for us.

June 4

The district is becoming more and more an abiding place for tanks, those noisy monsters of the new Armageddon. That residential cul-de-sac Sompting Avenue is now, for its sins, a regular home of rest for them. Many more take their pastime in a field near the new Territorial barracks in Upper Brighton Road, and more still make ponderous, ear-shattering perambulations about our streets – not only, alas, by day.

June 5

Flaming June. A lady from there remarked that London is looking very gay, quite risen from its ashes. Throngs of shoppers, and ladies' dresses very coloursome and pretty, but the shops appearing very ill-stocked, and shabby for lack of painting.

June 6

The heatwave continues. There is a curious lull in the war, just when we expected pandemonium. Here in England the unhappy Government, in prospect of a coal shortage, have to wrestle with disgruntled miners. F to the new Connaught Theatre to see *Robert's Wife*, a play dealing with clerical life, and very well pleased. Now, after a short season, these 'Court Players' are leaving Worthing, for shortness of takings, the public preferring the cinema.

June 8

Air-raid warnings arouse no emotion whatever now except that of annoyance. Nevertheless, the first of these, by its disturbance of sleep, causes me a heavy day. Browsed on the Green in the morning and gleaned a few cigarette cartons for salvage. The need of this is very urgent, but too many of the English still deafen their ears to the voice of the Government insisting upon it.

June 9

One notices that the new type, small brick and concrete, above ground air-raid shelters are still being erected in odd corners of the town. They are reinforced with steel rods or an inner lining of steel sheeting. When one hears the hum of a concrete mixer, this is the cause. For no other building is now permitted. It all indicates, rather depressingly, that in the opinion of the authorities, the end is still far off.

June 15

Today we went by the 12.20pm train from Worthing to Boscombe to stay at the *Elysium Hotel* there. Changed at Southampton where we found the station so dilapidated from bombing that most of the waiting rooms and offices had disappeared. Much of the platform was still roofless. The travelling was much more humdrum than we had expected. No crowding, and such passengers as there were mostly civilians.

June 16

On a stroll into Bournemouth and back we met hundreds of airmen from the Dominions, as well as RAF, about the streets. Also numerous women of the three services in their attractive uniforms of navy blue, sky blue and khaki respectively. All combined to provide an inspiring spectacle of our expanding war strength. An even more uncommon sight was the long string of female motorcyclists on their horrid spluttering machines.

June 20

This afternoon to Christchurch by bus. We sat in the sunshine beside the riverbank, just beneath the venerable walls of the Priory, where trees made a glorious vista.

June 22

Another perfect day. An air raid on Southampton last night. We were awakened by a warning siren, saw searchlights operating and heard the sound of bombs exploding in the distance and machine gun fire. There was also much rushing of planes overhead. However, this morning all thoughts of this raid were excluded by the melancholy news of the sudden capture by the Huns of Tobruk in Libya. Twenty five thousand men prisoners, and vast stores are lost in this disaster. The news caused anxious faces and hushed voices at the hotel breakfast. And, indeed, this Libyan campaign will form a dismal episode in our military history and suggests that we are as inferior to the Huns in military capacity as we are superior to the Italians.

June 23

Took tea at the house of F's new-found friend of long ago. She is paid by the Government 8/3. per week, her leg having been injured by a bomb out of Germany, and now shortened by half an inch. She threw herself flat on her face in the road when 14 houses close by were demolished in an air raid, and had a very narrow escape from death. We had a pleasant merry time with her, and marvellous good cheer for these sorry times.

June 28

As elsewhere, I have noticed a journal called *The Peace News* on sale here. It purports to present 'the Pacifist view' which advocates peace by negotiation. Happily, it is the view of only a tiny and harmless body of spineless and crack-brained cranks. What fully sane person could trust Hitler's bond?

June 29

Very fine. For us a day of trial. For we returned to Worthing and became engrossed in the toils of packing, paying, tipping and ration books, of wrestling with luggage, wrestling with train seats. We took nearly three hours to cover about 40 miles, including a change at poor battered Southampton. Crowded train – stifling heat – swarms of people cluttered with parcels, glistening, sweating, but still good-humoured. F slept bolt upright. After this restless fever the quiet and freshness of home seemed very sweet.

June 30

On a stroll this morning, I noted what change even a fortnight brings. The emergency water tank at the top corner of our road has rather mysteriously been demolished and our noble Green, which I had left literally so, was now brown. For this day completes a succession of very dry months and there is a general wilting of vegetation.

July 2

Sevastopol in the Crimea is fallen to the Huns. Public opinion about this phase of the war in general was well summed up by a woman today who remarked in F's presence, 'I'm English, and them Huns are not civilised as we are. Yet they seem to know how to do things better than we do.'

July 3

This afternoon saw proceeding down the Channel three coastal merchant ships, each towing one or two large flat barges, like Thames barges. Which I have not seen before and suppose to be for economy of ships.

July 5

Sunny and hot. We hear from a police source that on a recent night as many as 36 Canadian warriors at once were deposited in the local police station.

July 9

Men say that barges are being collected at Littlehampton for the invasion of the continent. It has been officially stated that we and the Americans will invade it sometime this year and so set up a second front against Hitler, to help the Russians. This talk about barges probably explains what I saw and noted on the 3rd.

July 13

Sat on the Green this morning reading my paper. A rare indulgence. The Russians seem faced with disaster. If the Russians, who are tougher than we are, cannot beat the Huns, what chance have we of doing so? The Americans are not yet ready either with men or ships.

July 16

After lunch sat out on a seat in Montague Place. The seats were filled with people sitting, like so many caged birds of prey, in stolid contemplative gloom. Their silence in these stagnant war days is monumental. I can think of only two possible occurrences capable of arousing them – a big success for our arms, or a bombing – in Montague Place!

July 17

Discussing the recent series of innocuous air-raid warnings with Phyllis she said that her husband says that they arise from reconnaissance planes which the Huns send over to see what we are doing, and whether there are any of our barges about. That mention of barges again is interesting. One feels that there is much going on that the citizen is not allowed to know about.

July 21

To Horsham by bus for a trip. We found Horsham to be a commonplace, bustling, small county town of narrow streets. The only notable thing about it seemed to be a disused church used as a wartime foodstore by the Ministry of Food, and Stuart's Rooms where we enjoyed a most refreshing tea and pleasing courtesy. There were many Canadian soldiers in the streets. Canadians, in fact, were visible in all the pretty villages on our route. They seemed to have entered into occupation of all Sussex, to the complete exclusion of our troops, save a few details.

July 24

All motoring for other than business reasons has now been stopped. This has caused a remarkable disappearance of cars from the Worthing streets, which in the afternoon seem almost deserted save for the occasional passage of a military lorry.

July 25

Chocolate and other sweets are to be rationed after today. Each citizen, irrespective of age or sex, is to receive but 2oz per week. Up to now we two have only occasionally failed to ensure a daily consumption of that amount. We have had to go hunting, but have had to exercise persistent activity in a failing market. It is a hard blow. Abstainers feel the grievance that drink and tobacco remain unrationed, but these are untouchables! Long queues outside sweetshops now – for the last time!

July 27

I heard explosions of four bombs in quick succession but some distance off. Heard later that bombs had fallen on Horsham. A few fatal casualties. There were eight at Littlehampton a few days ago. Worthing seems lucky.

24 *The scene opposite the Museum and Art Gallery, Chapel Road, in 1944. Mr and Mrs Harriss often caught the bus from this stop.*

July 29

A cogent statement in the paper today, which Air Marshal Harris has broadcast to the Huns in their own language. It points out the overwhelming scourging by bombing each of the German cities is about to receive and suggests they should overthrow the Nazi government and make peace. This seems excellent propaganda.

July 31

Our niece spent the day with us. She brought along her offspring Gerald, now approaching his 8th summer. Gerald is estimable and intelligent. And moreover a keen observer of life; yet six hours of him made us realise how infinitely tiring the presence of a child can be. We repaired to Steyne Gardens where he pretended for a long time to be a railway train subject to the rather embarrassing condition that I undertook the role of porter. His mother remarked on the difficulty of controlling boys with their fathers away on military service.

August 2

Sunday. Thunder accompanied by heavy rain. The droning of our bombers overhead, on their way to Germany, about midnight, is very noticeable now that our aerial offensive is assuming great proportions. I was awakened by what sounded like a procession of bren gun carriers passing along a neighbouring street. These little vehicles, on caterpillar wheels, make a shattering noise, being, for their size, even more offensively inarticulate than the strident tanks.

August 3

All the talk of the town is about the Rector of Broadwater having, in an address to young people, stated that a judgement is coming upon Germany and also Russia for their attitude to the word of God; that Russia is an anti-God country. People take it very ill that this Rector should assume so much against our braver Russian ally.

August 4

Enjoyed a long afternoon on or near the seafront. If we have to look through barbed wire and between concrete blocks, we can still imbibe the sweet sea breezes. Many people abroad but many shops remained closed.

August 5

Enemy raids are increasing again, though the number of bombers they use is now only small. Our retaliation, or rather, I should say, provocation, is terrific. The latest, 12 acres of factories laid waste at Dusseldorf, by hundreds of bombers.

August 6

The German drive into the Caucasus becomes more and more devastating. They have destroyed most of the corn and draw very near to the first of the oil centres. Their armoured Panzer divisions are a terror of the war. It appears that nothing devised can stop them.

Certainly the Russians cannot. It is an odd war that leaves over a million trained men in this country as silent spectators of their ally's disaster. The Second Front – when?

August 9

A fourth winter of war is beginning to cast its shadow. Found a young man on Broadwater Green haranguing a score of languid citizens against the Rector's recent pronouncement of Heaven's condemnation of the Russians for godlessness. All are with him as to that, yet I fear he is a representative of 'Communist infiltration'.

August 10

After 11pm last night there were sounds of bombs exploding and the sky became illuminated with flares and tracer bullets. There was considerable gunfire, all this in the direction of Hove. Then it all ended with a crash which sounded much nearer. People emerged from homes in our road and talked excitedly. Pyrotechnically it was probably the most stimulating raid which has yet touched Worthing. Heard this morning that a German bomber had crashed near to Worthing Hospital, upon the house of a lady doctor. Luckily the house was unoccupied. Crew of five all dead. Half-a-dozen Canadian soldiers in adjoining house were affected with burns, three of whom are dead. Which sad affair has distressed poor F much and brought her to tears. To the barber's, where the chief barber expressed his confident opinion that the war would end in October through the Huns cracking under the British-American bombing, which seems a bold prophecy.

August 12

It is said that there is about to be a Great Praying for better weather, our food being at hazard. Here in Worthing, for the past year or more, the mere whisper of 'biscuits' has availed to cause an instant queue to spring from nowhere.

August 13

After lunch at Mitchell's, F took a bus with old Miss S and journeyed to High Salvington, Worthing's elevated Tripper's Paradise.

August 14

After completing my shopping in the village, I strolled to the Green where the sun shone warmly through a large cloud and the new-mown grass was fragrant after the recent rains. I found a children's service in progress beneath the shadow of the trees. In a horseshoe of seats were sitting rows of colourfully dressed holiday children varied by the occasional bath chair of some mature but interested invalid. Two or three evangelists stood facing the company. With them sat a comely maiden, perhaps in her 18th year, pale and fair, who cast an air of distinction upon the motley gathering. As I approached they were singing a hymn and the quavering voices of the children floated across the broad expanse accompanied only by the drowsy hum of the distant mower. It was a pretty scene, calculated to induce a momentary forgetfulness of all the hurtful realities which now encompass us.

August 15

Workmen with oxyacetylene burners are removing all the iron railings about the squares and residential roads of Worthing, to be used for munitions of war.

August 17

Mr Morrison, the Home Secretary, has ordained that each householder shall place in his porch a container or containers to hold no less than four gallons of water, against the casting on us by the Huns of incendiary bombs. Containers are hard to come by nowadays. However, we are fortunate in finding two retired slop pails which will do.

August 19

The day opened in lively fashion with the 618th air-raid warning, 5.44am to 6.04am. There was much rushing about of planes very near. Then several bursts of machine gun fire, and we saw in the distance a cloud of black smoke followed by flame. A Hun plane had apparently been brought down. For we then saw our planes, in twos and threes, moving away in the opposite direction – going home for breakfast. The Huns have lately become much more active again over this country. But they are still using only a very few planes at a time. It would seem that they cannot spare more owing to their Russian entanglement.

August 20

The reason for the unusual air activity yesterday has now become manifest. At dawn, and for the subsequent nine hours, our combined forces were making a most gallant hit-and-run raid on Dieppe. The newspaper makes the usual attempt to write it up as a success, but it seems more than doubtful whether history will call it so. Our losses have been great, so have the enemy's. In return for them we have gained valuable experience, that is all. The Huns were taken by surprise, but, as usual, they were not rattled. Our men, who returned, did so, we are told 'in the brightest spirits'.

August 22

This afternoon we walked out past the hospital and inspected the ruins of two semi-detached houses into which a German bomber crashed as reported on the 10th. The whole frontage has been sliced off, and the front gardens, of considerable size, are a mass of bricks and plaster. Shrubs and also trees, some of which lie uprooted, were not only scorched but killed, evidence of the fearful heat from the burning petrol.

August 23

One finds no enthusiasm among those whom one meets as to the Dieppe raid. Only the RAF gave more than it received. Any result on land was pitifully small in view of the heavy losses. There is a sad hollowness about all this printed gush. A 'triumph' indeed.

August 24

The Government keeps warning all of a serious shortage of coal next winter, and urging all to stint themselves on pain of rationing if they don't. Yet nine million tons per annum are being lost through avoidable absenteeism of the miners, in spite of appeals to their patriotism and £25 million pa added to their wages. Such is democracy in excelsis. This spirit bodes ill for that New Jerusalem which so many optimists seem to expect to find in this country after the war.

August 28

I hear that there are about 200 invasion barges at Shoreham, being some of those used in the raid on Dieppe. Hove was rather badly bombed last Monday, the 24th, a row of houses being destroyed, and there were, unhappily, many casualties.

August 29

Our aircraft have been very active overhead. It's a common sight to see a couple of squadrons of fighters proceeding across the Channel to shoot and be shot at.

August 30

We are finding very irksome on these sultry days the necessity of closing up the house soon after 8pm, on account of the blackout. The milk is to be on ration again after a temporary release – three pints each per week. We have been consuming since April five-and-a-quarter pints each!

August 31

It is very impressive to observe the absence of railings and gates along all the streets. In many instances they have been torn from their sockets, leaving cracked and gaping masonry. The streets look despoiled and shabby. Yet it all passes as matter of course. There is no adverse comment. An infantry battalion marched into town this morning. They came down Broadwater Road three abreast, in succession of platoons. For the most part short in stature and none too muscular, though looking fit, evidently English, not Colonial. At intervals of about 50 yards, the platoons seemed to succeed one another endlessly, drab men in steel hats wearing camouflaged waterproofs. Shoppers stopped shopping to gaze, but universal khaki, and the extinction of mounted officers, have taken all the spectacle out of war.

September 1

Occupied most of the day in purchasing fruit for jam, and then making and jarring up 14lb of it. We had saved some sugar out of our ration, and felt it well to supplement our rationed 1lb each per month of 'sweet spread' against a difficult winter for feeding. It is nearly 20 years since we made jam at home, and we thought never to do it again. But this war is no respecter of human intentions.

September 3

The third anniversary of the outbreak of war, and the day of the 7th Great Praying against the Huns, who continue to be triumphant everywhere. We stand at bay waiting for the Americans to prepare and train. But this nation was never more united and determined for the undoing of the Nazis, and all the cranks and pacifists lie discomfited and silent in their holes. Which is very well.

September 4

After lunch F pronounced for a trip, so we went on the bus to Brighton. The intervening maritime region of Shoreham and Southwick always hideous with the erections and processes of industry, and the traditional squalor of dockland, looked especially desolate with so many of their little shops closed. The war has hit small traders very hard. Brighton front is in no better case, for there can be seen rows of smaller eating houses, which normally cater for trippers, empty, and 'To Let'. Western Road, however, and streets adjacent, seem as bustling and prosperous as ever. F was surprised at the abundant stocks of fabrics.

September 10

Very fine. Slight NE breeze. A grand day. Perhaps not even spring can equal autumn. The shops are filled with a glut of plums and damsons. Saw workmen removing for salvage railings from tombs in Christ Church graveyard. Now that body snatching is out of fashion they have no practical use. So they are better away, especially now that they go in so good a cause.

September 11

An anxious, anguished world watches the long-drawn fight for Stalingrad. For the Huns are breaking into the inner defences, and it seems that it must fall, though the Russians fight like heroes.

September 14

All about Broadwater we are beset now with these juggernauts of battle called tanks. There is, I think, nothing to likely inculcate hatred and disgust of war as these leviathans. They are monstrous, inexpressibly noisy and hideous, without any redeeming feature, a real reproach to mankind.

September 18

It has been a rather depressing day, as autumn does tend to be, however, as F cogently remarked, 'It is one day less of those which we have to go through, however long the war lasts.' Great history is in the making, but to those elders who sit and wait the time seems very long, time wasted out of our fast dwindling span.

September 23

One notices that it is becoming more and more common to see women smoking in the street. Women so doing always appear raffish or sluttish, and for most it is but a pose. The practice in general is one more sign of our national decadence.

September 24

To WH Smith's to lunch in the hope of a cut of roast meat.

September 25

To Brighton by bus as escort to F, who is troubled about procuring raiment. Clothing of any worthy quality is becoming scarce and very dear. Since many buses have been taken off in order to save petrol, tyres and crews, bus riding tends to become a purgatory. The buses are rushed by crowds, who 'strap-hang' for miles, but the public is good-humoured, even when left behind, as often happens.

September 26

Our convoys to Russia are hard pressed to fend off attacks by Hun aircraft based on Norway. It is very sad to see how our Navy, with its glorious history, is no longer a supreme unit. It is no longer sufficient unto itself. It can never rule the seas again. Ships must dodge or hide, or expect disaster, anywhere within the constantly increasing range of the deadly air weapon. In fact, the future of fighting ships is a dark one. It seems that navies may even become obsolete.

September 30

This was an occasion of a rather exciting event. I was in South Street when a plane suddenly came over with a roar from the sea, and passed northwards across Warwick Street. It was very low, perhaps 200ft up. Then I saw a black cylinder appear in a horizontal position in its wake, to become hidden by housetops. A few seconds later there was a terrific explosion and clouds of smoke arose some 400 yards away. I only then realised it was a raid by a German bomber. Then, too late, the siren sounded. It being noon, the shopping hour, there were many people in the streets but these showed curiosity rather than alarm. I heard, however, that all in Boots the Chemist's in South Street, both staff and customers, were made to lie down on the floor. It appears that the electricity works were slightly damaged, and another bomb fell in East Worthing near Onslow Court. Altogether there were only a score of casualties, and these of a minor kind.

October 1

We visited the district of the electricity works and viewed the damage from yesterday's bombing. A score of small houses had their roofs perforated, and there were many windows blown out, but structural damage was only slight. This area also comprises the gas works and, a little strangely, the hospital, and has become an attraction to the roaming Hun. I observed a printed notice in a window: 'Important, there are two persons sleeping here. And two cats.' This is to inform any rescue party as to what to look for in the event of the house being demolished. It has a grim side to it. They are brave people who live in that part of town.

October 2

Crowds of people on the front basking on seats in the sun. The crews of the great anti-aircraft guns sat around their charges in their shirt sleeves, a picture of idyllic ease in the bright blue sky.

October 7

Very dull and close. Mist early. Rain at eve. 667th air-raid warning 11.05 to 11.15pm. Early closing day. Very few pedestrians abroad this afternoon and almost the only cars those of the camouflaged military kind.

October 8

Dull with heavy showers. Fine afternoon. It was remarkable to notice how the sudden change to fair weather brought out our aircraft, just as the sun entices bees from their hives. In the recent clouded days there have been none visible, but this afternoon the sky seemed full of them, bombers and fighters, filling the air with their droning. Some were going about their exercises, and others on daylight swoops against the enemy in France and the Low Countries. F to the Plaza cinema to see a Welsh mining village drama entitled *How Green Is My Valley?* by Emlyn Williams. She returned warmly enthusiastic, being Welsh herself. The play included some beautiful singing.

October 10

After lunch F sought escape from the W gale in *Twinkle*, a review at the new Connaught Theatre, and found it to be the best thing of its kind she had ever seen. Pretty dancing intermingled with excellent comic pieces by one Clarkson Rose.

October 11

'I was so hungry last night when I went to bed,' remarked F 'that when I got to sleep I actually dreamed that I went to a pastrycook's, and asked what they had and they said, "we have only a pair of white silk knickers." I said "they will do" and took them and I believe I remember crunching them!' And what has my Lord Woolton to say to that?

October 13

We are dreading the fourth winter of war, now in prospect. The past two have been formidable, but this time we have to face the additional distress in a shortage of fuel, and deprivation of all but an infinitesimal allowance of sweets.

October 15

There is much talk of the rudeness of girl shop assistants. These hussies tend to be very young, for otherwise they would be pressed for the war, and often trade upon their present indispensability – a temporary one!

October 19

The sun shining through a slight haze transfigured with a pearly light the perspectives of the streets, and the foliage of the trees now beautiful in the varied colours of decay. Sat in the Steyne Gardens and found a great content.

October 26

Just before 11am we heard explosions seeming to be a mixture of bombs and anti-aircraft fire, but we could see nothing. Soon after 11.30 there were more. At 12.30 there was a renewal of the same, but louder. This sorry din continued, with fluctuations, for 20 minutes, and we felt as though we were in a battle. It was the worst experience we have had here in this war. We did not see any planes. F became much distressed, nobly anxious for unknown sufferers, and nervous about what

25   *'What a dismal sight the once trim promenade presents,' wrote Mr Harriss on 24 October 1944. The scene outside the Lido.*

might befall ourselves at any moment. Men say that bombs have fallen on Brighton and Hove but that Worthing has escaped.

October 30

Purchased 1lb of oranges, which I have not had a chance of doing for over a year, though there have been, from time to time, a few for children only.

October 31

Whilst this morning I was, for the first time this autumn, getting in my coal, I heard a loudspeaker van in an adjoining street crying out for non-ferrous metals to help the war. A drive for these is now in progress here. Depots have been opened in various empty shops, to which patriots have been bringing all manner of aluminium, brass, copper and lead bric-a-brac such as firescreens, fenders, plant bowls, ornaments and even sporting trophies.

November 5

Glorious news from Egypt. After 12 days of very difficult fighting against the enemy's prepared defences, the 8th Army, under Generals Alexander and Montgomery, has penetrated them. The enemy is routed and on the run. These are indeed glad tidings. It is very long since Britain heard anything so good. For this success probably represents the turn of the tide of the war. But there was no sign of excitement in Worthing.

November 6

It is a curious sight of the war to see crowded footways with the roads almost deserted. For the restrictions on motoring are now so severe that civil traffic is limited to a few business cars and the omnibuses. Now that the Japanese have captured all our rubber plantations there is no rubber available for private motorists' tyres. The shopping bustle, such as it is, is now over early in the day. For shops close at 5.30pm. Quite late enough since no one wishes to be out in the blackout (now descending before 6pm). It seems long years since we saw night turn into day by the cheerful blaze of countless electric lights. Now our days are short and gloomy.

November 8

In the east the 8th Army is chasing the beaten remnants of the German-Italian army across the desert. More than 60,000 prisoners taken and vast booty. British spirits, until now brooding and sullen, have been transformed. All is gladness and expectancy.

November 12

Morocco and Algeria have surrendered to the Americans, who are having a race with the Huns to secure Tunisia. The Huns have occupied the whole of France, descending to the Riviera. The air is full of rumours.

November 13

This was a noisy day due to the rattle of machine guns at training on the Downs, and the practice by the anti-aircraft guns on the front.

November 15

Sunday. This morning the church bells throughout the land, reserved in silence for more than three years past to sound the tocsin [alarm] of invasion when it comes, were released to celebrate the great victory in Egypt. This by direction of our rulers, and the now unfamiliar tinkling was pleasant in our ears.

November 16

I have been looking into a contemporary history of the Franco-German War of 1870, where the writer attributes the French collapse then to decadence due to licentiousness, frivolity, cynicism and disunion. Will in future historians attribute the present French collapse to precisely the same cause? To tea at WH Smith, where, having asked for biscuits, they brought me one all by itself on a plate.

November 19

A long forlorn queue at the fishmongers in Broadwater this morning. But there was nothing on the slabs and vinegar offered the only visible commerce. Yet the people seemed buoyed up by the hope that some fish would arrive by the next train.

November 20

This afternoon there was a continual passing of planes over Worthing, mostly large two-engined bombers. Some went over too high to be visible but there was no mistaking their note. There was also to be seen a meagre spidery little plane which tows after it a target for airmen in fighter planes to practise shooting at. This target resembles a long white sleeve floating in the air at the end of a rope.

November 23

A large greengrocer's shop in Brighton Road has been closed owing to the owner having had to join the Army. Even principal shopping streets now show blanks, and lesser ones so many closed premises that they look as though a pestilence has passed over them.

November 25

The Russians seem to have gained a decisive victory at Stalingrad. 35,000 prisoners taken and as many Huns killed. The siege appears to be ended. This success, coupled with the Anglo-American successes in North Africa, seems to show that the tide of the war has definitely turned against Hitler at last, so that men shall no longer cry 'Hitler always wins'.

November 28

There is much concern locally about the licence of the soldiery. A century and a half of unmarried expectant mothers recently taken to a single clinic. And the reputed fathers tend to disappear. The recent lechery is to be expected in our present social disruption, but what is called 'a broader attitude to matters of sex' must do nothing to lessen it.

December 4

The great sandbag fortification which blocked most of the pavement at the junction of Montague Street with Montague Place, and had begun to dissolve in decay, has been entirely removed. This has also happened elsewhere in the town. Whereby it appears that the fear of an invasion of Worthing by the Huns is now abated.

December 10

A feature of the moment is the sudden springing up all over the town of second-hand furniture and bric-a-brac shops, which find hermitage among the many premises now empty owing to the cruel exigencies of the war. Their wares are mostly of an essentially depressing and grubby aspect, but their hopeful displays are based, of course, upon the stark fact that the supply of new goods is stopped. I hear of a poulterer who, desiring 300 turkeys for his Xmas trade, can count on obtaining but 13! We have not tasted poultry of any kind for years. It is either too dear, or, usually, there is none.

December 11

Most people were awakened by an explosion at about 4am, which is said to have been from a bomb dropped into the sea.

December 14

We can no longer buy China tea, since that unhappy country is now entirely cut off from Europe owing to the military successes of the pestilent Japanese.

December 16

All the cat and dog meat shops seem to have closed now. Yet there is a greater abundance of meat paste in the shops for humans than for a long time past. Which is very strange. Entertained two neighbours to four o'clock tea. They were very agreeable. We provided for their sustenance a sultana cake, some rock cakes, and some Petit Buerre biscuits – procured from early foraging; but no bread and butter, for we could not, out of our scanty rations, spare any butter, margarine or jam.

26   *Goring seafront - a wasteland, defended with barbed wire and mines.*

December 17

We live constantly among tragedy. Only the other day one of the waitresses at the Assembly Hall, living with her mother in Brighton, had a message that her mother had suddenly been killed by a bomb. Then, a friend of ours at Littlehampton just died from shock following a bombing there. A fortnight ago a girl of 16 was killed in the street by an anti-aircraft shell which had gone astray. This morning Matilda [the new home help] arrived full of news of an accident whereby a local soldier has had his brains blown out through some other not knowing, or not remembering, that his rifle was loaded.

December 18

Yesterday at 4.30pm the town was shaken by a violent explosion so that we were startled, and then marvelled, at what it might be. We found today that the military destroyed a German mine seen floating near the pier. There are many casualties among glass windows in Montague Street and district.

December 19

There was another heavy explosion at 10.05am, which I suppose to have been from a mine in the sea. It set all the dogs in the town a-barking.

December 20

Our window cleaner has been pressed for making munitions. He is the third of that occupation operating in our road to go, or be pressed, into King's service since the war began. And now F is talking about our windows, which are gone a month without cleaning.

December 21

These days of long darkness in the morning and in the evening, when no man may show a light, make for sad living. Strange and not so cheerful was the sight of a greengrocer's shop in a principal street, in Xmas week, displaying no fruit of any kind!

December 22

Austerity marks the shops this Xmas. One sees none of the tinsel festoons, cotton wool 'snow', imitation holly or coloured glass balls. Toys are scarce and consist mostly of primitive shapes cut out of wood and painted. Dolls have rag faces. Prices are scandalously dear. To our great content the leading eating houses, by common agreement, have put up notices: 'Dogs not admitted.'

December 24

Some frenzied rushing about after victuals to cover three days, upon two of which we must lunch at home. Masses of people on the same errand, but little available; for there has been no increase in rations to honour this formerly festive season. And so, at last, in the evening, there was peace.

December 25

A grey sky. Calm. Mild. Admiral Darlan, late commander, under the collaborator Marshal Petain, of all the French military, naval and air forces (such as they are), also a collaborator with the

Huns so long as he thought they would win, and bitter enemy of England, has been assassinated in Algiers. General de Gaulle [leader of the Free French] must have been singing in his bath this morning, comments F.

December 26

This was kept as a public holiday for all, in the traditional way. There were no newspapers, no post and the public library was closed. So I hated it, and I imagine nobody enjoyed it much. Only in the cinema or tavern was true joy to be found.

December 30

Fine, but a black frost all day. F to pantomime at the new Connaught Theatre, *The Babes in the Wood*. A very good show very well patronised.

December 31

The last day of another year of war, which we two are much blessed to have reached without mishap and in good health. 1942 has been a year of stubborn endurance and much disappointment. The Allies are still unable to effect an invasion of Europe which is the inevitable prelude to victory. The recent successes in North Africa gave a transient fillip to gloomy spirits.

1943

January 2

A violent gale last night. This morning I noticed a flight of four biplanes moving in formation eastwards high above the crest of the Downs, a sight which I have not seen before during this war. For military aeroplanes, save for an occasional trainer, seem now to be always monoplanes.

January 3

Heard from a friend who has had no news of his officer son since the 14th of February last. On the 15th his regiment capitulated at Singapore after fighting against hopeless odds. Is he safe as a prisoner of the Japanese, no enviable fate, or dead? It is a cruel suspense for his parents.

January 9

Fiendishly cold SE wind. F, as a regular patron of cinemas, has noticed the derisive laughter of the crowd when the Italians are mentioned there. Certainly their activities in the present war have been the reverse of glorious. Such spontaneous popular demonstrations are very interesting to a student of current opinion.

January 11

Fine and mild with fresh SW wind. It was a day to make one cast off winter's cobwebs and realise the call of the wild. However, this carried me no further than the front, where, in the afternoon, it was warm enough to sit out. There was a lively sea running, but this was easier to hear than to observe, owing to the intervening forest of barbed wire. Here and there could be seen a little knot of military gathered about the anti-aircraft gun, keeping their unending watch.

January 12

There was a loud explosion at about 6am, which we heard later arose from a mine in the sea. These explosions are very damaging to shop windows, even at considerable distances. One sees more and more of them partially boarded up, either as a precaution, or to cover up damage not now readily repairable. I was shocked to observe a grocer's manager hold up a slab of bacon against a lady customer's face, that she might inhale its fragrance.

January 16

By the 10am bus into Worthing to procure sausage rolls for the weekend – if possible. For these are unrationed, demand none of our precious points, and introduce a gleam of variety into our drab home diet of cheese and fish paste. But they are limited in production and limited to each customer, and soon disappear before the hungry multitude. Today I was lucky. Hurried to the end of Montague Street, dared to ask for six, and was given them. Veni! Vidi! Vici!

January 18

On Saturday night our bombers carried out a heavy raid on Berlin. The Huns were caught napping, great damage was done, and the RAF lost only one machine. Now they have retaliated on London, but in a half-hearted way. London has been immune since May 1941. However, the days of German ascendancy in the air are over, and the worst that can happen now will be but a pale reflection of 1940-1.

January 20

The wonderful Russians have now relieved Leningrad, which has been besieged by the Huns since August 1941. So Leningrad, Moscow and Stalingrad, three key cities of the Soviet Republic, are all safe, though after infinite blood [has been shed]. Lest we base too great hopes on the vast German losses, it will give us pause when we reflect that each year there is a fresh brood of young Huns, amounting to half a million, 'coming forth for slaughter'.

January 21

There was a sudden explosion last night at about 11.10pm. It caused doors to shake, dogs to bark, and F to 'feel funny inside'. Men say that it was a mine in the sea off Beach House, and there were many more windows broken along Warwick Street and Brighton Road. Today we saw workmen repairing them with wooden boards or cardboard against the day when it can be done with glass.

January 22

There is much bother about mines off the foreshore and it is said that the Admiralty has been asked to deal with some which have been seen. An explosion being expected at any time, this afternoon people were ordered away from the western part of the front. But nothing happened.

January 24

The capture of Tripoli is announced. That implies a wonderful march by General Montgomery's Army from distant El Alamein, and the end of Italy's colonial empire. But elation is damped by another warning by our experts of the continual gravity of the U-boat menace.

January 26

The Russians continue their triumphant advance, relieving more and more of their towns and villages from the contagion of the Hun. We take it all very coolly, but imagine pleasant Kent, Surrey or Sussex overrun, and their familiar towns daily coming back into the map; rescued but ruined, and lacking many citizens, murdered or carried into captivity. Truly, despite air attack, the sea is still our salvation.

January 27

To the front to view the damage by blast from the recent mines there. There was another explosion yesterday. The damage is really stupendous. For a quarter of a mile from Montague Place westwards there is hardly a window left in the long row of lofty hotels and boarding houses. The glass is gone, and in many instances the frames are also broken. Even doors in some places are burst in. The spectacle suggests a bombardment.

February 2

Our will o'the wisp PM, who, after mysterious disappearance, was revealed on Casablanca, again vanished; to emerge in Turkey and now in Cairo! Was it to persuade the Turks into the war now that the Huns are facing disaster? The Turks have been much wooed by both sides throughout the conflict. There is an anxious side to the PM's aerial travels. Suppose he crashed. His extinction would be irreparable. For there is no outstanding figure to replace him. He is all too obviously a whale amongst the minnows.

February 5

I was not surprised to hear that the RAF visited Italy last night, because I heard the bombers passing over earlier, say 7pm. They had a long way to go and return. For Germany they leave much later, about 10pm.

February 7

Sunday. There was such a commotion in our street this morning with the Home Guard rushing about, clopping on the pavement with their ammunition boots. They kept firing off their rifles (unloaded) on corners, pretending that the Germans were come, causing F to comment disrespectfully, 'I bet they would run a lot faster if the Germans really did come.'

February 8

727th air-raid warning 2.11pm. Though so short, this alarm represented a raid of dire import to Worthing. Just before the siren sounded I, in the public library, heard the crashing rush of a plane which came over so slow that it seemed almost to touch the roof, and a short sharp explosion. Descending to the ground floor, I found a crowd in the porch watching billowing white smoke arising in the distance in the direction of Homefield Park. Poor F, who was caught alone in Chatsworth Road, saw what looked like a parachute descending with fire about it. This she feared was a bomb about to burst. But men say it was a flare dropped by the RAF. But why? It appears that a German plane was shot down after dropping bombs in the Sugden Road and Lyndhurst Road districts; considerable damage and 43 casualties including eight fatal – all women.

February 10

We had just sat down to tea when the siren sounded. Soon afterwards a miniature battle in the air developed. Planes rushed about, machine guns rattled, there was a salvo of bombs; then more firing followed by another salvo of bombs; later a third. But poor F ran into the bowels of the house, agitated about our own safety.

February 11

Worthing did not suffer in yesterday's alarms, though it is said Lancing did. In the afternoon we visited the area damaged here on the previous day. These melancholy expeditions bring tears to F's eyes. Yet she says, 'One likes to go.' Saw the remains of half-a-dozen houses which had been levelled to dust, with black-bereted ARP workers probing the wreckage for what could be saved. Dozens more had lost windows and part of their roofs. The events of the past two days have caused a good deal of nervousness and foreboding among ladies no longer young. Thus one we met had arranged to leave the town. Another has been advised to go to bed in her day clothes, but is in a quandary since she cannot sleep so! A third decided not to use her theatre tickets bought for today.

February 12

Most of us are jubilant about the successes of the Russian Colossus, but F sees a darker side to them, remarking, 'Mark me, there will be trouble with the Russians after the war.'

February 15

F, on her usual progress along the devastated front this afternoon, was diverted by watching our latest arrived Canadians being put through physical exercises, which included making wheelbarrows of one another. The Canadians have a song, topical of the war, which is become very popular. The refrain of it is, 'Praise the Lord, and pass the ammunition; pass the ammunition and we'll all be free.' F has taken to singing it too, and as much as possible in the bass of fighting men. Which is very comical to listen to.

February 19

To tea at Mitchell's. Sat opposite a lady with a pretty little girl who addressed her as 'mummy' and brandished uncouth dolls for our regard. Having presently inquired of our waitress, received reply, 'The lady has adopted her, and she seems very happy. She is only two-and-a-half years old. Her father was killed in the war. Her mother has married again and does not want her.'

February 24

Three dogs killed by a landmine near the pier. A Great Dane scavenging on the beach with two friends of lesser breed set it off. There are still too many dogs in Worthing, but as to this Great Dane, he was of noble appearance and a public figure in our streets, so we mourn our loss. F left her umbrella, a new one, in the rack at the Assembly Hall yesterday, and now it is clean gone. The third she has lost in a public place since the war began. There seems to be at this present a beastly dishonesty rampant among the people. This loss is more serious in that umbrellas can no longer be bought, but luckily I have two.

February 26

Last night from 9pm into the small hours the stillness was broken by the roar and rattle of military vehicles on the main roads at the back of Broadwater. And today found long rows of tanks on the front and adjacent roads, evidently newly arrived, dozens of them. Many sturdy muscular short men in khaki 'slops' and black berets were investigating and probing their [the tanks'] bowels.

March 1

By day and by night, more than ever before, the RAF keep bombing Germany; and about this district there is more and more rolling of tanks. It would seem that at last great events are afoot. Down by the front, near the *Kingsway Hotel*, the military have displayed a great map showing the southern ports. Maps are forbidden to be sold in shops.

March 3

Our streets are strangely quiet, for the tanks have all departed in the night.

March 8

743rd air-raid warning 12.20 to 1.40am. This awakened me from my first sleep, and I did not sleep again until after 2am, so today I have felt heavy and weary. This raid came very near. Planes kept passing and there were reports of guns and bombs. I could see flashes in the direction of Shoreham, and heard through the wall of semi-detachment, vague talking of disturbed neighbours. Everyone was aroused, wondering how much nearer the bombs were going to fall. One really felt that home, and perhaps life, were at hazard. However, once again, for Worthing at least, all is well.

March 9

After tea, when sitting out on the front, close to Montague Place, we suffered our worst scare of the war to date. The raid siren sounded. There was scarcely anyone in view except three old ladies who at once rose and walked sedately away. We, remaining seated, as most do now, smiled our contempt and made a reference to 'jitters'. And then, in an instant, more near to us, followed a crashing of bombs and bursts of machine gun fire. I saw a plane race out to sea and then a great spout of water shoot up from an explosion in the sea. It was just west of the bandstand, about 200 yards away. Under the official rules for such occasions, we threw ourselves flat down on the ground. The crashes continued for about a minute, and lying there on our bellies amid it all, I wondered what it would feel like to receive a machine gun bullet in the back. An old-fashioned gentleman, who, with his wife, was lying in front of us, I suppose by way of reassurance, cried out, 'We got it like this every day in London. You'll be alright. They cannot hit you unless your time has come.' And then he broke into singing a hymn. But we were little comforted, being deeply apprehensive lest our time HAD come. However, mercifully, as always here, the raid crisis was soon over, and it left no visible trace save some distant smoke rolling out to sea. Then F had a laughing fit which lasted throughout most of our walk back to Broadwater. But I think this was a nervous reaction after the shock she had undergone.

March 10

The raid yesterday was even more serious than we had thought. There was a crowd outside the Town Hall this morning reading the list of casualties. There are six persons dead, three missing (probably dead) and a score injured (most slightly). It is of course human to magnify the importance of an attack on one's own locality. This was actually only one of the small 'hit-and-run' raids on coastal districts by dozens of planes or less which are an everyday occurrence somewhere or other. They don't affect the war effort, though bringing dire distress to stricken homes.

March 13

Daily Telegraph is now but a four-page paper on three days out of six, and six pages on the others; this for lack of newsprint. However, we now have an egg each every other week, and the milk ration is increased from two to two-and-a-half pints per week. Still no fish in Broadwater but winkles.

March 14

748th air-raid warning 12.15 to 1.30am. 749th 6.40 to 7.50pm. For the third time in a week it was a real local raid and not merely a warning. After hearing some distant bombing I looked out. It was not dark for the moon was only partially obscured by clouds. Then, all of a sudden, the whole sky was illuminated with a white flash followed by tongues of reddish flame shooting upwards, and there was a deafening explosion. Darkness and silence immediately supervened. All was over – a bomb had fallen on Grove Road, about a quarter of a mile away. The casualties were two killed and four seriously injured, with a dozen slightly. A miracle that there were not more. Much devastation in the fine residential district of Upper Brighton Road. We went to see the damage, but soon came away, since poor F, already shaken by recent happenings, was so overcome in realising the distress of the people. On heaped up ruins of a house an undaunted wight had fixed a staff from which a Union Jack was flying; and gangs of men were busy up and down the affected roads doing urgent patching up.

March 15

Most of the shop windows in W Broadwater are out, the effect of 'blast' from yesterday's bombing in Grove Road. There is also dreadful damage to roofs along Upper Brighton Road. The explosion was caused by a landmine, that is to say a kind of large bomb which is released from a plane and falls attached to a parachute.

March 19

Biscuits, already only occasionally attainable, are cut by a further 50 per cent. Thus are the little comforts of the defenceless whittled away. But what a hullabaloo there would be if there were a similar cut in drink and tobacco.

March 24

Paper serviettes at tea have just ceased to be supplied at Mitchell's eating house. Since, nearly three years ago, the making of these was forbidden, the management must be said to have put up a brave fight against the inevitable. They will still supply them at lunch.

March 26

Noticed over 40 people in the fish queue in Broadwater this morning. Sitting next to me at lunch at Khong's was a man of some 70 summers, who was in sorrow at the small helpings of meat in eating houses now. He said his weight had decreased from 15 to 12 stones since the war began.

March 30

A well-to-do lady of our acquaintance in a great talking about the recent hit-and-run raids of German bombers against the town, though they have been trivial compared with those against many other towns. She says she will leave, as some have already done, and has been talking in a way to dismay them too. This sort of thing is contemptible. If she cannot help being a coward let her go away quietly without this spreading of alarm.

April 2

To the Odeon cinema to see *Desert Victory*, the official film presenting the El Alamein battle and the subsequent defence of Tripoli. The raucous canned music obligatory to the film was a torment, as were the usual heat and smoky atmosphere of the crowded cinema.

April 6

A vile NW wind, strong and cutting. We listened for a time in the afternoon to a fine silver band of the Royal Canadian Air Force performing in Montague Place. But the climate was so atrocious that there were only about 50 people present. Red-eyed and weary we sought tea at Mitchell's where we found happiness at last.

27   *Inside the Lido, sandbagged against bomb blasts.*

April 9

Today is my 61st birthday. For me birthdays are becoming but a memento mori. No longer for me gifts, and the cake with numbered candles. However, health being still good, if not robust, I believe myself to be happier than at any previous period of adult life. In youth I was too hard worked, distracted with vain hopes, impecunious and snubbed. In middle age easier in purse, yet pressed with affairs almost beyond my strength. Now my time is my own. I am glad to be out of the stream of life; only too pleased to watch the world go by.

April 14

From 9.30 until 11 last night, or later, there was at intervals the enormous drumming of bombers overhead. It was altogether beyond ordinary. They went over in waves during the calm clear night. One wave was continuous for over 20 minutes, many hundreds of planes must have been engaged in an attack, which, I have learnt today, took them to Italy. The noise recalled to me the passage of German planes on the way to London during the worst hours of the Battle of Britain. I felt excited. It seemed a night on which history was being made.

April 16

To Chichester after lunch, by bus, to seek a hotel for a fortnight's holiday in June. Found the *Dolphin and Anchor*, hard by the cathedral, apparently very suitable. This bright little country town felt all bustle and people – many of them, of both sexes, in uniforms.

April 17

774th air-raid warning 12.38 to 1.38am, and afterwards could get little sleep. And so a heavy day with aching head. It is remarkable that, for the first season since the war began, there are no packets of seeds displayed in the shops. Gone are the little envelopes with the optimistic coloured pictures of what you are to expect. Vegetable seeds remain on sale, as usual, for all are adjured to grow vegetables for our sustenance.

April 20

As I write, at 6.40pm, more than a dozen RAF planes have roared and flashed past in a loose succession at rooftop height, on some deadly errand across Channel. F commented severely, 'I don't think they ought to be allowed to go so low, upsetting people.'

April 21

This morning obtained, unexpectedly, at our baker's, half a pound of digestive biscuits. Oh, the joy of it! We are still limited to a miserable two-and-a-half pints of milk per week each.

April 22

Today being the eve of the Easter holiday, there was the usual scramble to get in supplies. In Broadwater there was a fish queue of twice the usual length. There was a long queue, too, at the stores opposite. Everywhere there were queues at the cake shops, which were soon sold out. Public holidays in our present straits are nothing but a curse to householders.

April 25

Heard news of the passing of a dear friend of many years. One who walked humbly and was kind. And now, as we hope, she has gone to rejoin her husband for whom she longed. It is best so. The pain is ours. Such is life.

April 30

The shortage of labourers has extended now to newspaper boys. It is become common to see a notice outside newspaper shops: 'Boys or girls required for paper rounds.' Our road is at present being served by a very sprightly little maid. She comes as early as 7am, assisted from door to door by a neat bicycle. She is dressed in a navy blue mackintosh with 'pixie' hood, beneath which fair curls are parted over an engaging, purposeful little countenance. Her sturdy legs are bare save for white ankle socks. She may have seen 14 summers and performs her task in a quiet and dashing style. A bright contrast to the sullen indifference of her male predecessor!

May 3

F still unwell [and] did not venture out. I did, inquiring at seven shops for calves' foot jelly for her, but could not find any. The way of the invalid is now hard.

May 5

Cold and dull early but the gale had abated. F still kept house. I, after lunching out alone off fish cakes followed by raisin pudding, became violently sick soon after 4pm. Which has made me feel a wreck.

May 6

My upset yesterday evening brought on a neuralgia which prevented me from getting any sleep. At 2.45am I was sick again, and now have no appetite. I have not felt so ill for years. However, both to eating house for lunching – another one! But in my state I could face neither their 'haricot mutton' or 'cod mornay', so went straight to the 'sweet', which was prunes and some disgusting semolina stuff oversweetened with saccharin. Food everywhere is at its lowest ebb. There is nothing nice.

May 8

Cold and violent SW gale, with heavy downpours, all day. One of the worst storms I have ever known. It was hard to keep one's feet in the streets. Much damage in the gardens. Tulips were ruined and no birds sang.

May 14

High summer has come upon us all in a flash. House temperature at 8am 61 degrees, a rise of nine degrees since the 11th. Spent part of the morning reading newspaper on Broadwater Green – an outstanding privilege of retirement. How I used to grudge a fine spring morning caged in an office.

May 16

Very fine. There were big parades of the Home Guard today in celebration of their third anniversary. They have improved greatly in appearance since their early days. They look now a set of powerful and workmanlike soldiery, quite capable of dealing with any enemy parachute troops. At first they included too large a proportion of old men, but these have been weeded out, and a proportion of young conscripts added.

May 17

787th air-raid warning 12.05 to 12.15am; 788th 12.50 to 1.12am. In the midst of the last there was a loud bomb explosion which sounded unpleasantly near. I slept again soon after the 'All Clear' but the double interruption of sleep left us jaded at breakfast time. As people were out in the sunshine this morning doing their shopping the sky seemed full of planes.

May 18

I was astonished to see about the town today a street musician playing on a miniature banjo. Such a sight has not been seen since the war provided jobs, and good jobs, for all. He was not old, and might surely have been doing something more useful in the present shortage of workers.

May 21

This afternoon I chanced to be one of a small crowd outside Beach House to witness the arrival of the young widowed Duchess of Kent, who came to make an ambulance inspection. 'There is also with her another Duchess of some kind,' remarked a lady. This second one was, I presume, her Grace of Norfolk. The pair, escorted by the mayor and police, made a smiling progress through the avenue of ambulances and picturesque little girls dressed as nurses, and were soon lost to view within the premises. The royal Duchess wore the dismal black uniform of the Order of St John, inevitable for the occasion, but little becoming.

May 27

Busy with small business. It fell to me to mend sunblind, repair umbrella stand, scrape out 'fur' from the kettles, clean out drawers of writing table, convert a pearl necklace for F, whereby from one dangling at bosom length it might become two chokers, renew blackout paper, clean out garden shed.

May 28

Weighing myself today, on a reliable machine, the same I was weighed on on October 1, 1941, I was startled to find that I now weigh but 8st and 12lb as against 10st then. Allowing, perhaps, some trifle for possible difference of raiment, it is still a great decrease, and can only be due to the poor diet. I have never weighed so little since I became a grown man. And, indeed, it would seem if the war continues much longer I may grow light enough to qualify for a horse jockey.

May 29

We were in Chapel Road, outside the public library. Two vapour trails of unseen enemy planes, and there was a sound of firing. There was a call to take shelter, which was done – on the run! But nothing untoward happened. Later in the afternoon that prolonged booming became audible in the sky from invisible planes, which I have come to recognise as indicating a sortie by the famous American Flying Fortresses. Daily bombing is their speciality, and they fly very high. They are a tremendous menace to the Huns.

May 30

Sat out on Broadwater Green this morning, but we were not allowed to forget the war. In the distance artillery boomed forth at practice. Out in the mid-Green a couple of the RAF regiment were attendant upon a Bofors gun, alert to destroy any intruding Fokker Wulf planes, at one side a party of Royal Engineers was repairing a military telephone line, while at intervals there constantly circulated around the three surrounding highways military lorries, anti-tank guns and tanks themselves, hoisted on their gargantuan drays and carriers.

May 31

Had F weighed. She also has lost a stone since October 1, 1941, that is to say since rationing became really severe. She weighs now but 6st and 10lb. Our loss of weight is accompanied by a frequent sense of over-fatigue.

June 1

803rd air-raid warning 1.35 to 2.26am. Horrid to be awakened by the shrill siren! Felt flat and weary on rising at 7am, and throughout the day. Still we fared better than the unhappy wight beside us at lunch. Had to turn out twice to report himself at an air-raid station: quite in vain as usual; for the raiders went towards London.

June 5

The anti-aircraft guns did not disturb our rest last night, as they have been doing, with their practising; so we were afflicted by the siren instead. There does seem something fatuous and wrong in spoiling the sleep of a whole district for nothing in this way. Purchased half a pound of 'Petit Beurre' biscuits. It is a red letter day when one can do that. For there is a dire shortage of biscuits.

June 6

F remarked this morning, 'My nerves are bad. The war is wearing me down. It is killing me inch by inch. All the sad news is too much for me.' This attitude is distressing in one so normally cheerful. Today she is specially smitten because a civilian plane has been barbarously shot down by the Huns, with the loss of the 17 people on board, including Leslie Howard, talented actor and film producer.

June 10

In the afternoon, F, for a treat, took me out to the suburb called The Pantiles, at West Worthing, where there is a very dainty tea house. We had home-made scones and two cakes each, with tea, all excellent for but 1s. 10d. It is a self-contained district with its own pretty new line of shops; and even the people appeared more fresh and ornamental than the familiar Worthing crowd. So, after our refreshment, we sat out on a seat there, and enjoyed the pure air scented with newly cut grass, and around us the cheerful scene of villadom alight with many coloured flowers. The sense of novelty supplied the illusion that we were arrived in a hitherto unknown resort for a holiday.

June 11

Purchased a pair of outdoor shoes, spurred thereto by the ominous appearance in the shops of foot gear with wooden soles. The Fascists in Italy have forbidden women to wear trousers so, there is, after all, something good in Fascism.

June 13

The RAF carried out their biggest raid of the war on Friday night, when near 1,000 planes bombed Dusseldorf and Munster. 42 unhappily lost. Next day the Americans followed suit with a daylight high altitude visit to Wilhelmshaven. When we were out walking this morning in Forest Road some Canadian tank soldiers quartered there were playing at catch with one of their great clumsy baseballs, as they love to do. But a catcher missing, the ball hit a girl on a bicycle so that she fell off and could not resume, being assisted home. And F, indignant, insisted on delivering a chiding harangue to the company of sheepish guilty Canadians, whose spokesman replied with admirably contrite words.

June 16

Soon after 10am came a heavy shower of hail, and, an hour later, a thunderstorm. There was a terrific report with a blinding flash of lightning. Men say that an RAF plane flying over the district was struck and brought down. The pilot escaped death but was injured.

June 17

Our ration books being due to expire, I to the town hall and obtained new ones. Detained only ten minutes, this time, for a change, the business being very well done. Yet I am truly glad that this worry is over once more.

June 19

Sky mostly overcast. W wind still strong and cold. Much engaged in the petty worries incident to leaving home [for a holiday in Chichester], cutting off bread and milk supplies, newspapers, etc – with due provision for their resumption when the agony of the holiday is over. One feels a guilt about going away in wartime, but this grows less as the years lengthen out; for we are not immortal and can only live our lives once.

June 20

At about 11.30pm last night could be heard the engine hum of a vast number of our bombers going over for an attack on the continent. They seemed to pass in a continuous armada for more than half an hour. It is most impressive to lie in bed and hear that concentrated deep-toned droning in the silence of the night. In 1940 we used to hear the same noise; but more fearfully, for then the planes were German – going the other way!

June 21

Journeyed to Chichester to obtain a fortnight's respite from the domestic round. Put up at the *Dolphin and Anchor Hotel*, a fine old rambling house.

June 22

Last night we were awakened by an air-raid warning about 2am, which lasted half an hour – disappointing on this our first night in this secluded cathedral town where we had expected unbroken repose. This afternoon we went by bus to little Bosham. Some interesting Saxon work in the church. Here is an inlet of the sea, which we found blue and sparkling in the sun and breeze; and around it a hamlet mostly of modern villas peeping out prettily enough among luxuriant saplings and undergrowth. Here, too, was peace, and a company of small children romping on a grass plat over against the waterside.

June 23

We find Chichester a very pleasant ancient city; lively and well equipped, and with good shops for its size. Having, indeed, but 16,000 of population, it seems to be a town which makes a little go a long way. Our hotel is very spacious and comfortable, though the meals necessarily reflect the rigour of the times.

June 25

Hotel life in wartime – at breakfast we had only one teaspoon between us, and on our applying to the waitress for a second, received the reply, 'We are very short. We are getting down to having only one for two people.' By bus to Southsea. The Southdown bus services, though slightly curtailed, remain excellent here as at Worthing. The devastation at Portsmouth caused by bombing was a melancholy spectacle. The little Royal Naval girls, called Wrens, were everywhere about and pretty to see in their jaunty 'Jack Tar' caps, white blouses and blue shirts with black silk hoses.

June 26

At the hotel today we ate tough boiled pudding, tough pastry and tough beef. Which is very ill. It is a misfortune for the management (and indeed for us!) that they can provide no fish but cod; and no stewing fruit but little mawkish white cherries. This afternoon to a military band playing, Greek dancing, etc, in the garden of the Bishop's Palace. There was also an exhibition of tumbling by high school girls; very well done. We paid 1s. each. All this was to aid local cripples. Altogether an agreeable, blameless entertainment in a fair and venerable setting.

June 27

To matins at the cathedral. The interior, not impressive through lack of spaciousness, is now deteriorated by many of its coloured windows being boarded up against the Huns.

June 28

A great flight of our bombers outwards at midnight, and this afternoon, as we sat in the Priory Park recreation ground, beside the beautiful little ancient chapel there, the air seemed alive with planes. They came and went in all directions, bombers and fighters too. It was like a tattoo, a circus of the sky. I have never before in the war seen anything of the kind of so great a scale or so continuous.

June 30

To Petworth by bus. Glorious country around it, but an ugly village sprawling on a hill surmounted by an ugly church built of sandstone now mainly black. The interior was largely blacked out against the Huns, and seemed very cavernous and grim. Thence to the beautiful little RC church, which contains some fine modern glass. There was recently a terrible bombing tragedy at Petworth. A school hit, and 30 children, with the headteacher, killed.

July 1

For us just an idle day in summertime. We began it with a rather sad sight – a long column of young men marching from the railway station, under escort, to the barracks. These were young conscripts going for training. They were mainly still in civilian dress. Some of them looked disconsolate, and none showed spirit; which is, I suppose, the way with pressed men. For it is hard to be snatched, unwilling, out of the comforts of family life into the doubtful amenities of the barrack room, with a more doubtful prospect to follow.

July 2

Very fine. We went again to Midhurst. We met a lorry full of Italian prisoners returning from work on the land. They wore greenish clothing curiously patched in brown, as a hindrance to escape. It seems they are in excellent heart, having taken to singing so lustily that they have had to be restrained! Well, one could understand them singing on being out of Italy in its present predicament.

July 3

It was pleasant, in the middle of evening, to sit beneath the lime trees [opposite the cathedral]. Evening parade in Chichester is now an animated and picturesque occasion, a panorama of uniforms and bright summer dresses. There are soldiers (here, too, mostly Canadian), fleetmen, airmen (Dominion as well as our own), navy girls, army girls, land girls, fire girls, police girls – all mingled with the general population. It is a scene, primarily, of sparkling youth, very novel and colourful against the mellow background of this venerable city; a scene unequalled in all of the centuries since first the Romans set out its four square streets. Yet it is a scene which we nevertheless trust will, in no long time, vanish like the rainbow.

July 5

Today consisted of the distresses of getting clear of the hotel, travelling with luggage, and unpacking it on arrival home. So ends one more annual holiday – a very pleasant one and remarkable for the fact that during the whole fortnight no rain fell. Personally, I am always glad when this exodus is over; for it is unsettling, and I dislike being unsettled. What will have happened in Europe by the time another holiday goes around?

July 8

Cool and unsettled. Thunder showers in the afternoon, with hail. The Great Pause [in the war] is broken by a vast battle which has begun between the Huns and the Russians on the Kursk salient. The Huns, according to their enemies, have sustained fantastic losses in planes and tanks, but have gained a little ground. And the battle continues in the large indefinite way of Russian battles.

July 10

At 7am we were treated to an inspiring display of bombers overhead. I counted 40 of these great planes passing slowly, majestically by; irregularly placed, silver against the blue. Behind them lingered, intensely white, the long spiral train of filmy exhaust vapours. At 7.30pm they were followed by a covey of 17 more.

July 11

It appears that what we witnessed overhead yesterday was an Anglo-American expedition of bombing airfields at Caen and Abbeville and other parts of northern France. Happily, only two planes are missing. But today comes much more sensational news. For the invasion of Sicily by Anglo-American forces has begun! This is a most portentous event.

July 12

I enjoyed a leisurely stroll about the town after many inclement days. Worthing, whose sole industry, apart from horticulture and the nurture of the aged, has suddenly become a producer of ships and boats. I counted a score of these laid out ready for delivery in the municipal car park near to the railway bridge. They were painted blue-grey and fitted with looped ropes along the gunwale for victims of the sea to take hold of. They were earmarked to contain 40 persons, save a few fitted with motors and screws, which leave spaces available for 36 only. These long grey shapes speak eloquently of the necessities of the U-boat menace; at last, it would seem, near to being mastered.

July 14

Between 7am and 7.30am many American Flying Fortresses passed over in the direction of the French coast. Their engines filled the sky with a deep booming sound. I saw 16 of them in a mass each emitting a separate line of exhaust vapour, as through drawing with chalk on the blue of the sky. At a little distance behind, these lines coalesced into a single giant snow white bar across the heavens, which gleamed in the morning sunshine; it was a very beautiful sight.

July 15

There is a good deal of public concern about the heavy losses of the RAF in their night raids over Germany. They lose an average of about 25 great bombers on each one, and carry out two or three raids a week. And each lost bomber carries half a dozen or more of the highly trained cream of the nation; heroes in the fullest sense. Yet the spirit of the force seems unaffected. Which is very wonderful.

July 17

Bought at the leading grocers' one quarter of a lb of 'chopped ham' for the weekend, being what the Americans send us and call 'Spam'.

July 19

As we were sitting on a seat overlooking Broadwater Green yesterday F remarked, 'Matilda says these Commandos who have just come into the town are a very superior kind of soldier. Their landladies are given 30 shillings per week for each of them, so that they can have more meat.'

July 20

The American air force carried out a very heavy raid on Rome. This is the first time the Eternal City has received such a visit, which was confined to railways and factories. The Anglo-American army has already gained half of Sicily. The Russians are more than holding their own. One begins to feel a mild excitement, and to dwell on the possibility of a happier way of life after the war. For the pendulum at last is obviously swinging very much in the favour of the Allies.

July 23

Same drab weather. I was on the front this afternoon, and it presented a truly melancholy picture. For the sky was grey, the battered stucco houses were grey, the road was grey, and so were the great synthetic monoliths which, with the rusty labyrinth of barbed wire, obscure one's sight of the sea. And it was almost deserted by man, save for one redeeming exception. This was a little flaxen-haired girl in a scarlet jacket, proud and sedate on the box seat of a go-cart drawn by a Shetland pony, which passed up and down the desolate road. It is remarkable that, after nearly four years of war and exploding mines, there should still be this go-cart and two or three riding ponies plying for hire on the front. But where are the crowds of '39?

July 25

Sunday. We now regularly hear the church bells again after years of silence. This afternoon it was warm enough to sit out in the garden in comfort. But I was fretted by the discharge of various ordnance, the din of planes and tanks, and by the undulating cacophany of the air-raid siren. For there is no Peace in our time.

July 30

This holiday time, there being no ban on visitors as in former war years, there are considerably more strangers to be seen abroad. Their presence arouses mixed feelings among the natives, for while, on the one hand, they bring money into the town, on the other, they consume victuals and raiment already insufficient. After luncheon to the children's bathing pool by the Beach House, where a pandemonium of young and small people yelling, jumping and flinging about the water in the hot sunshine, whilst parents lay watching in deckchairs in the shade of the surrounding trees. It was indeed a striking spectacle of ardent, joyful young life in an ideal setting. It seemed, in present conditions, almost dreamlike – a peep back into the carefree seaside existence before the war came.

August 3

There were more holidaymakers abroad than for years past. Eating houses had long waiting queues; and, after fruitless attempts to lunch at any of our usual haunts, we did so at a tavern refectory off fried cod and chips with marrow. The waiter, rushing frantically about to satisfy the demands of the multitude, was unable or unwilling to bring us even a drink of water; but, since the sweat was rising out of his face, out of compassion we forgave him.

August 7

Our wireless set having, after five years of uninterrupted utterance, become suddenly dumb, today an expert, of appearance below military age, called to examine it. Like a physician, he was solemn: he was mysterious, and he said nothing. Like a physician he probed here and there, and used an instrument with earphones, much like a stethoscope. Then at last he pronounced his diagnosis. A condenser was 'gone', and so the patient must be removed to his workshop for a week.

August 8

Sunday, mainly cloudy. W gale. We seem to have been more cursed with wind this summer than in any that I can remember.

August 10

All the world seems on holiday. There has been nothing like it seen in Worthing since the war began. The crowds in shop queues and eating houses have become a real trial to nerves; and, as a resident, I shall be glad when August is out.

August 12

On the front this afternoon anti-aircraft guns were practising against a target towed by a plane. A nervous woman asked if the plane was a German so I was glad to reassure her. She came from Portsmouth; had there been bombed out three times, and had lost three relatives in Birmingham through bombing. So her nervousness was very excusable.

August 15

Put aside for salvage two of my prize books which I have preserved for 50 years. Sentiment has hitherto prevented me. But a recent Government appeal has lain on my conscience. After all, I shall never want to read them again, and they are relics of my preparatory schooling. They are *Fair*

Women And Brave Men by Charlotte Yonge, and *In Greek Waters*, by G.A. Henty. Typical pasturage for young minds in their day, though never ranking with the classics.

August 16

We heard very distant explosions, gunfire from time to time, both distant and near, and occasional droning of planes. Worthing was unscathed, though today the front opposite Steyne Gardens was roped off, and Police notices were displayed intimating 'Unexploded Bomb – Keep Clear'. Some houses nearby have been evacuated.

August 17

The ban on visitors to the South Coast has been reimposed in various places, it is believed here. But, since this time it has been done secretly, there is at present much uncertainty. It is clear, however, that great troop movements are in progress. For the first time in the war balloon barrages have appeared in this district. I saw one today apparently over the barracks in Upper Brighton Road now occupied by part of the Canadian Tank Regiment; and another to the east of the town in the direction of Shoreham. Today there is great news: the Huns have evacuated the whole of Sicily.

August 18

825th air-raid warning 11.55pm to 12.15am. A horrid breaking of one's first sleep! It was a calm clear night of enchanting beauty. We had a few bad moments of expectancy; but nothing happened except that a distant explosion shook the house a trifle. People are flat about the capture of Sicily because, after all the talk in the newspapers about putting the Huns 'in the bag', they seem to have all escaped to the mainland.

August 20

As the days shorten we are increasingly oppressed by the blackout regulations. It is irksome at 8.30pm to have to shut out the cool evening air from a sun-baked house. But it is that or sitting in darkness; for not a chink of light may show. We have a new uniformed postwoman who hath not, thank God, adopted the revolting trousered appearance of her predecessor. One respects her for her smart blue skirt with the official red stripe on the side.

August 21

Most of the visitors departed today. They have, for a week or two, added colour to our streets, and contributed to an arresting picture of contrasting peace and war. Little families in the bright filmy garments of summer have rambled and browsed everywhere about; whilst even more tanks rumble along or line the streets, and planes pass overhead. These war children, what a spectacle of health and beauty they provide! Children never looked so well before. Since they no longer receive from parents, between meals, questionable cakes and sweets of yore – these being no longer usually obtainable – pallor and spots are banished away, and kindly Hygeia rules over them unhampered.

August 27

Stood in a great queue of 100 or so in Montague Street, for a full half hour, to gain 4lb of damsons. The only distraction occurred when someone dropped a sixpence. The queue writhed and broke, individuals bowed themselves and sniffed, but no soul acknowledged to have retrieved it.

August 30

Found two pairs of kippers displayed in the village fish shop, and secured one of them. A rare windfall! Be it remembered that in this war lobsters and crabs have disappeared entirely. Which is very sad. For although there is really nothing cheerful in being a boiled lobster, nevertheless his rosy carcass on a slab seemed always decorative and cheering.

August 31

This morning, soon after 7.15, several squadrons of RAF fighters roared and rushed past the house at rooftop height, going east. This was an unusual and startling occurrence, even for this war. Now, as I write, at 4.45pm, the vault of heaven is filled with the ominous booming note of the American Flying Fortresses setting forth on a raid – dozens of them. People run out into their front gardens, crying out 'can you see them?' and the answer is 'no, they are too high up,' quite lost in the blue. Can anything be more tantalising?

September 3

This was the fourth anniversary of the outbreak of war, and celebrated by a Great Praying. Different sects at each their own prayings at their own times; and there was one at the Assembly Hall, for all sorts and conditions, altogether, at noon.

September 4

Today we have the great news that the invasion of Italy has begun. General Montgomery's famous 8th Army has made a successful landing at many points. So the Allies are once more on the continent of Europe; and the tide of liberation of tortured peoples seems at last to be surging back, as we trust and believe, in irresistible flood.

September 5

It was a pretty and rare sight to see, as I did on rising, six goldfinches ranged side by side drinking at the bird bath. These bright-plumaged little birds are very timid and cannot endure the human eye upon them. For as soon as they perceive it, which is usually instant, they are up and away in a flash; so different from the bold robin, always ready to stand his ground.

September 6

The Anglo-American air attack grew even greater the last evening. As I lay in bed reading *Tom Jones*, there was a constant succession of bombers going over for nearly an hour. And this morning, as I dressed, still more flights were passing. Our general attitude to the war now is one of weariness. Yet we are thus reminded that these are great days. Very likely in time to come ardent souls will deplore that they were born too late to share them! The ban on visitors to Brighton is making Worthing unpleasant by the diversion of visitors hither. So there is crush in the buses, crush in the eating houses, and crush in the streets – already purgatorial with the numbers of military lorries, and the infernal noise and rushing about of military motor dispatch riders. Yet we often find solace on fine evenings in sitting in flower-bordered Denton Gardens and watching our visitors perform on the putting green there.

September 8

It seems that at Brighton a citizen may not possess a telescope, nay even opera glasses, without a special permit. One from there sitting on a public seat in Montague Place remarked that Brighton is being made a centre of preparation for the coming invasion of the continent. 'It lies conveniently between two harbours,' he said, 'Newhaven and Shoreham, and has many squares suitable for the collection of stores. Barges are daily passing along the coast.' It seems to me that this fellow might, by saying so much, be bringing himself within the prickly embrace of the Defence Regulations.

September 9

Today we have the best news since the war began. Italy has surrendered! So now the forces of righteousness can concentrate upon the elimination of the foul Hun. There is a general joy in consequence – heartfelt if restrained, in the manner of the British people. Fair women murmured, 'what lovely news!' The load of everyone seems suddenly lighter; and the end of the road so much nearer.

September 10

The situation in Italy remains obscure and peculiar. The Allies are in possession of 'the toe', but there are believed to be nearly 300,000 Huns in different parts of the country, mixed up with perhaps twice as many of the hapless Italian troops now nominally 'surrendered'. It seems a problem as to how the two armies will be sorted out, and how they will deal with one another in the meanwhile.

September 12

The surrender of Italy seems infinitely significant. For it is recognition by an erstwhile friend of hitherto invincible Germany that they must lose the war and the Allies win it. Hitler calls this action a betrayal. So it is, but it is more than that; it is abandonment of the sinking German ship. No wonder we throw up our caps!

September 13

Much thunder and rain last night. Today thundery showers with bright intervals. Intensely close and warm. This afternoon I was seeking alleviation on a seat under the trees in Steyne Gardens when a little white-haired ivory-faced elf of some five years of age suddenly addressed me, with anguished looks. 'Have you seen another cat, besides this one; a grown-up cat?' The visible cat she referred to was a lank ginger beast, which I had noticed nosing about in the bushes, and seemed to be little more than a kitten. On receiving my negative reply, she continued, 'His name is Jacky, and he's lost his mother. I cannot find him anywhere, and I am afraid he will be run over.' I tried to console her by expressing my conviction that Jacky was well able to look after himself, whereupon she disappeared, with, I fear, little comfort.

September 15

My barber has lost his last assistant, who hath been pressed for the war. However, luckily for him, he is reserved for that novel and potent mystery 'Radiolocation'. And so he will not have to 'run with the bayonet' as F puts it. In the result, my barber has abandoned the shaving of 'gents', and now will only shear them, which he finds more lucrative.

September 16

There is anxiety about a great battle at Salerno, near Naples, between the Allied 5th Army under the American General Clark and the Huns. Hitler's men, no longer diluted with any Italian element, make a terrible enemy.

September 17

For the first time, I observed a woman butcher's assistant. She was engaged at a greasy counter, removing imported carcasses from their muslin shrouds. It seemed, for a woman, an enterprise more heroic than nice.

September 18

There is great relief and thankfulness today at the outcome of the hard-fought battle at Salerno. The Huns are in full retreat. For a time, indeed, it seemed that the Allied army was fated to a second Dunkirk. And it was clearly what the Great Duke [of Wellington] would have called 'a damned close-run thing'.

September 20

This afternoon we tramped about Worthing in vain, trying to purchase chocolate, a few biscuits, or powdered milk. The way of the [alcohol] abstainer is very hard now. He has a continued struggle to obtain the smallest allowances of his modest comforts. He does not receive fair treatment as compared with a tavern knight.

September 21

Very cold for the time of year. The cold made us feel miserable. Winter seemed to have arrived all of a sudden. A fifth winter of war conditions is a depressing prospect. Nevertheless, we dread it less this time since the war situation is so infinitely better. Hope of peace is stirring lustily within us at last. Britons are having to subsist largely on American synthetic meats, which they regard with a good deal of scorn. These meats differ one from another hardly perceptibly, yet bear various fancy names, whereof the best known is 'Spam'.

September 22

A great speech by the PM in the Commons. He took the occasion specially to emphasise his determination to destroy Prussian militarism completely, once and for all. Which is very well.

September 24

To Brighton by bus for a trip. Brighton looked shabby and sad, just as it did when I last visited it six months ago, save that there are now more naval men about, and more airmen, the latter mostly in the dark blue uniforms of the Australian Air Force. Tea at Fuller's in East Street, where it was stimulating to sit, amid a great mass of the undistinguished, cheek by jowl with a full Admiral in all his glory. It has dawned on me today, after looking at a menu, that the expression Spam, indicating certain American meat, is onomatopoeic, and not pure fancy. Spam means spiced ham! But how many realise it?

September 26

Today in England is being celebrated the Battle of Britain – by processions of the uniformed male and female; services in churches; sounding brass and tinkling cymbals; standards in the breeze. And, indeed, that great gallant event emerges more and more as one of the outstanding milestones on the broad highway of Time. If we had lost it?

October 4

The sky last night was wonderfully alight with stars. It seemed to glow and flash with a glorious riot of scintillating constellations – a spectacle of serene unfathomable loveliness and mystery, which seemed to bid the war-weary soul look up and be refreshed. Today, the town is all agog with the 'Aid to China' fund. Whist drive, public garden party, concerts, flag day. Also, as 'open sesame' to compassionate purses, public placards illustrating unhappy Chinese in profundis, hounded by the atrocious Japanese. The Chinese tribulation has been long drawn, and bitter, and they deserve all that we can send them.

October 5

From 7 to 8 last evening there was a continuous procession of RAF bombers going over to the continent. They made a tremendous din. 'I don't like hearing that,' remarked F, 'It makes me feel so sad when I think of the poor young men who will not return.'

October 8

Brilliant day, with hot sun. To the barber's for a haircut. For lack of males he hath engaged a fair assistant for auxiliary services; who tucked me up before the operation, and combed my hair and unshrouded me after it, which was a mighty novel experience, yet by no means disagreeable. The barber sprung about from one reclining patron to another, performing lightning snippings. In the evening to a concert performance of *Merrie England* at the Assembly Hall, by the Municipal Choir with four hired soloists. It was very well done. The ladies of the Municipal Choir wore very long white dresses, as I believe is their custom, and looked like a set of ghosts.

October 9

Poor F suffered from an indigestion in the night and this morning her cold was heavy. Then she was tempted by the sunshine into the town and had a bad fall, though no bones broken, I thank God.

So today for her it has been by no means 'Merrie England'. Put out another of my 'Prep School' prizes for salvage to help the war, *St Bartholomew's Eve* by Henty. These old books and the onset of autumn make me ponder on how people grow old and die, and the world rolls remorselessly on. It is 50 years since my kind and admirable preceptress handed me that volume amid the plaudits of my fellows. She was silver-haired then and majestic in bonnet and dolman, and must be long since with God. And now, in no long time, I, her grateful pupil, will follow her – and the world rolls remorselessly on.

October 13

There were only five persons killed in air raids over Britain in September, the lowest figure since May 1940. Excellent both in the saving of life and the growing weakness of the German air force.

October 14

A lady at our eating house had the hardihood to ask for a second helping of apple tart. Such gluttony has been unknown for years and is contrary to the Food Regulations. The request was firmly refused by the astonished waitress in the hushed silence of those within earshot.

October 16

The Americans have lost 60 Flying Fortresses, carrying 592 men, on a daylight raid. The raid was successful in its object of doing crippling industrial damage, and the Huns lost 100 fighters. Nevertheless people here feel a sense of shock. The price seems too high. I have been reading again Sergt Bourgogne's memoirs of *Napoleon's Retreat From Moscow*. It is a vivid and absorbing work. I wonder whether Hitler has read it now that his men are repeating the same enterprise!

October 17

840th air-raid warning 1.45 to 2.08am. Heard a few distant bomb explosions. 841st, 2.47 to 3.07am. These came at a dire time of night for sleepers, but one must not complain after a total respite for ten days. 842nd, 8.15 to 8.33am. There were some sharp bursts of anti-aircraft fire to disconcert our getting of breakfast, but the Hun, if near, was invisible to us.

October 19

For the past year or so the fashionable fair have been wearing coats with great square puffed shoulders, their coats looking on them as though suspended on wooden coat-hangers rather than on flesh and bone.

October 24

I observed from the remains with which they litter the streets, scorning considerations of salvage, that the Canadian soldiery enjoy not only their own special brands of cigarettes but also of sweetmeats. Thus on a short walk I met with rejected coverings as follows: 'Adams' Chiclets' (chewing gum, these), 'Robinson's Butternut Krisps', 'Neilson's Malted Milk Candy Bar', and – most seductive of all – 'Neilson's Chocolate Rosebuds'. All these delights normally unknown in the Motherland.

October 27

On the front this afternoon it was warm enough for summer. Watched a battery of Canadian anti-aircraft gunners whose guns and lorries were parked in Montague Place. These men were of the French variety, short, sturdy and sallow, with dark eyes. They were cleaning up generally in a leisurely fashion; and spoke French to one another while seeming to have English enough to establish contacts with the passing fair [women]. F to Brighton to buy a hat. It is a silly fashion now of small flat saucer shapes worn on one ear. 'I went into such a grand-looking shop,' she said. 'The assistant said, "Would you care for a beret? How would you like this nice Montgomery?"' Now a Montgomery is named after the famous general, the hero of Alamein, and adopter of the beret in preference to the conventional headgear of his rank. Such is fame!

October 31

I notice that the military have with their vehicles sheared off another stretch of Broadwater Churchyard wall. In their dashing way they frequently effect these demolitions. Nobody seems to care; c'est la guerre! And the taxpayer pays. The road, it is true, is dangerously narrow and is long overdue for widening.

November 3

Same drizzle early and late, but a grand afternoon which I spent on the dilapidated front, browsing in the sun, as did diverse soldiers, airmen, early closing shop people and flocks of seagulls. I wish the Allies would start a second Front in Europe if only to rid us of the swarms of military motorcyclists who make day hideous with their rushing helter-skelter about the best shopping area of Worthing, shattering nerves with a din like the firing of machine guns.

November 5

Dull and colder. The curse of the blackout is fully upon us again. At the moment, it begins at 6pm and continues until 7am; and of course it becomes daily longer. Guy Fawkes Day. The 5th without fireworks.

November 6

Suits and coats are worrying us. For we have reached a stage in the war when pockets, linings, buttonholes, hanging tags, are in rapid dissolution. Yet it is most difficult to get them repaired. Two or three shops, realising the need, have opened in the town to do nothing else. Yet they are overwhelmed with the stacks of garments.

November 9

I think there is too much talk, in speeches and press, about 'a better Britain after the war', and I fear inevitable and dangerous disappointment. For what our democracy intends is merely a greater material prosperity for individuals, the desire for which is natural and intense. But it is clear that there is no corresponding ambition for improved standards of conduct. So I expect only the same old political dogfight as before, and that embittered by a shortage of goods.

November 10

Saw a lady of fashion in the town with blue hair!, a pretty pastel shade. God intended it to be grey. She was so proud of it that she wore no hat. And, indeed, I have never seen the like before. Even other women smiled.

November 12

Milord Woolton hath resigned his office of Food Controller on appointment to the greater one of Minister of Reconstruction. As Food Controller we have found his administration able enough, but unsympathetic. Yet he had become an institution in our lives. So we felt a tinge of regret at his going.

November 14

Our Canadian tank soldiers have suddenly and secretly departed like all their predecessors. No longer are our streets lined with long rows of their gaunt charges in repose. Now, apart from a few anti-aircraft soldiers, our garrison appears to consist solely of Canadian Highlanders, perhaps half a battalion of them.

November 17

Crockery is in such short supply that at one principal restaurant in Worthing they are using old cups previously withdrawn from use on account of broken handles. The jagged remains are ground near flush with the cups; which, however, the patrons must handle delicately against the heat of the beverage within.

November 22

Heard at the grocer's that a stick of bombs fell into the sea off the west of the town on Saturday evening. Here in Broadwater we heard an explosion which shook our doors.

November 23

People throng the cosy teashops – the only relaxation for most, save the cinema. Though fare is of the plainest it is solacing to feed in company. At home there is isolation, for rationing makes entertainment almost impossible, and the difficulties of travel prevent meetings with friends at a distance.

November 24

It is very remarkable where a large proportion of people in Worthing's streets now are in the sixties of age or more – due mainly to the claims of the war on those younger.

November 25

Berlin has been undergoing a week of terrific raids by the RAF. It does one's heart good to read of the devastation of the German Olympus. Never was there such retribution for bullies and torturers. They know now what it feels like to the defenceless.

November 28

Extremely warm for time of year – so warm as to occasion headache and loss of appetite. Without informing us yesterday, the milkman today has abandoned Sunday delivery. So the remains of Saturday's pint must stretch over today and also tomorrow's breakfast to our great annoyance. But in times of scarcity consumers are little considered.

November 29

My cobbler, who for sometime has been refusing more repairs through pressure of business, has now put up a notice to say that he can do no more soling until he can get leather. After tea to Woolworths to buy a pocket diary and a tube of Seccotine glue, but they had neither. Before the war they [diaries] sold for one-and-a-half pence. This year they had a few at ten-and-a-half pence. These were quickly sold out.

November 30

Two or three familiar figures here have recently been removed by Death. It seems hard to have endured the travail of the war for so long, and not to see the end, the only compensation. I trust I may be spared to see it and to complete this record. Sometimes I worry somewhat about this as the war seems always to prolong itself. Met a lady social worker who deplored the increase of drinking among young women, and the undoing thereby of country girls brought into the great cities by the employments of the time.

December 2

To the barber's, where the presence of one of the celebrated 8th Army made a point of interest. He had campaigned all through North Africa, from Alamein to Tunis, Sicily and Italy, and looked none the worse for it. It is believed (but this is very secret) that most of the original units of this Army are being brought home to provide a stiffening of veterans for the Army which is designed to open the eternally discussed Second Front in Europe.

December 4

Coals are so short owing to strikes and absenteeism among the miners, and to some having gone into the Army, that young men are taken by ballot and put to the coal face, whether they be dustmen or dukes. Which indeed shocks the conscience and sounds like sending slaves to the galleys.

December 11

It continues bitterly cold. This morning on rising, I found about an inch of snow on the ground and there were some slight showers of snow during the day. I was interested in hearing that many people in London consider that the PM's recent 69th birthday celebrations in Tehran were unsuited to the seriousness of the hour. He is still popular, but not so popular as he was. At cinemas, F reports, there is less applause on his appearances on screen, but rather laughter. For he is, as a lady remarked, 'a good showman,' and comes on the scene with an air of boyishness. Down here, though people are thoroughly tired of the war, there seems less nervous irritability than there was a year ago.

December 14

Life seems just a miserable contest with the cold. All the soldiers one sees now, officers and men alike, wear the Army 'battledress', which is a most unlovely and disfiguring drab uniform. I cannot think it will long survive the war.

December 15

Dull morning, sunshine in the afternoon. There was some kind of military inspection at Broadwater Green this morning. The ground was marked out with little blue and white flags, and there seemed to be quite two battalions present. There was a band of brass, and, alternatively, a band of bagpipes. The troops were tall Canadians of the Scottish kind, and the long columns of men marching in 'threes', in greatcoats and steel hats, looked impressive. The sight was unusual here, for one rarely sees about Worthing more than a half company of soldiers at a time. Nevertheless, the British public was not interested, and went on with its shopping. The bitter cold provided an excuse. For the first time since the war began, Mitchell's failed to provide paper serviettes at lunch, though their manufacture has been forbidden for about three years past. Mitchell's must use hundreds each day. It has been a magnificent effort to keep the serviettes flying.

December 16

Dark and cold. I was engaged over one hour 'doing out' kitchen scullery and larder. So into town and lunch at an eating house off tough rabbit's leg (yet quite a special treat in these days!) and a shiny boiled pudding. 867th air-raid warning 5.47 to 6.30am. In addition to the ordinary siren, for the first time we were treated to the alarming 'cuckoo siren', which is sounded only when there is imminent danger, and is an innovation only two weeks old. It was justified in the present instance by the immediate explosion of a bomb not far away, and apparently then by a still nearer crash. Altogether it was a most upsetting manner of being brought to the beginning of another day. I have not found anyone who knows where the bomb fell, so Worthing town must be unscathed; but the ensuing crash was caused merely by a falling, owing to vibration, of a blackout screen measuring 5ft by 4ft from our scullery window on to the tiled floor.

December 22

Two elderly women were knocked over, and I fear fatally hurt, in Chapel Road today, one by a military lorry, and the other by a military motor bicycle. We did not see the accidents, but we saw the victims laid out in the road and thence transferred to an ambulance, with attendant doctors, ambulance girls, police, etc.

December 23

This is a bleak Xmastide. The only mitigation appears to be a larger supply of biscuits.

December 24

This Xmas people look glum and weary. There is widespread extortion in the sale of children's toys, which are few and primitive. There are no decorations, no poultry in the shops, and very little meat. Tried six shops seeking one quarter of a pound of cut tongue for F's Xmas dinner but failed. So she must be content with cheese. I have some equivocal sausage rolls which I shall eat, but she will have none of them. Dried fruit is scarce, and there are no apples or oranges. Cakes are of the plainest. Of course no bananas or lemons.

December 25

Saturday. Xmas Day. Dull, calm and mild. I awoke with neuralgia; and the Ideal Boiler stove went out in smoke. So I had to clean out the flue, with aching head. Later we walked abroad and were amused to see about 50 soldiers eagerly storming a tavern directly it opened its doors at noon. To abstainers it is very strange to observe the spell which strong waters cast over so many of the English.

December 27

Few people abroad. Lunched off cod steaks and mince pie at the *Albion Tavern* in Montague Street, our accustomed eating houses being closed. All this very well served, with vegetables, at 2s. 6d. per head. Just as we were about to leave we heard the news on the wireless of the sinking by ships of the Royal Navy of the German battleship *Scharnhorst*.

December 28

A pea soup sky and a coldness which seemed to penetrate the bones. We felt tired and depressed. The prospect in Worthing was still that of a dismal bank holiday. For the principal shops were still closed, and some of them will remain so for about a week.

December 29

Paid to the milkman for Xmas box 2s. 6d. Such largesse in these days attracts the imputation of bribery; yet I bestowed it solely in recognition of so much 'sad mechanic exercise' faithfully performed. To the infant laundryman 1s, who accepted it with a gratitude polite, if short of fervent. Perhaps he expected 2s.

December 31

So ends this year which, though it has seen the turn of the tide of war, has been a profoundly disappointing one to the civilian populations of Great Britain and the oppressed nations of Europe. For we had been frequently led by our rulers to expect that the climax of war would be reached this year, yet that climax is still to come. There seems, however, to be a general opinion that 1944 will see the end of the German War. How we trust it may be so!

1944

January 1

Cloud with bright intervals. A very pleasant opening of the year. Our eating house at lunch full of people wishing one another a happy new year. Also of children about to be taken to the pantomime, to wit *Cinderella*, at the new Connaught Theatre.

January 2

When I awoke at 7am I lay listening at intervals to the droning of the RAF night bombers returning from a raid on Germany. These the fortunate ones. Now that the Allies have attained supremacy in the air the German beast is getting horribly hammered, and, we must hope, is acquiring at last a proper distaste for war. The influenza epidemic is subsiding, happily much sooner than was expected.

January 4

At lunch at Mitchell's two women, not very young, even smoked cigarettes as they took their soup. Which was to me a horrid sight. And indeed, this nation, with its self-indulgence and licence, seems to be heading on straight for the fate of Old Rome.

January 9

On a stroll about Broadwater I noticed how all the soldiery have disappeared. The new Territorial barracks and the various mansions about it, where for years past they have had their habitations, are suddenly all empty. Where are they now? Are they gone to invade Europe? No man knows. No man may know. But Broadwater seems like a deserted village.

January 12

The Huns seem to be husbanding their aircraft to meet the coming invasion which the Allies, at last casting secrecy to the winds, are now trumpeting over the Earth. When and where will it come? The World has never before faced a question so fraught with immeasurable destiny.

January 14

We are receiving between us seven pints of milk per week, although the official allowance is now but four pints. At which boon we marvel greatly – the more so since this favour began before we gave the milkman his Xmas box. But we shall make no complaint.

January 15

I see from the newspapers that a large force of American bombers went over yesterday afternoon to bomb targets in France, and gained a 4-1 victory over enemy planes. When I was opposite the Town Hall at 2.30pm I saw some of them, two squadrons in spearhead formation, quite a beautiful sight, cream-coloured against the azure sky. They moved deliberately, inexorably, in fateful majesty. Bombers are the mastiffs as fighters are the terriers of the air.

January 17

There have been four pantomimes in Worthing this season, two professional and two amateur. The former were *Cinderella* and *Babes in the Wood*; the latter *Snow White* and one I forget. This may seem excessive, but people are now ready to invest their cash on any entertainments which may help them to forget the drab present.

January 19

There is a great deal of minor illness in the district, which everybody except the Ministry of Food attributes to the poor diet. No eggs, no fruit, and little milk, not to mention other shortages, must

28   *'VD - A great evil and a grave menace.' This eye-catching poster, pictured in 1944, overlooked the southern entrance to the 'Quashetts' pedestrian tunnel under the railway line.*

make the difficulties at this season. 'How we keep meeting! We seem to follow one another about!' remarked a gushing lady. Alas, we do. It is a penalty of this eating house life. And to think that the whole force of our ingenuity is daily directed towards avoiding her!

January 20

Our laundry has sent us a notice that all laundries in the South East area have been warned to expect a large allocation of military work in the near future, and when this occurs one collection of civilian work in every four will have to be abandoned. This is interesting as perhaps a first indication of an early Allied descent upon the continent from hereabouts.

January 31

To the barber's. He said the Home Guard are being instructed in special duties against the departure of the Regular Army to invade the continent. I suppose that this year invasion will really happen. I asked him whether, in these days of salvage, anything was done with the hair he cut from people. He replied no, now it was too short to be of any use, though many years ago, when hair was worn longer, clippings were in great demand among builders for reinforcing plaster for ceilings. Oranges on sale to adults for the first time in two or three years. This season everybody is to have 1lb per month; which is very pleasant, and due to the Navy's success over U-boats. These oranges were Jaffas.

February 1

We are offended at the widespread practice of women decorating their faces at public luncheon tables. F [said] 'How absurd. Why don't they wait till they get to the cloakroom. Disgusting I call it.' Alas, it is but one more instance of that decline in manners and morals which marks the beginning of our national decadence. Berlin has been the depository of about 5,000 bombs in the last four nights. Half the city is in ruins. One feels a certain pity for the civilian victims. What a ghastly price to pay for having voted for the wrong man!

February 2

The Huns, unhappily, share our own virtues of toughness and courage, and are, besides, harder and better disciplined. So why should we expect them to surrender quickly?

February 4

There was sunshine all day save for a temporary darkness caused by a freakish snow blizzard which sprang up with astonishing suddenness at 10.15am, and was accompanied by a clap of thunder and lightning. It passed after a quarter of an hour and the sun emerged again. Really a curiosity of the weather. It is engaging to see how the soldiers throng the coffee houses in Broadwater in the morning. Indeed, a soldier's first thought on going off duty seems to be to eat and drink. This is the more remarkable since they are given generous rations – much better than ours. They seem to have a kind of 'let out' in the middle of the morning and then these shops become packed with a khaki-clad swarm – artillery, infantry, commandos, Signal Corps, and the rest. And their conduct is admirable, showing, despite the press, every courtesy to the civilians and offering no undue attentions to the female staff.

February 5

Very fine. Frost early. The fine weather occasioned intense aerial activity all during the day. As, at 9.30am, I hurried past Broadwater Green on my way home three squadrons of fighters dashed over returning from the East. Then at 10.15am there were many more bombers overhead, but this time going East. These were so high up as to be scarcely visible were it not for the vapour trails. These, as the planes proceeded in bodies of half a dozen or more, in close line abreast, draped the sky with parallel lines of gossamer which gleamed in the sun's rays and presently coalesced into a broad white band across the sky.

February 6

The news from Russia is very favourable. On the northern and central part of the immense front the Huns seem near to disaster; they are losing ground and also fortified places every day. But in the south they still hold the Crimea and quite half of the fertile Ukraine. However, our appetite for Russian gains has been soured by the grasping and even hostile attitude of the Russian government towards our friends the Poles. The Russians are demanding about half of pre-war Poland for themselves. This is an extremely ugly situation. People are saying that as between Russians and Huns, Stalin and Hitler, there is little to choose. We shall see.

February 10

Mainly fine, but a strong and bitter NW wind. I was indeed sorry for the Broadwater fish queue, lashed by the blast as it was. Fresh fish has been very scarce since Xmas, though dried cod and 'red herrings' have always been with us.

February 13

A raw dark day. F fell to discussing the best way of committing suicide. There are various ways, but we held to the gas oven. The subject demonstrates the influence of climate on the human spirit.

February 18

Ten divisions of German troops have been surrounded and annihilated by Stalin's wonderful armies. A really stunning blow at last. It is sad to note that some 7,000 British and Dominion troops have been killed in Sicily since September 3. We seem as a nation somewhat insensitive to our losses. Yet, perhaps, in order to endure a long war it is best so.

February 20

888th ARW 9.40 to 10.40. I went out for an hour at midday but the wind brought tears to my eyes. Did a little tailoring in the afternoon. We are driven frequently now, sometimes by shame at their enormity, to undertake refurbishments ourselves for which we formerly sought professional assistance.

February 21

It was a night of great disturbance for, in addition to the sirens sounding at the worst possible period for sleepers, there was an immense passage of RAF bombers to the continent between 1 and

2am. The din of them was deep and soul stirring. It dominated one's whole consciousness as one lay in the darkness, and went on and on, remorselessly, interminably. The night bombing armadas, fortunately, do not often pass our way. For poor F, with her too active imagination, finds her mind obsessed with the hazard to the crews, and suffers almost the anguish of a mother as she hears the planes go by. On the previous night the RAF made another great raid, losing 79 heavy bombers, their highest casualties of the war so far. That means 500 men lost.

February 23

The PM has just stated that the Navy and RAF have each lost in dead about 40,000 men since the war began. An awful toll which few, I think, realised. I did not.

February 24

Amid much firing we heard a distant explosion which seems to have been that of a bomb dropped on Kemp Town, Brighton. It killed 20 people. I am troubled at F's alarm whilst these raids are on, if there be firing. It is pitiful to witness. Her nerves are very tender. Unfortunately, poor dear, her emotions can destroy her reasoning power while danger is near.

February 27

Sunday. On our midday stroll we found a poor, ill-clad urchin standing in the cold outside a public house. In answer to our inquiry as to what he did there, he replied, 'Waiting for mum and dad.' Here is a chance for social reform. I sometimes think that beer should be delivered to the people's homes daily with milk. This would promote the well being of countless young children who at present stand and wait; and help to eliminate tavern over-drinking.

February 29

After years of absence, lemons are reappearing in the shops. I expressed surprise to F that Col Llewellyn, new Food Controller, had not taken an early opportunity of making contact with the people by a broadcast, as the great men are wont to do. 'That,' she replied, 'is because there is nothing to say. He knows that things are so bad that the least said the better. After all, it is better for him to keep quiet rather than go before a microphone and wriggle, as Lord Woolton used to do.'

March 2

Many planes passed overhead, and many guns here fired at them. The Huns were making another raid on London. The present raids are more serious than the 'nuisance raids' of the past year or two.

March 4

Voices in the Becket bun queue. The bun van was half-an-hour late on arriving at the shop. Present also, but not interested, was a lordly black and white spaniel wearing a smart khaki jacket adorned with brass military buttons and sergeant's stripes. 'It is a pity there is so much drinking among the Canadian boys here, but some of them say they do it because they have nowhere but the pubs to go to.' 'Yes, I know those whom the girls bring home are glad to find somewhere cosy and a fire. But they do eat!'

March 5

Uncle Stalin has asked for a share of the surrendered Italian warships, and will be given it, and deserves it – if only in return for his army's great killing of Germans. But is this battling world merely exchanging the Nazi Colossus for a Russian one? Uncle Stalin clearly intends to make his weight felt.

March 7

This afternoon, not for the first time, I had to call for silence at the Reference Library; on this occasion to check the persistent prattle of the presiding nymph with a strolling soldier, apparently a suitor. I could not read for the visitation of it. I am timid, but prolonged provocation is a powerful stimulant to valour. So I lifted up my voice among the company and he departed. She then followed, to commune with him outside.

March 9

Met a man today who claimed to have information that the invasion of the continent is to begin next week. The fury of the air assault on the north of France and on Germany during the past week suggests that this may be correct. I trust it is; for there must be a beginning before there can be an end.

March 14

899th air-raid warning 12.50 to 1.22am. Soon after the siren sounded a plane made a shattering noise as it passed very low over our house. Then there was a great crash followed by anti-aircraft fire. The crash represented a bomb explosion about a quarter of a mile away, but the bomb fell on open ground and did no harm. There were 961 killed in air raids on Britain last month. That is a terrible record – the worst for nearly three years.

March 15

There were 50 people rendered homeless at Lancing in yesterday's raid. Luckily, however, only incendiary bombs seem to have been dropped there; so, although there was damage, there were no casualties.

March 18

There was again frost early, and I became cold and tired standing from 9.40 to 10.20am in the weekend Becket bun queue. A wartime queue such as this, whose frequenters meet regularly and become mutually familiar figures, is not without its sense of romance, its glow of comradeship. One feels, too, that it is something special in a transient episode of existence, which we had better try to realise before it passes away forever.

March 19

Today and of late there have been many veterans of our Army now in Italy abroad about the town – sturdy warriors wearing the black berets of the Royal Armoured Corps and displaying

29   *The view of the Pier Pavilion and pier from the Lido in 1944.*

the ribbon of the North Africa Star. I suppose them to be destined to go across Channel to very hard tasks soon.

March 23

A ban on egress from and entry into all places within a belt of coastline from Cornwall to The Wash is to be imposed from the 1st [of April] for reasons of military security.

March 25

We had a very noisy time [last night] with many planes passing over towards London. Poor F badly scared by the noise of the anti-aircraft fire. To Brighton by bus, in rather a jaded state, to meet my brother-in-law on his annual visit. We passed by Shoreham Harbour and the maritime fastness of grimy Southwick and Portslade. Rather strangely we saw no sign anywhere either of bomb damage or of shipping preparations for the Second Front. At Brighton our relative was not at the rendezvous, his train being much delayed by reason of bombs on the tracks in the night's air raid. So to lunch, a bad one, and afterwards we found him on the front. Sat there looking at the sea through festoons of barbed wire, and listening to the rumble of artillery at practice on the Downs; and the rush of military lorries and the tramp of armed men along the road behind us. Far fewer Canadians in Brighton now, but hundreds of tall Australian airmen in their rather ugly dark blue uniforms – very brave young men far from kith and kin. To tea at Fuller's where are still to be found daintiness and courtesy. You pay a little more than elsewhere, but even paying is made a pleasure at Fuller's.

March 31

We found ourselves too tired after lunch to make our accustomed pilgrimage on Friday to The Pantiles, West Worthing; and we were glad enough to seek repose on the shabby, shattered, litter-strewn front, now mostly in the occupation of French-Canadian soldiery.

April 14

For a long time past there has been much French-Canadian soldiery here, lodged in the many now disused tenements on the front, and their guns and equipment parked in Montague Place and other roadways.

April 16

A blessed rain fell from dawn until 3pm, though it came untowardly for a church parade of local organisations at Broadwater Church – especially for a number of unhappy little girl guides assembling on the street corner, under a forlorn banner.

April 17

I noticed as I walked abroad that the road signposts, removed three years ago for the confusion of possible invading Huns, have all been replaced in the boldest fashion. Which is very significant and cheering. It is invasion the other way about that occupies men's thoughts now. But when? when? when?

April 18

In a longing for pastures new we lunched at Wendy's in Broadwater. A crone presently entered whom we recognised as a most conscienceless 'crasher' in lunch queues. A little ferrety-faced woman, there had been two or three sharp exchanges in the past between her and F but now she came up and greeted her affably enough, remarking, somewhat cryptically, 'I don't want you to think I minded being seen speaking to you!' Whereat, F not well pleased; and are still wondering what she meant.

April 19

I was awakened at 12.30am by a tremendous droning of planes which continued for over an hour. This was the RAF going over to the continent. After the alarm sounded there were the addition of German planes going over to London. It was a bad day for poor F apart from that. For she tramped the town to find a dressmaker ready to make her a dress; visited four, and failed! As she returned exhausted, with bag of material still in hand, the bus stopped unaccountably. 'This bus has gone wrong,' explained the conductress, 'there will be another along presently!' In the next bus a man crammed himself against her. 'I think that gentleman is drunk,' whispered a lady warningly. 'I don't care,' was F's response. For by now she was past caring.

April 20

Here in Worthing we have so far seen very little of the hosts of the USA, now in training in Great Britain. But even here the sight of their various vehicles is becoming increasingly common. These are painted a lighter grey than our Army's, seem to eschew camouflage, and bear on the side a large white star. Also, all but the smallest run on six wheels instead of the four usual with us. One feels very kindly towards their robust, workmanlike crews who have come so far to help us; and one appreciates the view that they are really 'only Englishmen gone a little wrong'. But they do not look like Englishmen, having mostly dark eyes and swarthy, colourless, but very alert countenances.

April 21

We were kept awake between 2 and 3am by the continuous passage of RAF planes overhead going to France to bomb railway targets there. Sometimes one thinks that the invasion of the continent is really coming, though one cannot rule out a giant bluff directed at the enemy's nerves.

April 22

A cloudless spring day. The loveliness of the burgeoning foliage seemed suddenly to thrust itself upon the grateful senses. The mulberry and the walnut among all trees still stood aloof, waving bare branches. After breakfast, as usual on Saturday, I hastened to join the queue by 'The Becket' and for the first time found standing there in the sunshine too warm instead of too cold.

April 23

Nephew GP, now Temporary Lieutenant, RA, called unexpectedly. Discourse sadly hobbled by the subjects we most wished to discuss, eg. the war and his part in it, being barred by official regulations – lest the enemy be assisted. He might not disclose even where he is residing; nor post a letter in a public Post Office, nor telephone.

April 27

To the barber's for a haircut. He observed that the Second Front would be started now in a very few days, everyone, British, USA, Russians, Italians and the French, will attack at once. Well, barbers are apt to know!

April 29

Here regiments come and go, unheralded, mysteriously. The other day it was the Somersets; today it is the Royal Scots Fusiliers. Men say they come to gain experience of tank warfare, which is provided for them on the adjacent Downs. Watched these Scots parading on Broadwater Green this morning. They looked smart and hefty warriors; their marching very good, as good as I have seen anywhere, in their various evolutions. But, alas, military exercises no longer provide a spectacle. The khaki uniform is ugly, and one so misses the embellishment of mounted field officers once so conspicuous.

May 1

A perfect May day. Nature is rioting forth, though the soil begins to cry out for rain. Summer life has arrived once more. Another year is beginning to glide away too fast – and still the armies wait.

May 2

Still fine, but W wind foul and cold. To the Post Office and paid ten shillings to renew our wireless licence; which we grudge, for the programmes were never so poor and silly. And besides, our machine ails somewhat, and we cannot find an artificer to amend it.

May 9

Deadly cold at night and magnificent sunshine throughout a long day. Saw on the front, extending from Splash Point in the east to the *Beach Hotel* in the west, a distance of half-a-mile, a line of military vehicles – tanks, then ambulance waggons, and bren gun carriers. These last belonged to the Royal Scots Fusiliers, some of whom were engaged in groups threading strips of green and fawn cloth through netting, to provide camouflage to throw over their vehicles. In adjacent side streets were parked more tanks. For the first time for three years there seems to be no Canadian soldiers in Worthing. The tank soldiers are now 'Monty's men', from Italy and N Africa; then there are a few Commandos, the Royal Scots and some RA in charge of anti-aircraft guns. The Scots, I notice, are displaying on many of their vehicles the great white star which I had hitherto thought to be peculiar to the American Army, which is very baffling.

May 11

A perfect day; a day upon which the fancy turns to thoughts of first class cricket – but alas! To those who cannot see any end to the war without the opening of a Second Front the present moment, I think, brings a feeling of painful expectation, of tension similar to that eerie sensation of August 1939, when we saw the shadows hourly deepening, and had the thought always at the back of consciousness, 'When will it come?' This mental tension engenders feelings of unsettlement and impatience, now aggravated by an intense desire for peace.

May 14

The day here very peaceful save for an inspection of the Home Guard on Broadwater Green. They looked fit for very effective service now that the old men have been weeded out. On my evening stroll I make a good haul of cigarette cartons to help the war. I estimate that I am recovering over 500 in the course of a year.

May 15

As we were passing down Chapel Road into South Street just before noon we met three soldiers who were requiring all pedestrians to produce their identity cards. This was a complete surprise, but luckily we had ours with us, as did near everyone, in accordance with the Regulations. This is the first time we have been asked for our cards since the early weeks of the war. It was doubtless done to check the effectiveness of the ban on visitors.

May 19

After long communing sold my christening spoon and fork to a silversmith for 15 shillings. Now, in the shortage of all metals, one meets requests for the sale of old gold and silver at every turn – so I was tempted.

May 20

'Your trousers are dreadful,' remarked F, 'they are a disgrace. All baggy and shiny at the knees. I don't like you being seen in them. I know we are told that shabbiness does not matter now. But that sort of thing can be carried too far. It is quite time this war ended, or we shall all be in rags!'

May 21

The news of the Allied attack in Italy is soberly good. Cassino, now a heap of rubble, is taken after it had held up the advance for over five months, and the armies have moved forward against the next defence line of the Huns. 'Oh, how I should like,' quoth F, as she chomped her dinner of clammy, tasteless war cheese, 'a good dinner of fowl and bacon, with stuffing and bread sauce and vegetables; and a nice piece of rich cake at tea!' Ah, those memories of long ago!

May 22

Despite their special difficulties it would appear that these are brave days for caterers; for patrons are brought down now to accepting almost anything which makes some sort of a show on the plate, and crowd in everywhere. This is because: 1, It seems unpatriotic and greedy to object to even the smallest helping; 2, The patrons have usually nothing at home; 3, They know they cannot do any better elsewhere; 4, There is now a shortage of eating houses. This applies to the 'popular' restaurants. Money still talks; and those able and willing to pay heavily can still obtain more satisfying refreshments.

May 25

We found much people assembled about the Town Hall, and a whisper abroad that General Montgomery, GOC all British forces for the Second Front, who is the popular hero of the war, was coming. Clerks were craning their necks out of the Town Hall windows; councillors and public were ranged about the steps, and we took our stand on the opposite side of the road beside an assemblage of schoolgirls who were bubbling with excitement. Then presently the great man came slowly along, sitting, with other officers, in a small military car. Shy Saxon cheers sounded fainter, sped by the high wind. But he smiled and raised a hand in salute – though, to general disappointment, he did not stop or speak. However, he passed within a yard or two of us. He looked in the best of health, his bronzed face keen and alert, yet kindly, with an expression as though he never had a care in the world. In profile especially he bears a striking likeness to the great Erasmus as pictured by Holbein, and he has adopted a like fashion of headgear in his black beret. F enthusiastic and, indeed, it is a day which neither of us will forget.

May 26

To the barber's, which resembles an ancient coffee shop for news. Today I gleaned these gems – 'All leave for the local soldiery is stopped as from tomorrow', 'The war is expected to be finished off within six months', 'Yesterday was General Montgomery's last local inspection. The 8th Army hate him.' The last, at least, I take leave to doubt.

May 27

The Food Ministry have unleashed upon us some American boiled bacon, in addition to the usual bacon ration. Yet it is nearly all fat and such as many cannot stomach in the heat, tasting of oil paint somewhat. Weighed myself. Scaled 9st and 5lb against 8st 12lb at this date a year ago. Which is very well. For I seem to have arrested my original decay under the rationing. We are now told the white star is to be used on all Allied vehicles employed in the invasion of Europe.

May 28

A grand sweltering day. An extraordinary jump from temperate to torrid which will mark this festival for many a year. After a dinner of parched cheese I felt I would give all Col Llewellyn's boiled bacon fat for half-a-pound of prunes. There have been none on sale for weeks, nor any other fruit save sultanas. This heat creates a longing for fruit. On an evening stroll up Hill Barn Lane and around into Forest Road, I directed two soldiers who found themselves lost in a strange land. The courtesy of the military men is so engaging that it is a pleasure to help them.

May 29

Just before 11.30pm, as we were peacefully composing ourselves to sleep, we were alarmed all of a sudden by the unheralded crash of a deafening explosion. It was followed by the sound of a passing plane, and then by the belated siren. Wardens and others appeared in the street, exchanging remarks, but we could gather no audible information. Poor F very agitated and in sad anxiety for those possibly bombed and not without reason. For when morning was come I inquired of the milkman. 'A bomb fell on the camp at Sompting, two mile away,' was his reply. 'Was anyone killed?' 'Five, I believe.' 'Were they soldiers?' 'No, girls.' He spoke with no more emotion than if they had been goats. But as for F, the tragedy of it quite upset her day.

May 31

I can gather no certain news about the bombing of war girls at Sompting Camp on Sunday. Some say they are Air Girls and some say ATS, and I have heard the death stated as five, four, eight and none! The authorities are always reticent about such matters; and the general public are become too case-hardened to care much, I fear.

June 3

We were awakened soon after 1.30am, by heavy gunfire near at hand, which continued about an hour. This was only a military 'exercise'. Since it was long after 3am before I could get to sleep again, we felt wretched today in consequence.

June 4

We went on our constitutional this morning and proceeded down a long residential road lined throughout one side with Army Ordnance lorries containing mostly motor engines and great wooden cases bearing the magic names Austin and Chrysler; these were all parked ready for embarkation for the Second Front.

June 5

The Allied Army in Italy has occupied Rome, the Huns having evacuated at the last moment. It is providential that the Eternal City has thus escaped being fought over. This is great news; nevertheless, people here are not enthusiastic. I have noticed only two or three Union Jacks waving in celebration. The public, in fact, at this late stage, requires something of the kind much nearer home to arouse it from its lethargy of weariness. The tanks and their satellite vehicles from the famous 8th Army, which have had their habitation here for the past few months, this afternoon emerged from the side streets where they have been parked, and rattled and lurched and scrambled along Warwick Street, up Chapel Road, and away out of town bound, as we suppose, for what is vaguely called the Second Front. There was a thin line of spectators on the pavements, with some exchanges between the crews and their acquaintances – mainly of the female sex. Well, they are a very fine orderly body of men, and we are sorry to lose them though not their huge noisy leviathans of war! The railway companies are advertising that still more trains are going to be taken off without notice; and forms are being displayed in the shops asking for volunteers to give blood for transfusions into the wounded, as was done earlier in the war. So it seems that the pot of preparation is filling up, and that the Second Front is not to be a hoax.

June 6

Cloudy with bright intervals. Cold NW wind. This is an historic day. The military stagnation which has persisted since the melancholy Dunkirk Evacuation four years ago has been ended at a stroke. Since 6am this morning Allied troops have been landing on the Normandy coast from Cherbourg to Le Havre – Le Havre where the British Army landed in 1914. We don't know more yet than that heavy fighting is in progress. So much we learnt in a lunch queue at noon, because, unlike the more curious majority, we do not listen in to the wireless news until 9pm. The unseasonably cold grim day has contributed to people appearing anxious and subdued; but most must have had in mind the heavy inevitable casualties. I hear that the troops are tired of doing nothing but route marching, and are glad to go. I am sure that many of them are eager to earn the right in the future to exclaim 'I also was of the Army of Liberation!' Most citizens about here had a disturbed night, for there was tremendous aerial activity in the small hours and up to 7am. It was so pronounced that I remember saying to myself, 'Has the Second Front started?' The day in Worthing has been unusually quiet; there have been reduced numbers of both military and civilians about the streets.

June 7

Miserably cold for the time of year. The initial Allied landings seem to have been brilliantly successful, and losses much less than expected. Now it is a matter of building up a sufficient mass of men and material to withstand the German counter-attack. Here, after yesterday's emotionalism, there has been a sense of anticlimax. We seem to have already adapted our minds to the new situation of there being once again an Allied army fighting just across the Channel.

June 8

Miserable weather for the Allied Expeditionary Force. About 6.15am an enormous armada of Allied bombers began passing overhead. I stood at my bedroom window, chilly in night attire, but enthralled. It was indeed a magnificent, inspiring sight. Coming from the NE and in no formal order, they were moving across this district towards the area of the great battle in the West. They might have been all the bombers in the world unleashed, rising continuously above the horizon and moving interminably in successive waves, black against the newly risen sun. And the empyrean reverberated with the thunder of a thousand engines in unison. The sky at this early hour (4.15am) was mainly clear, but there was a good deal of light, fleecy cloud and also much vapour streaming from the rear of the planes. At first this appeared golden in the sunrise, but as the sun gained altitude the gold became changed to white. There were magnificent effects of great criss-crossing trails, with vast whirls and streaks across the blue; and, near the sun, cloud-piercing rays of light such as one sees depicted in an Easter illumination. And so from the far horizon ever more planes emerged, cleaving the void in silent majesty. It was time now to dress, but, though I must not delay, in my excitement I could not resist frequent visits to the window to devour the spectacle again. By 7.30am the main body had passed into the SW, and the booming of their engines had declined to a distant rumbling; but a few planes continued to fly over until by 8 all was quiet again. Oh, what combative might does such a spectacle afford; a spectacle never before, nor, ever again, to be seen over England, which I have seen with my own eyes! What stupendous days are those we are living through.

June 9

Wind WSW, strong and cold. Drizzle all the morning and after 5pm. The vile weather has kept the sky clear of planes today, and provided rough seas for our carrier ships. Since the great news of the 6th one has become conscious of an entirely new outlook. The feeling of stolid endurance through the years has given way to a kind of stimulating expectancy, for now we are no longer marking time and many expect the war to be pressed on energetically to a conclusion.

June 10

The sensation of living seems quite different since the event of the 6th; and, moreover, that date seems already as though it were long ago, and the period before altogether dim. Which is very strange. In the meanwhile, of course, home problems remain with us in full force. Thus F laments, 'I have tried everywhere but cannot get a hat. It is devilish what they charge and I cannot find anything to suit me.' Hats are almost the only raiment remaining both unrationed and uncontrolled in price.

June 12

Rough seas keep adding to the difficulties of the Allied invasion of France. But the return of the sun has improved the opportunities of the airmen. We have seen many squadrons during the day setting out for, and returning from, the area of battle.

June 14

The invasion of France has had its repercussions here. Thus the Tank Corps and the Royal Scots have left us. So have, from the seafront, the great lorries, the tanks, the ambulance waggons and anti-tank guns. Montague Place is clear of war's panoply for the first time for years. Only the small fry of the Army vehicles is represented – bren gun carriers, small lorries, radio cars and impressed motor cars. The invasion has even directly affected civilians here, for we cannot now obtain any anthracite coals, since the military traffic on the railways to the southern ports has cut across and prevented transport hither of coals from S Wales.

June 16

Oh, the curse of the siren wailing all through the night. All this meant 12 separate disturbances. But all this turmoil amounted to very little locally – a very distant rumbling of gunfire at one time, and an alleged bomb explosion at Shoreham. We spent a wretched day with heads heavy from so great loss of sleep.

June 17

We now have an explanation of yesterday's disturbances. The Huns have begun to let loose upon us pilotless aircraft filled with explosives. It is entirely novel and very disquieting. These devilish machines are necessarily erratic and may land anywhere. One landed here last night in an allotment

30   *On 16 June 1944 Mr Harriss wrote, 'Oh, the curse of the siren wailing all through the night.' This is probably the infamous 'cuckoo' siren, on the Town Hall, which warned of imminent air attack.*

field north of the Upper Brighton Road and blew up. It was about a mile distant from our house, but the noise was terrific and we thought for a moment that we were about to be hit. Many houses nearby were damaged; a dozen people were injured, though by a miracle no one was killed. Poor F in piteous affright. This morning we walked up to view the place. Nothing but a crater in the soil was visible, all remains of the machine having been removed by the authorities. People today are rather gloomy about this new and sudden affliction, so incalculable – so full of menacing possibility. However, I am confident that the great men of science will soon discover a way of dealing with these machines.

June 18

These pilotless planes again; though none fell in this district. But at one time we heard a noise of a heavy anti-aircraft barrage from the seafront. What we are enduring now is in fact to us worse than at any previous period of the war.

June 20

Owing to departures for France, the cafe where I buy our daily bread seemed quite empty this morning. It is usually thronged with the British Army. However, many military still remain on the seashore. In Montague Place this afternoon there was a party doing physical exercise, leapfrogging and jumping about in the sunshine. They seemed to enjoy it.

June 22

Since the Invasion of France began I notice that the solitary aeroplane which, through the years of conflict, has partaken these skies towing a white sleeve-like target for our fighters and our AA gunners to practise their skills upon, has been withdrawn.

June 24

'This is the worse season for gardening I have ever known,' I heard a bus conductor remark. There are no strawberries, nor gooseberries, nor rhubarb in the shops; and as there are also no prunes, housewives are awkwardly placed. Doubtless, as last year, the Government are taking all the fresh fruit for jam. Eating houses make a show with Canadian tinned apples; and these, considering all they have been through, are remarkably good.

June 27

Cherbourg is fallen to the gallant Americans, so the Allies have an invasion port instead of those exposed beaches. It is harrowing to read day after day in the *Daily Telegraph* notices of the deaths of people, sometimes two or three in a family at once, 'by enemy action'. That, just now, indicates death by the flying bombs. I gather there have been terrible happenings in the southern suburbs of London, but all is kept secret.

June 28

The flying bombs are causing many people to sleep downstairs, and some even to leave the town. These little temporary panics have arisen before when anything bad has happened. They are usually quite illogical. Thus we have had one flying bomb drop here by chance, but it is utterly improbable that the Huns would direct these missiles at Worthing.

June 29

There is satisfactory news from Burma where our men, after sad privations and losses, seem gradually to be turning the tables on the barbarous Japanese. Yet, inevitably, that campaign arouses small public interest here. There is too much war on our own doorstep. Our accustomed waitress returned to duty at the eating house after two or three days absence to attend her husband, home on 'Embarkation Leave'. He sails today, no man may know whither.

June 30

Numerous alarms all relate to flying bombs, which present our defenders a still unsolved problem. Last night, one was shot down into the sea near here, exploding as it went. This is the best that can be hoped for, yet it resulted in the fracture by blast of many shop windows near the front.

July 2

A lady from London reported that the flying bombs are causing serious alarm there. They keep coming at intervals during day and night, and have caused havoc – notably in Tottenham Court Road, Kingsway and at the *Regent Palace Hotel*. Oxford Street in the usual crowded hours is now almost deserted.

July 3

A busy day of arranging for our departure tomorrow for a fortnight's visit to Chichester again. We planned to go to Winchester, but that being outside our county we may not penetrate the ban on visitors there. We rather exhausted Chichester last year; but there is little choice – it is either that or Brighton. F badly needs a change.

July 4

To Chichester by the 11.35am train. Arrived at the *Dolphin and Anchor* for lunch.

July 5

Started the day with a battle. How one hates to have to fight for one's rights. Yet, though we had booked suitable rooms for a fortnight, five weeks ago, now we were put into two little top floor rooms, F's opposite to the fire watcher's station, mine too small for the furniture and with a tiny square window, the top of which didn't open. Saw the manageress and took a very firm line. She, clearly beaten, made no defence; immediately found us two good rooms on the first floor. But it meant a wasted, exasperating morning transferring and rearranging our belongings. But tonight, at least, the fire watchers will cease from troubling F, and I shall enjoy fresh air. There was an air-raid warning in the early hours, and I heard a flying bomb pass overhead. The PM said in the Commons today that in the past three weeks about 2,750 have been sent over, causing about the same number of deaths.

July 7

After lunch we spent an hour in the Cathedral. We found it rather stuffy and depressing. The pressure of protracted warfare is reflected in the hotel. I asked for a second chair in my room for the better ordering of my clothes, and the handmaid could only supply one with the cane seat burst through. The wireless set is useless for want of repair, and the staircase clock hath his face veiled for the same cause; while the guests must bring their own towels. Nay, more – sometimes the bar exhibits a notice 'No Beer!' Yet this is accounted a first class house.

July 8

In the afternoon by bus to Bognor. The war has dealt harshly with Bognor, rendering it shabby and unkempt. But, apart from that, it is a resort suited more particularly to the very modern, the very young, and in general those easily pleased. The pier there is now occupied by the Royal Navy under the name of HMS *St Barbara*.

July 10

The food at the hotel is fair, representing of course the effort of those struggling against adversity. We seem to have struck an especially bad period for victuals. There is no meat but pork in the butchers' shops, and the supply of fish seems to have stopped again. Also, one sees no fruit about. Hence at the hotel there is much ado with omelettes, rhubarb and mushrooms. But there is often lobster or crab (probably tinned) for those who can abide crustaceans, and the usual American tinned stuff; occasionally chicken or turkey.

July 12

To Bosham by bus. We found the pretty creek cluttered up and disfigured mysteriously with vast new War Department works in progress. Great cranes and barges and huge iron caissons. It seemed like an invasion from Hell of this little rustic demure spot.

July 13

This little bustling country town presents a remarkable panorama of England at war – or rather of the Allied nations at war. The streets are gay and kaleidoscopic with uniforms. One sees British, Dominions', Polish, Czech, Belgian and French airmen; British, Dominions' and American soldiers; British, Dominions', American, Norwegian and French seamen. Then there are the multifarious Women's Services; Army (ATS), Navy (WRNS), Air Force (WAAF), motor transport, civil defence, fire service, auxiliary police, Land Army, and the Women's Voluntary Service (WVS) in dark green with red facings. The American seamen are garbed in navy blue uniforms very like that of the British and other navies, but the street patrol, set nightly to watch behaviour, adorns it with white biretta-like linen caps, and white belting and gaiters. All this array provides a very striking spectacle in this ancient centre of piety. The other day I even observed a French cavalry officer in a very dapper khaki suit, and tall light blue kepi with scarlet top.

July 14

We were awakened by the siren at 1.30am, and presently heard the eerie grinding note of a flying bomb passing right overhead. The window was illuminated by the jet of fire which these monsters emit from their tails. Perhaps I might have seen the machine itself, but I was too lazy to get out of bed. These things are vulgarly called 'doodlebugs', and yesterday I heard a waggish newsboy announce 'Evening Argus or doodlebug!' Nevertheless, they are too serious a matter for jesting. Nothing at all seems to be known at the hotel about the mysterious works at Bosham creek. Which is very strange. Mystery seems everywhere about us here. There is one wearing the uniform of an ordinary seaman of the Royal Navy who appears to be stationed in this hotel, and may often be seen on his knees before the empty fireplace in the lounge, match in hand, meticulously burning papers. What is his dark secret? There were 1,935 persons killed in Britain by enemy action in June; a ghastly increase due entirely to the flying bombs.

July 18

We returned to Broadwater by the 10.43am train – to our great content, for we love not hotel life.

July 19

The air activity yesterday proves to have been the RAF's biggest daylight operation of the war. The bombers went over to support a renewed offensive by General Montgomery in the Caen district, where he is now breaking out from the difficult countryside into the plain. We returned to Worthing to find all the soldiers gone, save a few details. There seems not a single military vehicle left on the front or in the other streets which have hitherto for years been parking places for them.

July 21

There has been an attempt to kill Hitler by a time-bomb. But it failed.

July 23

Poor F very nervous when one or more [of the pilotless bombs] passed closely overhead uttering their ominous grating cacophony. After the siren goes there is now an aggravated 'tension'. For one can never be certain when or where they will come to earth and explode. In the South of England, and especially in London, these flying bombs are casting a deep shadow over life. Oh, for a quiet night!

July 24

Last evening, a great convoy of Army lorries towing giant trailers passed through Broadwater on their way, I suppose, to the war port of Newhaven. They carried excavators, dredgers, cement mixers and other huge machines, and were probably intended for the repairing of Cherbourg Harbour. They came along at 50 pace intervals for about half an hour, great yellowish-grey monsters.

July 27

There is much disappointment at the slow progress being made in Normandy. Now the news is actually disturbing for the Army has even lost ground which had been gained.

July 29

Heard today from friends in Blackheath that the ceilings of all their 14 rooms were down through flying bombs. The family of four escaped physical injury in the basement, but one of them has had to be removed to a mental hospital.

July 31

Here we are evidently well situated for the preparations incidental to the Normandy campaign. This morning dozens of tanks rumbled through Broadwater, going west. Then, later on, I found the road along the front, and adjoining side roads, filled with vehicles of war stretching about a mile from the pier towards West Worthing. These were neither guns nor tanks but a miscellaneous collection of lorries containing materials and machines for assisting the advance. There were huge searchlights, bulldozers for clearing roads, observation cabins, tar boilers, cement mixers, steam rollers, and various strange monsters altogether baffling to the civilian mind. I thought it indeed fortunate that the Huns seem now too weak in the air to send manned bombers any more, for here was presented to them a most tempting target.

August 2

There seems to be a wave of optimism as to an early triumph spreading over the country. I noticed that the town electricians, in anticipation of peace, are re-equipping the streetlight standards, which have stood dismantled for the past four years.

August 4

The great circus of military road-making machines left this morning, going to the west to embark for Normandy. Their bronzed drivers, I thought, looked happy and expectant. The procession advanced from its bivouac on the seafront up the Broadwater Road, endlessly it seemed. Many morning shoppers stood and watched with wonder this passing to the battle area of this vast array of uncouth vehicles; its like never before seen in Worthing's prim thoroughfares, and, we must trust, never to be seen there again.

August 6

An American breakthrough of tanks in Normandy has cut off Brittany with the Germans there, and transformed the situation in the West. In the East, the Russians have penetrated into E Prussia. One is sensible of a growing excitement to one's inner consciousness.

August 7

An ideal bank holiday; but for Worthing a quiet one. Plenty of people abroad, but mostly residents. For the ban still operates against visitors, and we are considered too exposed to danger to receive evacuees. By way of outdoor recreation, there was a minor cricket match on famous Broadwater Green and the usual Grand Fete elsewhere – no excursions, no access to the beach. We stayed at home.

August 8

Summer has arrived very late this year. It is of the finest quality – the heat of the sun tempered by a divine freshness. We were at breakfast when we heard a flying bomb go over. Today, in Worthing, it was extremely difficult to realise that one of the greatest battles of the world was raging just across the Channel. The town has taken on its usual holiday aspect. Streets and public gardens were thronged with children and their parents enjoying themselves in idyllic conditions. I went to the Green to watch a village cricket match quite charming for its English scene, the canopy of blue, and the green area, the happy patient company sprawled in their deckchairs and 'the run getters stealing to and fro'.

31 *In 1944 pedestrians, including Mr Harriss, were once again allowed to walk on the promenade, which had been lined four years previously with giant concrete monoliths.*

August 9

We visited Beach House Gardens after tea. There was an orchestra playing there, the flowers were looking gay, and the place was swarming with local holidaymakers and children – all largely in the undress of the tropics. At the present stage of the war, I think people feel that they can let themselves go more than for years past. Most people expect a peace before Christmas.

August 11

Saw a queue of 120 people standing in Portland Road to buy plums.

August 16

As we were wending our way home from Worthing this evening a lorry full of soldiers passed us upon which they had chalked in large letters, 'Don't wave, we are only British.' This, I presume, was a sarcasm arising out of a jealousy of these warriors at what they considered more complaisance of the fair towards the Americans and Canadians.

August 19

It will be interesting hereafter to indicate here the influence of the war on the state of the population in Worthing – always a town with a predominance of elderly residents. Just now it seems to contain swarms of children, with the necessary mothers, and more elderly people than ever – some of them refugees from battered London. Young men are extremely few; and girls between 18 and 30 not numerous, though in their case the Conscription is less severe. In the middle ages women are well represented, men less so. But in the 'useless' ages over 60 there is a large army of both sexes. All this is strikingly illustrated in the field of sport. Thus the town's bowling greens are thronged, bowls being a game for the elderly; yet all through this fine weather the lawn tennis courts have been almost deserted.

August 20

The Battle of Normandy is won! The routed Huns are in disorderly flight; the Allies begin to cross the Seine, and we expect the news of the liberation of Paris. Truly these are historic days.

August 23

F purchased two hats for next winter at about one guinea each, a small expense for these days. She is jubilant, having been almost in despair; for never were women's hats in general so few, so dear, so silly and so small. The roads adjoining the seafront are become strangely quiet. For military men and military vehicles, so long in occupation there, are all departed. Strong points bristling with guns are now dismantled and derelict. One is conscious of a blessed sense of emancipation from the threat of the enemy.

August 24

Last evening we heard on the wireless that Paris and Marseilles had been recaptured, and Romania had made peace with the Allies. Events, indeed, seem to be tumbling over one another. But there was remarkably little excitement or comment about it in the town today. However, a few flags appeared on church buildings, and churches rang bells in a half-hearted way. Otherwise, the stolid South Saxons went glumly about their business as usual. Yet I think most felt a flow in their hearts. I did!

August 25

The ban imposed on visitors hither as from the April 1 has been removed; though, from the number of strangers about taking holiday, it would appear that since August began it has not been strictly enforced.

August 27

The flying bombs still cause many, though fewer, deaths. The Huns have sent over 7,250 of these missiles since the first one in the middle of June. Bulgaria has surrendered.

August 30

Worthing displays more of a holiday appearance than for years past. This afternoon there was a small circus performing between Beach House and the sea; the orchestra was playing in the public gardens nearby; while away to the east a small section of beach has even been reopened to the public by the military authority. And each of these delights has attracted numerous patrons.

September 5

At 3pm we witnessed an uncommon sight, a dozen great silvery Flying Fortresses on their return from a raid, sailed slowly, majestically, over Worthing, *en plein soleil*, at the uncommonly low altitude of only some 200ft. Beautiful and grand!

September 8

The dreaded flying bomb has been eliminated owing to the capture by the advancing Allies of its launching site in the Pas de Calais area. The Anglo-American armies now range themselves abreast along the German frontier for the final kill. And we and the rest who have sat so long in darkness can see a great light.

September 9

We bade farewell to a waitress who we have known long since, who is leaving shortly for Canada, having, like others of our damsels, married one of the warriors from that Dominion until recently residing here. We wished her happiness. There is a big risk about these war marriages.

September 10

Bulgaria requested an armistice six hours after Russia's declaration of war against her, which Russia has now granted. Which must constitute about the shortest 'war' on record. To complete the comedy, Bulgaria has proceeded to declare war on Germany. Well, every little helps.

September 12

We are so appreciating our undisturbed nights. With the flying bombs overcome, and the German air force no longer strong enough to bomb Britain, it seems probable that sirens and gunfire and explosions at night belong to the past and will not recur; though it is almost too good to believe. Anyhow, evacuated people are surging back to their houses in London notwithstanding official warning to the contrary.

September 13

We went by bus on a trip to Brighton, taking with us Miss P, a neighbour. I noticed at Brighton the fighting force much reduced, and of course trippers much increased, compared with six months ago. But Brighton, unlike more favoured Worthing, still mans her guns along the front, and refuses even partial access to the beach. In general the town looked very shabby and grim, though still little damaged by bombs.

September 14

In recent days there has been a rather mysterious influx into Worthing of military searchlights with their attendant lorries. They line the front from Splash Point in the east throughout its length far to the west. All this impedimenta is served by stalwart Royal Artillerymen, who seem hard put to it to fill up their time. Since enemy bombers ceased to come over searchlights have lost most of their usefulness.

32 *The pier, with a section blown out by Royal Engineers, in late 1944.*

September 16

It is rumoured today that the Huns have begun to dispatch their long threatened 'rocket' bombs against us; there has been damage by them to houses in Chiswick and Hammersmith.

September 20

Through F's kindly initiative we got into conversation at lunch at Mitchell's with two boys opposite, one of whom was going to Tonbridge School for his first term this week. Which made me feel very sentimental, for I underwent the same thrilling experience on a September day 48 years ago. The boy looked well equipped by nature to make the best of all the delights offered by my Alma Mater; and goes with happy anticipations which I am sure will not be disappointed. Would that I were going, too!

September 21

This afternoon I was enticed by glamour of the wild to explore a spacious disused quarry near Hill Barn Lane, of the kind beloved by blackberry pioneers; though I hoped rather to see some butterflies. My hope was realised by the appearance of a few Whites, a Small Copper, and a Clouded Yellow, a cluster of lordly Red Admirals and exquisite Tortoiseshells. This little Eden was gloriously warm and agreeably infrequented.

September 23

We are worried about the situation in Holland where, amid a great flourish of trumpets, a large British airborne force has been dropped near Arnhem. But it seems to have been encircled by the Germans, while a British army coming up from Belgium to join up with it is held up, about five miles away, by unexpectedly stubborn German resistance. People today are saying very little, but looking glum. 'Critical, but not hopeless,' one paper comments.

September 25

We are now allowed some relief from the blackout, but are still a little doubtful how far we may safely go. I have begun by removing some of the brown paper cowls from the interior electric lights. For five years I have not been able to see properly at evening meals. So even this minor alleviation is a joy. To my barber's. He said he was glad there were no longer any soldiers in Broadwater. For he had been doing up to 70 haircuts a day for them. Which made him so tired he could not sleep at night and it was breaking him down.

September 27

Greater aerial activity last night than for several weeks past; particularly in the small hours. Awakened by many planes returning from the continent between 6 and 7am. News from Arnhem is being withheld for security's sake.

September 28

All our airborne forces at Arnhem have been evacuated after ten days of very gallant fighting against odds, more than half being dead or prisoners. As I listened in to a broadcast recital by eyewitnesses of the soldiers' sufferings I felt the moisture well into my eyes. It has been a tragic business, though the sacrifice does seem, from a tactical point of view, to have been not altogether in vain. To Goring by bus, since F wanted to inspect and take tea at The Mulberry, a famous hostelry there. But the manageress would not give us tea, being doubtful whether she had enough victuals for her resident patrons.

October 1

Although the land of France was liberated some time ago, the Huns clung to the ports and were hard to dislodge. Today, however, battered Calais has fallen to the Allies; and there remain in enemy hands, I think, only Dunkirk, Lorient and St Nazaire – of any importance.

October 4

How I appreciate the blessing of continuous quiet nights. The war is going so well now that it seems probable that we have already heard that vile air-raid siren for the last time. The blackout, that other major curse, remains, though reduced in stringency.

October 5

A new bus on our route has seats of plain wooden slats instead of the normal stuffed cloth. 'We cannot get the material for the other kind,' explained the conductor.

October 7

Brought in, under pressure from F, the two enamelled slop pails which have stood for long in our porch, containing water against possible fire through assault of the enemy. They [have] become mausolea, through misadventure, of all manner of creeping things. I trust I am not acting in defiance of the Defence Regulations, which, however, are more elastic now.

October 9

We are much perturbed by news of the parlous state of Holland. There is much looting and inundation by the Huns, with the prospect of famine in large areas unless they are driven out within a month – which seems a very remote possibility. So far the advance of the Allied Armies in their direction has brought nothing but misery to the unhappy Dutch.

October 10

The Corporation's men have begun to remove the barbed wire from the seafront, but it will take a long time. F has lost her purse 'out'. It contained 8s. 6d. and a nice comb; but luckily, for once, neither her clothing coupons nor her glasses. So she dismisses the affair philosophically, with the doubtfully just commentary, 'The Lord hath dealt harshly with his servant F.'

October 11

In the afternoon, gale with a deluge of rain. F had her hat sent spinning down South Street, and one of our two irreplaceable umbrellas was blown in.

October 12

To Kendall's in the Arcade to have my umbrella, broken in the tempest, amended. But they would not take it, saying that there would be a queue formed for 'Gents' broken umbrellas at 9am on November 1, when a heavy quota I think would be expected, for amendment in a space of from 7-8 weeks! Could they supply a new one? No, their quota for the current month had been but one. Wherefore, on coming home, I was fain to take out needle and thread and effect my own reparations. And now I have an umbrella not pretty, yet, I trust, serviceable, at least for the rest of this now dwindling war. To my great content.

October 16

After lunch we went into W Worthing to collect F's purse which she left on a seat the other day, the same having been reported to the police by a finder honest, and of a condition above accepting a reward.

October 18

The gale continued [from day before], with heavy showers throughout the day. As so often since June 6 (Invasion Day) the elements seemed to be conspiring against operations of the Allied Armies on the Continent.

October 23

Dull morning; heavy rain from 1 to 3.15pm. Early by bus into the town. 'Father forgive them for they know not what they do!' exclaimed our conductress with good-humoured profanity, on being tendered half a crown in payment for a 1d. fare. On the whole these war substitute conductresses do very well in the present most exacting conditions of overcrowding.

October 24

This afternoon for the first time for over four years I took a walk along the promenade, which is now cleared of wire from Splash Point as far as the pier, though the chain of concrete blocks remains along the sea side of it. It was pleasant to watch again the tireless beauty of old Ocean upon the unheeding shore. But Lord, what a dismal sight the once trim promenade presents; rent and broken where the barbed wire and supports have been dragged away; and foul with weeds, and with the flotsam and jetsam of years lying everywhere about.

October 25

Walking with a friend on the front this afternoon, F found her curiosity aroused by the sight, unusual here, of 'crowds of officers'. I myself observed a Brigadier, as well as a full Colonel. I think it was some powwow or conference.

October 26

Felt cheap today through becoming cold in the night. The house is cold, but we are afraid to begin the kitchen boiler fire since coal is so very hard to obtain.

October 28

Yesterday, opposite the old Town Hall, a great white bulldog tried to stop a motor car – succeeded in stopping an elderly man on a bicycle. Man fell in the road; tactlessly kicked dog. Dog, resentful, sprung at him. Agitated spectators intrepidly dragged it off. Man shaken but, miraculously, not bitten. Just indignation and rushing of populace. Cries of 'It must be destroyed,' in which F, excited, joined. However, in the tumult and hubbub dog discreetly conjured away by its guardian up a side street. Then a policeman appeared.

November 1

Everyone is feeling depressed owing to the war situation. For the light of victory, which shone forth so brightly in September, has become lost in clouds again. The PM only suggested the spring or summer for the end of the German War. So the end eternally eludes us. The stubborn courage of the German soldier in defeat remains the dominating factor in the situation.

November 5

We have changed our Sunday newspaper, rejecting the crime-stressing *News of the World* in favour of the more eclectic *Sunday Times*, whose readers need not gather that they live in a wicked world.

November 6

Last evening at 7.35pm the Sabbath quiet was broken by the wail of the siren, signifying our 985th ARW, the first since the 24th. We heard a distant explosion, and men say that a flying bomb fell at Pulborough.

November 9

The hundreds of searchlight vehicles which have made the front their habitation for several weeks have suddenly disappeared. F.D. Roosevelt has been re-elected President of the USA for a fourth term. A unique honour for the world's greatest figure.

November 14

Visited the beach in the morning. People were sitting on the groynes on the east side of the pier, enjoying the sun and the lapping of the indefatigable waves. Just now, after the years of banishment from the shore, there is a novel, arresting pleasure in tramping the shingle again.

November 16

At the present moment there is procurable in Worthing neither toilet paper, envelopes, nor woollen stockings. It is very disappointing that, in spite of the U-boats having been mastered, there is no easing of the civilians' privations; but they rather become worse.

November 18

At this stage of the war, it is rare to see a motor car with a label which one has not seen before. Yet today I did. It had 'surgical unit' inscribed in red letters on the windscreen. It was a stylish-looking car, grey with scarlet facings, and appeared to be in the charge of two girls in khaki uniform. Rather strangely, it bore no Geneva cross.

November 19

The supply of milk on Sundays having been stopped without notice, we had only Saturday's dregs for meals today and Monday's breakfast. Luckily I had some milk powder in stock, but F will not touch it.

November 20

Very mild. Torrential rain until noon. Rain again after 4pm. Wind SW. Six Allied armies aligned along the German frontier from Holland to Switzerland have gone into the attack – with initial success. So talk about 'end of the War before Xmas' is being raised again. But I think the weather is, and will be, too bad for much to eventuate before March. F took me into Woolworths after tea. All things there still bright and beautiful after five years of war. No wonder the populace flocks thither; it prevents them becoming downhearted. I noticed, under a blaze of electric lights, a wonderful display of Xmas cards – many buyers of tin pastry pans for making mince pies – and a comely maiden, clad in white raiment, dispensing soft drinks.

November 25

The blue vault of the sky was overspread with a network of vapour trails from multitudes of planes which seemed to be moving from all points of the compass at once. It was a remarkable sight. Great white filmy streaks and arcs and wavy lines crossing and interlacing. And the air was full with a deep incessant droning, sounding, as it were, the knell of Hitler's Germany. People's glances were all attracted upwards; which is seldom the case at this late stage of the war.

November 27

Found to my disgust the carcass of a bluebottle fly in a 2lb jar of marmalade which I opened. But didn't tell F, who, still more temperamental, would not have eaten any of the legitimate, and now precious, contents, had she known.

November 28

SW gale accompanied by heavy rain 9am to 4pm. Mild. I went out only into the village to procure a loaf. 'That suit of yours looks awful,' remarked F in deprecation, 'you should send it down to the museum to be put into the case for "This Week's Treasure".' Well, the suit is only my 'working' one and ten years old, and so may claim indulgence.

November 29

A brilliant morning but some cloud in the afternoon. People have relapsed into their normal state of gloomy resignation about the war. With milk down to two-and-a-half pints per week, and no eggs, the food shortage is felt more than in the summer. Also, despite daily hysterical headlines in the newspapers, progress on our battlefronts is disappointingly slow. The Hun is tenacious and always rises from his ashes. Moreover, at the moment, we are further depressed by a shocking accident in Staffordshire, where a large RAF underground bomb store has suddenly exploded, doing immense damage and killing more than 150 people.

December 1

The bomb store disaster at Burton-on-Trent is not quite so extensive as was first reported. Deaths now said to be 59. 4,000 tons of bombs lost – enough for one major raid on Germany. There is, in view of this Xmas being the 6th of total warfare, a very surprising display of calendars and cards. But they are from three-four times as expensive as before the war, and greatly lacking in richness and design and execution. Most of the cards are crude and poor.

December 3

Today, the Home Guard paraded for the last time. The purpose of their enrolment – to meet German invaders – has passed. They have developed into a fine body of men.

December 4

Today workmen were engaged removing the dugout or military shooting box erected in 1940 outside the public library in Worthing as part of the defences to meet the invasion scare after the downfall of France. It was of quite a flimsy construction, all earth and timber, and intended to shelter troops firing at Huns advancing up the main street from the sea. In a very few years, I suppose, it will be altogether forgotten that such a shabby disfigurement of the handsome municipal buildings ever existed. However, down the street, in the circus opposite the old Town Hall, is a much more ambitious erection, a concrete fort made to contain guns. This for the present survives. It is disguised to represent a rustic store, with painted wares at the windows and painted creepers on the walls. And it bears a superscription indicating proprietorship in the remarkable name of Hyam Already!

33 *On 3 December 1944 Worthing Home Guard paraded for the last time on Broadwater Green. 'They have developed into a fine body of men,' said Harriss.*

34 *Colonel Frederick Stern, of Highdown, shakes hands with Worthing Home Guard veterans at their final parade on Broadwater Green.*

35 *The final salute for Worthing Home Guard on Broadwater Green prior to its disbanding.*

36 *Worthing Home Guard parades one last time.*

December 8

We are in the throes of the usual war winter milk famine. The 'non-priority' allowance is now cut to but two pints each per week, though a kindly milkman leaves us a total of six pints. We do not know why, for we have made no approaches to him. In this shortage the less fortunate jealously watch the bottles left for the fortunate. There is a powder termed 'household milk' from which the cream has been extracted which is supplied by the Government. It is used for puddings; and also for tea in tea houses, and spoils it. The tins are marked 'not to be used for babies', and, indeed, I would they were not to be used for me.

December 9

The war, they say, has killed Xmas in Germany. It has not done so here. Toys are scarce; but Xmas trees, holly wreaths and gaily dressed dolls – beaming with their lovely coy expressions on their wartime muslin faces – are here in plenty, though the last only at great price. Crowds throng the shops but find little to buy – so that a choosing of presents is become a torment.

December 14

11am at the fishmongers. 'The fish train has only got as far as Redhill so far,' announced the proprietor, 'so it won't reach Worthing till about 4, so there won't be any fish in the shop till 9am tomorrow.' Whereupon the queue melted sadly away.

December 16

Xmas gleanings: A huge queue in Marks and Spencer's and stretching away down the street outside, for nuts. A placard outside the pessimistic butcher's shop: 'Three things are certain – Death, Income Tax, and no chicken.'

December 18

Awakened at 4.30am by the thunder of many bombers passing overhead. This continued for a long while, and had to do, one supposes, with a great counter-offensive which the Huns have just opened on the Western Front. At about 6pm yesterday one of the bombers then mentioned exploded on the ground. We were very startled, fearing the noise was that of a flying bomb. However, it seems that a bomber, having engine trouble, crash-landed on the beach near Heene Terrace and exploded. The pilot is said to have been the only survivor of the crew [in fact none survived]. Great damage by blast to windows in that district as far as South Street, nearly a mile away. Altogether a very sad business.

December 21

The Huns continue a most violent offensive. It was an unpleasant surprise to find them still capable of initiating a battle on the grand scale. This attack is against the American part of the Allied line. Their front has been broken through and rendered fluid on a 25-mile stretch, with the Huns 30 miles into Belgium again. Some people here are very gloomy at the news, but I am very

37   *This is the ill-fated crew of the fully bomb-laden Lancaster bomber which crashed and exploded on Worthing beach, opposite Heene Terrace, in 1944. Streets in West Durrington were later named after the airmen, and a memorial plaque can today be seen on the pier.*

confident that at the present stage of the war this attack cannot be long sustained – it is the last throw of dictatorship in desperation.

December 23

This is Saturday. I no longer hurry off after breakfast to join the 'Becket' bun queue, as I regularly did last winter. If we want Bath buns – and, on account of their deterioration, we want them less and less – we find that we can obtain them after lunch, in the town. I regret this abandonment. For this war queue became a part of my life; I and the others in it became familiar and developed a comradeship. Now, for me, it is all over. It is gone away and can never be again. It is lost in the chaos of departed Time.

December 25

A memorable Xmas Day – perfect for the time of year. After a modest repast we walked out for an hour in the afternoon; which seemed, from the deserted streets, more than the rest of the local lieges felt capable of doing. After tea I went out alone to observe the beauty of the unclouded moon shining through the tracery of great trees. All was impressive solitude; and I thought of Xmas Days long gone by and their enchantments, and what a changed and solemn day Xmas becomes for those the measure of whose years is filling up.

December 26

Same weather but some fog in the afternoon. No newspapers, no one about; very stale bread. Life a struggle to make rations last until tomorrow – when the town – or most of it, returns to sanity.

December 28

The great German attack, after advancing for over ten miles, seems now to have been held up everywhere. Nevertheless, 1,000 square miles of luckless Belgium have been overrun again. This great contest – still in progress – is to be called 'The Battle of the Ardennes'.

December 30

We are becoming increasingly annoyed now by the expression 'Full Fruit Standard' which faces us on all our pots of bought jam. For in fact the jam contains so small a proportion of fruit that its flavour is hard to discern. What the label really means is that the jam contains the fullest amount of fruit that the Food Ministry permits, and the rest is glucose. Which is another instance of how the ever submissive public is humbugged in this war.

December 31

Frost all day in the shade. On a stroll in the morning out past the Green and along Offington Avenue, and back by Poulter's Lane, the prospect was one of peaceful solitude. And, indeed, now that all the soldiers are gone, and their habitations in her villadom deserted, Worthing seems further than ever from the throbbing heart of wartime activity. So ends another year of war, a year with its moments of triumph – moments when the Promised Land seemed very near – but a year which, contrary to the prognostications of experts, has ended in anticlimax and disappointment.

1945

January 1

It is cheering to feel that we are in a new year. Under present conditions one does not regret the departure of the old one. We are only too glad to be rid of it!

January 2

Mr Hyam Already's concrete fortress opposite the old Town Hall is being demolished by the agency of pneumatic drills – to the sore undoing of citizens' ears!

January 4

The Hyam Already fortress is found too strong for pneumatic drills, and stands scarred, still challenging demolition.

January 5

Same bitter weather. For some five hours from soon after 6pm we witnessed, for this area at least, an unique display of aerial activity; and the deep booming note which indicates the movement of many large bombers hardly ceased. Those that were visible from time to time were moving not only SE in the direction of the Ardennes battle – as was to be expected – but N and even SW. I suppose some were setting out and others returning; and the general effect resembled the wild confusion of a disturbed ants' nest.

January 8

From 7.10am there was another passing of great bombers. I saw some clusters of planes emitting trails which resembled streaks of golden rain as they caught the rays of the rising sun at early dawn. As, too, the planes still had their fore-cabins illuminated, each had the appearance of a fiery comet rushing through the air. A very beautiful sight which I have not observed before.

38   *A view of the old Town Hall, with an air-raid shelter in the foreground and the famous 'Hyam Already' pillbox on the roundabout.*

January 9

A considerable fall of snow. The ground and bare branches and undergrowth became a fairyland of white, presenting a sight unusual for Worthing.

January 13

Overcast. Bitter NE wind, freshening. The scarcity of woollen garments seems to be causing real distress, especially among the more elderly women. The dustman today pointed out to me a single snowdrop bloom in our front [garden]. It was the first he had seen, he said. Which I thought very nice of him; for one looks not for such pretty observations in the weary titans of the muckhill.

January 15

To my dentist, a filling having come out which he put in but a year ago. For the refilling he mulcted me 10s. 6d. 'Why he ought not to have charged!' cries F, 'don't you go to him again!' Yet, in dental affairs, a wight clings somewhat to the ill he knows!

January 16

Raw and hazy. To the coal merchant's to press for boiler fuel. This was for the third time. We are rationed to 5cwt per month, but cannot obtain near so much, nor, just now, any at all. This wrestling is very miserable and racking, for it is dreadful and menacing to be left without the boiler at this season. Coals in general are scarcer, and dearer, than at any time during the war.

January 17

There has been a tremendous change in the aspect of the war. The Russians, whose progress has for the past six months been disappointing, have suddenly begun a series of attacks along their whole front from the Baltic to the Carpathians, and have carried out deep penetrations. They seem in fact to have been waiting just to gather themselves for the kill; which their overwhelming numbers of men and machines, with the Anglo-American armies pressing hard in the West, suggest that they can now effect. The German morale remains wonderful, but it would seem, as we trust, that the odds against them are now beyond human bearing.

January 18

Warsaw, ill-fated Poland's capital, after five years of durance, is recaptured by the Russians from the Huns – a ruin.

January 20

The news from the Eastern Front continues to be very encouraging. I have never felt so light-hearted about the war.

January 22

F to the cinema and impressed by a display of the Ministry of Information showing what is being done with salvaged waste paper, to help the war.

January 23

Snow all day. Bitter E wind. I struggled out into the village to do urgent shopping with the snow flakes driving into my eyes and a slippery mess of freezing slush under my feet. On Broadwater Church noticeboard I read this not inappropriate text, 'O Lord, I am oppressed: undertake for me.' Upon which F made the macabre comment, 'This is a day which we shall not forget – that text might as well be "call the undertaker for me!"' For the rest [of the day] we sat in, and contrary to our adopted practice, ate all our meals at home.

39 *On 4 January 1945 Mr Harriss wrote, 'The Hyam Already fortress is found too strong for pneumatic drills.'*

January 24

Intensely cold. Yesterday's snowfall had ceased soon after dark, and provided a lovely spectacle in the silence of the night – a gleaming wilderness of white brooding in the pale glory of the Meridian moon.

January 26

The worst frost here within memory continues. Temperature in the hall at 10am only 38 degrees. We long for a thaw. Several hundred Russians have descended upon the town. They are dressed in the drab British battledress and lodged in empty houses or hotels on the front where our soldiers used to be. Men say that they have been engaged, as prisoners of war of the Huns, on forced labour in Germany, but liberated by the Allied Armies. They are mostly stocky, powerful-looking men, many of them resembling English of the sallow type; but the features of Tartar or Mongolian origin, some resembling Japanese. Parties of them were today marching about the Worthing streets in formation, singing weird airs with no little musical ability. These Bolsheviks have aroused much interest and curiosity among the local British, who regard them as though they were some strange kind of animal. Their officers look no higher class than the rank and file.

January 27

Two more inches of snow fell during the night to add to that already on the ground. I overslept, and then, after breakfast, in a hurry to go out to sweep away snow, forgot to shave! Luckily F, who notices most things, did not notice this, I being fair. I hope others at Mitchell's eating house didn't! I only discovered the fact myself on returning home to tea.

January 28

The Great Frost persists. It is very rare in these parts to see, as now, the countryside snowbound for days on end. This afternoon I went out upon the Downs by way of Hill Barn Lane and very pleasant it was plunging about in the sunlit, snow-clad solitude.

January 29

Fine at first, but it soon became a dark and bitter day, with slight sleet. Wind NE, later SW, but this, strange to say, brought no alleviation of the frost. We are very worried about coals, having but 1cwt left. Today yet another visit of stimulation to the coal merchant's. Found many others pleading before the coal damsel. She, radiating hope, with ready pen, inscribes the names and addresses of the most insistent on a special roll; who are thus pacified and depart in peace. But experience shows that nothing more will happen.

January 30

A further four inches of snow in the night, but this morning the Great Frost subsided into a most blessed thaw. A happy release. Today Hitler completes, scarcely celebrates!, his 12th year of power. And the misery of Europe has come full circle. Millions are without even fuel in this hardest of winters.

January 31

A day of cloud, fog, drizzle and slush. The hall temperature rose from 42 degrees yesterday to 48; to which great content. Yet we are not unscathed, for the supply of potatoes at our eating house has been cut by 75 per cent. Oranges have appeared in the shops (1lb for each citizen); and strangely glowing and colourful they look in the winter drabness to those who have been denied them for so very long.

February 3

The Russian soldiers in Worthing are the lions of the moment. Many of them are quartered in the *Marine Hotel* on the front, long since commandeered by the Government as military barracks – and fallen into consequent decay. Today they were to be seen sunning themselves outside the entrance, swarming in circles around a comrade dancing a 'pas seul' to the unlovely notes of the accordion. Others were marching about in companies singing their outlandish semi-barbaric songs. In a few cases one notices contacts between them and local inhabitants; but language is a formidable bar. Nevertheless, all are drawn to them, for all here feel it is the Russian nation which is winning the war for us, though the part played and to be played by these particular representatives of it remains obscure.

February 4

The eyes of the world are fixed on Berlin, for so long its storm-centre, but now awaiting the *coup de grace* from more than a million Russians aligned along the Oder, while Anglo-American bombers in thousands blast it from above. At last the Huns, too, are learning to hate war.

February 5

Spent much of the morning on top of a pair of steps at the laborious task of removing blackout curtains which on a day of wrath in September '39 I had hung upon the curtains of peace. The present moderating of blackout regulations permits this. Or at least I trust so!

February 6

These are great days for marrying. A winsome serving miss of our acquaintance, having been jilted by a Canadian warrior, found another lover and has married him in time to use the dress and cake provided for her expected marriage with the first! And so she is consoled.

February 7

Deposited blackout curtains in the town salvage dump by the Rivoli cinema. The Russians are across the Oder on a 50-mile front. Which marks the final phase of Nazidom. It opens, indeed, a prospect so bright that a lady here, indoors with a sprained leg, was lamenting lest she should not be out in time to buy her flags for Peace!

February 12

2cwt of boiler coal has been delivered to us just as we had but a scuttleful left. A very small mercy, yet it will allay our anguish until March.

February 15

It demonstrates how long this war has been in progress that one notices so many young women who started it as maids now married and trailing after them families of two or three children. Viewed at the museum an admirable exhibition of Victorian valentines – relics of a pretty and harmless custom now dead, like much else of that era that was worthy of a better fate.

February 16

Our Russian guests have suddenly departed. They wore British battledress but without badges, and had no weapons nor equipment of any kind; yet they were soldiers. What were they doing in this galley? I wonder what they, and not least the inscrutable Mongolian part of them, thought of our many local women – those in sloppy trousers and monkey coats, with painted faces and sucking on cigarettes as they usher children along the streets.

February 20

Crowds flocked on to the newly liberated beach and promenade to the east of the pier. To the barber's, where I learnt some particulars about the local Russians. It seems they were originally soldiers who were taken prisoner in the German drive into Russia. The Huns used them as slaves in western Germany where they were ultimately liberated in the course of the Anglo-American advance. Then they were brought to England, and have been at Aldershot for the past six months recuperating. Those here came from there for a short holiday.

February 22

F induced me, unwilling, to accompany her to a house decorator's to arrange for some interior work to be done chez nous. I was further depressed by the intimation that owing to the changing cost of paint and other materials Mr X does not give estimates now. 'Changing' here is of course a euphemism for 'increasing'.

February 23

Worthing remains utterly war-battered, but changes towards a peaceful ensemble have already begun. Thus the whole of the promenade is now clear of barbed wire, though the line of cement blocks on the beach verge remains for the present; as does, too, an occasional scarlet and white noticeboard, 'Beware of mines'. Then, as regards personnel, nearly all the hitherto very numerous fire service men have departed from the many posts about the town where, from the first day of the war, they were always present in readiness to deal with the expected conflagrations from incendiary bombs which, by the mercy of God, never here occurred. Sometimes a score of these dark blue liveried figures might be seen performing elementary military evolutions in the streets nearby, or, more frequently, beguiling their tedium by playing at ball.

February 24

A further party of Russians are come to the town. They aroused much interest as they marched 'in threes' through the streets, or stood outside their appointed habitations on the front. This because, unlike the first party, these wore strange brown dress with great green patches affixed (such as I have seen worn by our Italian prisoners of war), their headdress being sometimes round Cossack caps and sometimes flat peaked kepis worn by German soldiers. 'Look at them! They come all tired, straight from their slavery,' remarked a sympathetic lady. But their sleek, well-fed appearance belied this; and their motley suits were just a temporary issue, for battledress was in course of being supplied to them. As I looked upon these poor outcasts, the thought came to me of the pathetic upset and destruction of social ties throughout the world caused by the German Beast, and the absolute need of eradicating him for ever.

February 25

We are suddenly thrown into a state of great expectancy. The Americans have begun a great attack in the West, while the Russians approaching Berlin gather themselves for the final leap.

March 1

With the surge of Spring stimulating us we made an expedition by bus to The Pantiles, West Worthing, which is a pretty, bright, self-contained locality with a separate existence from its bustling parent. Took tea there and walked back, three miles. There was much booming of planes invisible through cloud. The Huns are now experiencing a hideous Calvary indeed. My mind goes back to August 1914 with the Berlin Crowd madly cheering for war. What do they think of war now?

March 2

I have noticed an increasing habit of womenfolk of officers and men in the fighting services to wear their men's regimental and other official badges in the form of an enamelled brooch; and a very pretty custom it seems, and helps to maintain the martial spirit at home. Our Russian guests appear to have mastered at least one English phrase – and that readily acceptable to their hosts. Thus I heard one remark with a grin 'We 'ate the Germans!' The Red Flag with the hammer and sickle is flying from the top of the *Warnes Hotel*, as the present headquarters of these Bolsheviks – which is very strange to see.

March 3

The house temperature at 9am has fallen from 51 to 44 degrees in two days, so we were glad to light our kitchen stove again after five days of abstinence. We are trying to make our last 2cwt of anthracite suffice for what remains of the cold season rather than be partakers in the miserable struggle to obtain coal. Kind-hearted lady to defiant four-year-old on the front, 'You musn't try to get through that barbed wire little boy, it will hurt you'. 'I don't care.' 'Or you may be blown up by a mine!' 'I don't care.' 'If you do I shall fetch a policeman.' 'I don't care.' But by this time the kind-hearted lady had come to the conclusion that she didn't care either, and departed disillusioned.

March 7

The house decorator called; but having only two painters left to him out of ten – both over 70 and one afraid to climb ladders – he couldn't do our work before July!

March 8

The Russians have struck their flag at Warnes and departed. Today, in place of hundreds, there was not one to be seen abroad. They were a simple, good-natured-seeming set of men, and had begun a lively if necessarily mainly inarticulate fraternization with the local street urchins. Their visit has inspired us with a sense of utter novelty. Now they are gone; and I suppose I shall never set eyes on a Russian again.

March 9

A brilliant day brought brilliant news. The Americans, by a sudden unexpected thrust, have crossed the Rhine by a bridge providentially left unblown, and established a firm bridgehead on the eastern bank. Further, the Russians have resumed their advance on Berlin, now less than 30 miles distant. It is evident that the Huns are now so short of good troops that they are unable to make effective counter-attacks. People here keep asking one another, 'How long will the war last now?' Everyone is experiencing an insatiable craving for more and more news.

March 10

I was astonished to hear a lady remark to her companion, as I passed them in the street, 'I don't think we could have had worse treatment than we have had from the Americans. They want the trade, they want the airports, they want to collar everything.' I disagree emphatically. We must remember that they are now by far the strongest nation in the world. I am profoundly grateful to them for the way they have fed and equipped us, and for their magnificent military contribution, in this war.

March 13

As I was enjoying the sunshine in Denton Gardens, I saw for 20 minutes many four-engined bombers passing over on one of their persistent raids on Germany.

March 16

New restaurants are springing up like mushrooms in Worthing. Catering is become very lucrative. Unfortunately, in this multitude of eating houses there is not more to eat, though ices and icing on cakes are to be permitted again. There is a little more fish about, but meat is shorter than ever, and the cheese ration is reduced from three to two ounces per week.

March 21

At Mitchell's eating house there is now appointed a special janitor to control the lunch queue which floods the shop below. A hard-bitten man in a black beret, he is become familiar to thousands as he stands between shop and stairs uttering his cries of 'Will you keep the gangway clear, please.'

March 23

To Littlehampton by bus. All the great Green there between town and sea is wired off from the public for military occasions.

March 24

There were many bombers passing over the district today. Just before noon they presented a majestic sight as they moved over the crowds in Chapel Road intent upon their weekend shopping. But few people looked up.

March 27

On my travels this afternoon I looked and saw a great company near the Pier Pavilion engaged in removing the concrete defence blocks from the promenade; a hard business of rollers and levers and a long, low lorry. There are about 360 of these six-ton adamantine monoliths.

March 29

The German Western Front is broken and crumbling; and authorities seem to agree that a general collapse is at hand, with the official end of the war expected in the course of next month. But now that the day of deliverance is just round the corner no one seems in the least excited about it. We are too old now to throw up our caps until it happens.

March 30

Good Friday. No newspaper in the morning. As usual on Friday, I did out the kitchen and scullery whilst F did noble work upstairs. Then, since Mitchell's was closed, we went elsewhere and had the kind of lunch which is more beneficial to the caterer than to the customer. 'I'd sooner starve at home and just have air than go there again. Many pigs get better swill than that coffee,' quoth F. Then, since we could not walk about all the afternoon, and the public library was closed, we went

40   *On 27 March 1945 Mr Harriss witnessed workmen starting to remove the giant concrete blocks from the front.*

to the Dome cinema to see Cedric Hardwicke and Anna Neagle in *Nell Gwyn* but I enjoyed more an admirable newsreel of the historic crossing of the Rhine.

March 31

A bewildering great crowd about the streets of Worthing. Great queues at the fish shops in pursuit of a poor supply. The people seemed quiet, kindly and impassive as is the British wont. They probably feel more light-hearted than they have been for years past; but the desperate matter of provisioning over the Easter holiday left little room for thought about history in the making on the continent. Many were hugging triumphantly to their bosoms rolls of highly coloured floor mats surprisingly being retailed by some trader in Montague Street, for such things are now usually unobtainable.

April 1

Easter Sunday: A most evil day. Drizzle from early dawn until noon, and again after 4pm. All the time SW gale. We did not go out. Sought for and brought out against the coming Peace our Union Jack flag which we bought for HM the King's coronation.

April 4

Cloudy and cold. Thinking I may err and miss something in life by my persistent neglect of the drama, this afternoon I consented to accompany F to the new Connaught Theatre to see *The Importance of Being Earnest*, that celebrated farce by O. Wilde – and mighty clever it is with its tricks and turns. Yet [it] demands good acting which here it had not. So we were little amused. Hemmed in by people, cramped on a hard seat, with head hot and feet cold and a gentleman performing 'a trumpet voluntary' with nose and 'kerchief behind my neck, I was more than glad to emerge and range freely again.

April 5

Finished reading *A Life of Cecil Rhodes*, by J.G. McDonald. Most interesting. The last and supreme among Empire builders. I can remember the thrill at home of his great pioneering days in S Africa. Is it a sign of national decadence that we no longer think imperially?

April 7

Airborne Forces' Week began in Worthing. Milord Winterton, our MP, opened it this morning with a speech, standing rather forlornly beside the mayor on the steps beneath the cracked portico of the old Town Hall. He remarked that the audience was small and looked rather dreary, for which there was now no need. Which they resented – for they were standing in a bitter wind, wanted to get on with their shopping, and knew that he only wanted money. He himself did not look happy. It was indeed a cold-blooded business both for him and them. This speech was milord's swansong; for the constituency is to be divided for the coming Election, and he will then stand for Horsham only.

April 8

Thought for the day: It seems a strong argument against survival after death that the dead are beyond number – yet so are the stars in the heavens; and each hath its appointed place.

April 9

House temperature at 8am only 49 degrees. I am today 63 – too old for such frigid mornings! One sees more and more notices in shop windows requiring skilled hands, shop assistants, and even errand boys. Also for charwomen, 1/6d. per hour is offered for this last, but they are almost unobtainable.

April 13

I was indeed shocked on taking up the newspaper this morning to read of the sudden death, at the age of 63, of President Roosevelt, the greatest figure in the world today. This is a calamity for all the Allied nations. One admired him for his able and indefatigable conduct of the greatest affairs; for his courage in physical infirmity, his eloquence, urbanity and sense of humour. He was a beneficent friend to the British Commonwealth, and has died in sight of the Promised Land, a martyr to the cause of Humanity.

April 15

The sun almost of summer heat, but without summer's oppression. So far this month, one is happy to record, no bombs have arrived. This because the rapid advance of the Allies in Holland and N Germany has overrun so many of their sources of origin.

April 16

Though the warplanes still pass overhead, if we accept scarcities, life about Worthing is steadily resuming the peacetime normal. Today Lord George Sanger's Circus is in Beach House Gardens, little children mob the vendors of creamless ice cream, contented crowds are lounging on the promenade, and the War Inquiry Bureau in Chapel Road has closed its doors.

April 17

Same perfect weather. The hottest April period for 40 years. From all directions the Allied Armies seem to be closing in for 'the kill'. No wonder there was a crowd waiting for the evening papers outside the Arcade this afternoon.

April 18

We are not allowed altogether to forget the war. Thus last night we were awakened about 12 by a violent burst of cannonading on the Downs. F frightened, but it was just an exercise. We have suffered from them before.

April 19

As the Anglo-American Armies advance into Germany one receives impressions of good and bad. Thus many of our prisoners are being liberated and restored to their families after years of most irksome captivity, but the awful secrets of the civilian concentration camps for Jews and Poles and anti-Nazis are being revealed. The Germans seem to be by nature cruel beyond possibility of exaggeration.

April 20

The lesser blackout of recent months, popularly called the 'Dimout', is abolished as from Monday next save for a belt five miles deep around the coast. We, unhappily, are within that belt.

April 24

F to the Rivoli cinema to see *Since You Went Away*, and returned charmed and enthusiastic. Many wept – she among them, I rather suppose. The principals included Claudette Colbert and Shirley Temple (the former American child prodigy now almost a woman).

April 25

Some shops are exhibiting flags for vending to celebrate 'Victory', now inevitable soon.

April 26

Poor F very much moved by the awful illustrations now appearing in the newspapers depicting victims of the murderous atrocities perpetrated wholesale by the Nazi Germans in their concentration camps. I much hope that for her sake, and even for my own, these pictures will soon cease to appear; though it is right they should appear – for seeing is believing; and remembering.

April 27

The war seems to be moving rapidly to a tremendous and final climax. The Russians have completely encircled Berlin and have battered their way half through it. The British have captured the great port of Bremen. There is no sign of effective German resistance anywhere.

April 28

The news today is sensational. It is reported that the Americans and Russians have met on the Elbe, in central Germany. Also Musso has been arrested (for the second time) by Italian partisans, who have seized Milan for the Allies. I am afraid the Italians will kill Musso now.

April 29

The newspapers are full of rumours. Peace feelers by Himmler, Hitler dying of cerebral haemorrhage. Hitler and Goebbels shot dead. Hitler continuing to direct the defence of Berlin in person. What are we to believe?

April 30

The Italian patriots have, as expected, lost no time in executing Musso.

May 2

We heard on the wireless last night, at 10.30, the dramatic news of the death of Hitler at his post in Berlin. The news, in German, was followed by the strains of the Austrian [underlined] National Anthem, a deep-toned brass band, which sounded very beautiful and moving – but seemed grotesque in celebration of the passing of such a villain. Hitler has filled the European bill so exclusively and so long that one feels a sense of loss of the familiar – of the removal of an all-pervading deputy Satan. It is very remarkable that he and Musso should both have mounted the dragon on almost the same day.

May 3

The Russians have captured Berlin, with over 100,000 prisoners! Further, the German Army in Italy and Southern Austria has surrendered. Field Marshal Montgomery's men have taken Lubeck and mighty Hamburg. In fact prodigious events are tumbling over one another so as to lose significance by their very multiplication. Hereafter this will be reckoned among the greatest of days. Yet the British here and now are taking this long-deferred triumph with absolute calmness, in fact, to outward appearance at least, even with apathy.

May 5

The German Armies in NW Germany, Holland and Denmark have surrendered to FM Montgomery at 8am today! The Great Deliverance has arrived! Never again shall I watch the armadas of bombers making their majestic progress towards the Western Front. The newspapers have ceased to insert their daily war maps; for the war is over! There is nothing of the German dominion left. Here is history being made.

41 *The scene outside the Town Hall on VE Day, photographed from the bombed-out shell of Mitchell's.*

May 7

A few flags have appeared about the streets, and loudspeakers and a dais for speakers outside the Town Hall. But the great news has not yet come through.

May 8

Yesterday the Huns signed terms of unconditional surrender at a schoolhouse in Rheims. Germany lies helpless at the mercy of the Allies, broken and ruined. So today we have been celebrating the first of two ordained VE days as they are called – meaning Victory in Europe; for the shadow of the Japanese war still stands over us, dark if remote. We were present outside the Town Hall when, at 11am, the mayor gave a short conventional address and the Salvation Army Band played two or three hymns followed by the National Anthem. Then we spent the rest of the day on or about the front, as did others in their thousands. The news of Peace has of course produced a glow of satisfaction, but it has lacked the element of surprise. So the joy was of a subdued order. People had to find their entertainment in watching the moving throng, for the only diversion was the

42 *Mr Harris and his wife were close by as the mayor addressed crowds outside the Town Hall, Chapel Road, on VE Day.*

43 *VE Day crowds outside the Town Hall in Chapel Road. Somewhere among them is Mr Harriss and his wife.*

occasional passing of a car emitting 'canned music' provided by the local authority. But there were Army lorries wherein not only members of the Forces, but also a multitude of juveniles enjoyed rides about the streets. Flags flew from most of the buildings; flags were carried and waved; whilst here and there women, children and even dogs appeared decorated in red, white and blue. 'Wave your flag, sonny' remarked a very young infantry officer to one of his too numerous offspring.

May 9

The PM has just completed five years in office; and such years. The pilot who warned of the storm, and weathered it, received a supremely well-observed ovation in London last night. Today, the 2nd VE Day and second general holiday passed here very like yesterday, though with a diminished effervescence. The same good-humoured populace trailed aimlessly about; the same canned music occasionally brayed; but lorry-riding civilians had apparently been stopped. In Montague Place a mute evangelist stood forlornly, extending to passing eyes placards notifying 'Christ died for us; he is rejected by us,' and so forth; while some sinners danced to the strains of The Lambeth Walk. It is very strange, I think, that neither today, nor yesterday were there any peals of bells audible here; for bells add greatly to the gaiety of national celebrations.

May 10

The German war is over. Today the guns are silent overseas, and the passing bomber, now infrequent, conveys, instead of missiles of wrath, good things to fill the hungry. We faced domestic life against a forgotten background, and began to peer – not without apprehension – down the blessed avenue of Peace. Today, with relief tinged with mild regret, I abandon my long-drawn task of saving from oblivion some passing incidents of days supremely great. In doing so, I cannot but reflect on the good fortune of us two in our war experiences; how we have not only survived injury, but have also been spared illness, ruin by bomb, billeting of soldiers, billeting of evacuees (save only the she-pedagogue for one week), and fire watching – all evil things. For which and other mercies we are truly thankful. Yet we have touched unprecedented events, so that as memories grow dim, I trust that this record may have an interest for many. And so I close my book.

Mr Harriss made one more entry, to record the end of the Japanese war in the Far East.

August 15 and 16

Japan, urged by the new awful and irresistible Atomic Bomb, and by the addition of the Russian Armies to the Allied phalanx encircling her, both only in the course of last week, has suddenly surrendered – much sooner than one expected. It is glorious to feel that in consequence the whole world is now at peace again. But many of us are not so happy as we had thought to be. This is because, since my last entry, our great war leader Churchill has been tremendously defeated in a General Election – which to many seems shocking and disgraceful. But it is all too clear that, though through years of peril he had the huzzas of our fickle populace, he never had their hearts. These two days are called, in the jargon of the moment, VJ days; and they too are appointed public holidays. This second celebration of Peace is in the way of anticlimax, and has lacked the *eclat* of the German Peace. There have been fewer flags waving and no ebullience among the multitude. On the seafront there have been just the normal August crowds – but nothing to distinguish these days from any others. In the past three months there has been no improvement in living conditions, save that there is more petrol, and therefore a great increase in motor cars. Labour and coal remains almost unobtainable and rationed food has been actually reduced, though there is some compensation for this in an increasing supply of fish. Under such circumstances V days are nothing but a curse to householders. Yesterday there was a heavy rain. Food shops opened only for an hour or two, resulting in frenzied shopping with long queues. Today, happily, has been fine; but taking into account the disorganisation of normal existence they have caused, not to mention their boredom, I am truly glad that there will be no more V days in my time!

Index